A Macroeconomic Analysis of Profit

Based on the observation of economic reality, this book provides for the foundations of a new structure of national payment systems. Specifically, to this end, a rigorous accounting for money transactions, savings, and invested profit is suggested, with a major aim to settle sustainable lending levels.

Profit lies at the heart of economic activities. Indeed, companies, from small to large, seek net gains to remunerate shareholders and to increase their assets. Yet, economists are far from sharing a common theory of profit. Using mathematical tools and a discursive approach, this book contributes to the debates in such regard, in the attempt to provide new answers to old economic issues. What is macroeconomic profit? Is there any relationship between wages, lending, and profit?

This book is an accessible resource for economists and financial experts as well as global economics students, researchers, academics, and historians alike. It will challenge policy-makers and professionals and lead them on a thought-provoking journey through the realm of macroeconomics.

Andrea Carrera is Professor of Economics at Schiller International University, Madrid campus, Spain. He has gained academic and business experience in both Europe and North America. He has lectured on and authored a number of scientific articles in economics, and he has worked for large and medium-sized companies. Andrea holds a PhD (Switzerland) and an MPhil (Spain) in economics. He loves 20th-century history, languages, food, and hiking with good friends.

Routledge Frontiers of Political Economy

Economics for an Information Age
Money-Bargaining, Support-Bargaining and the Information Interface
Patrick Spread

The Pedagogy of Economic, Political and Social Crises
Dynamics, Construals and Lessons
Edited by Bob Jessop and Karim Knio

Commodity
The Global Commodity System in the 21st Century
Photis Lysandrou

Uncertainty and Economics
A Paradigmatic Perspective
Christian Müller-Kademann

Discourse Analysis and Austerity
Critical Studies from Economics and Linguistics
Edited by Kate Power, Tanweer Ali and Eva Lebdušková

The Dark Places of Business Enterprise
Reinstating Social Costs in Institutional Economics
Pietro Frigato and Francisco J. Santos Arteaga

Economic Woman
Gendering Economic Inequality in the Age of Capital
Frances Raday

A Macroeconomic Analysis of Profit
Andrea Carrera

For more information about this series, please visit: www.routledge.com/books/series/SE0345

A Macroeconomic Analysis of Profit

Andrea Carrera

Routledge
Taylor & Francis Group
LONDON AND NEW YORK

First published 2019
by Routledge
2 Park Square, Milton Park, Abingdon, Oxon OX14 4RN

and by Routledge
605 Third Avenue, New York, NY 10017

First issued in paperback 2020

Routledge is an imprint of the Taylor & Francis Group, an informa business

British Library Cataloguing-in-Publication Data
A catalogue record for this book is available from the British Library

Library of Congress Cataloging-in-Publication Data
Names: Carrera, Andrea, 1986– author.
Title: A macroeconomic analysis of profit/Andrea Carrera.
Description: 1 Edition. | New York, NY : Routledge, 2019. | Includes bibliographical references and index.
Identifiers: LCCN 2018058380 (print) | LCCN 2018060582 (ebook) | ISBN 9781351213356 (eBook) | ISBN 9780815380351 (hardback : alk. paper) | ISBN 9781351213356 (ebk)
Subjects: LCSH: Profit. | Wages. | Loans. | Banks and banking.
Classification: LCC HB601 (ebook) | LCC HB601. C327 2019 (print) | DDC 338.5/16—dc23
LC record available at https://lccn.loc.gov/2018058380

ISBN 13: 978-0-367-73058-1 (pbk)
ISBN 13: 978-0-8153-8035-1 (hbk)

Typeset in Sabon
by Apex CoVantage, LLC

Contents

Figures

Tables

Foreword

The existence of profits is a fact nobody can deny. Yet, economists' search for a satisfactory theory of profits has been going on for a long time, and it is only recently that a full explanation of their formation and expenditure has been provided. The Classics, confronted with the law of exchange establishing the necessary equivalence between the terms of any relative exchange, could not explain the formation of positive profits in a way consistent with their labor theory of value. If the exchange value of goods is determined by the labor necessary for their production, and if the payment of wages corresponds to the purchase of labor, no difference can ever occur between the amount firms pay to workers as wages and the amount firms earn through the sale of produced output. For the Classics, the law of exchange takes the form of the necessary equality between values and prices, and if the payment of labor is identified with the purchase of produced output by firms, it is immediately clear that firms cannot derive any positive profit from the sale of this same output to consumers. Purchased by firms at a price equal to its value expressed in labor terms, products can be sold to consumers only at the same price: profit is necessarily nil both for any single firm and for the set of firms.

Marx's attempt to avoid this result by introducing a distinction between labor and labor power fails, because profit (surplus value), formed as the difference between the value of labor's output and the value of labor power, takes the form of a stock of goods that is doomed to remain unsold. The only income available in Marx's system being equal to the value of labor power, namely to what we would call today the value of wage-goods, profit-goods, which are obtained at zero cost by firms thanks to surplus labor, are unsalable. The logical impossibility to explain the monetary realization of surplus value calls thus for the rejection of Marx's ingenious attempt to explain profit as a surplus value and confirms the difficulty of reconciling the law of exchange with the existence of profit.

The law of exchange is also at the center of Walras's general equilibrium analysis, which is logically incompatible with the existence of firms' profits.

In general equilibrium, prices are equal to costs, and firms cannot derive any positive profit from the sale of their products. The economy analyzed by Walras and his followers is an economy of exchange, which implies the essential unity between the market for products and the market for productive services. As is the case of the market for products, where produced goods are purchased by consumers, on the market for productive services the latter are purchased by firms: in general equilibrium analysis, every monetary transaction is a purchase. It thus follows that firms act as simple intermediaries between two kinds of purchases occurring on two markets that are necessarily connected: the exchange between products and productive services results from the purchase of the latter and the sale of the former. As intermediaries, firms transmit what they get, and no profit can emerge in a system fundamentally unable to extend to the economy of production.

Keynes's great intuition about profits concerns their inclusion into national income; that is, given that human labor is the unique macroeconomic factor of production, into wages. According to Keynes, national income is identically given by the amount of nominal wages paid to workers and by the sum of real wages and real profits. The first relationship concerns the formation of national income, while the second refers to its subdivision between wage-earners and firms, and to its final expenditure in the purchase of wage-goods and profit-goods. In this theoretical framework, profits are formed in the market for products through the sale of wage-goods at a mark-up. Yet, this explanation of profit is still incomplete if not altogether unsatisfactory, because it is apparently not substantially different from James Steuart's attempt to derive profits from the process of circulation. The claim that profits can be explained by introducing a positive difference between prices and values leads to a contradiction, because it is tantamount to saying that values and prices are two distinct units of measure of produced output. Measured in terms of value at the moment of its production, output would be measured in terms of prices at the moment of its sale, and the two measures would be distinct and different. This would imply also that the value of money, its purchasing power, would differ according to whether it is determined on the market for productive factors or on the market for products, even though money's purchasing power is given by the same physical output. As these arguments clearly show, the identity between values and prices (or law of exchange) is not an assumption that can be accepted or rejected at pleasure, but a logical constraint within which profits must be explained.

This difficult problem requires a difficult solution, because if the law of exchange was applied rigidly and no degrees of freedom were allowed, the identity of values and prices would be incompatible with the formation of profits. If, in each instant of continuous time, prices could not differ from values, profits could never form; in particular, they could never be derived from wages as Keynes suggested.

Schmitt's macroeconomic analysis of money's circular flow allows for a new approach to the problem of profit. Banks issue money as an asset-liability, a purely numerical means of exchange that cannot finance net purchases. Money is a mere intermediary through which payments are conveyed, and it is never their object. It is through an instantaneous circular flow that money plays its role. If banks could issue money as a net asset, money could be given up in exchange for real goods and would represent the very object of monetary payments and not simply their vehicular means. However, in the real world, neither banks nor any other economic agent or institution have the supernatural, metaphysical power to create something positive out of nothing. The asset-liability nature of bank money as expressed by double-entry bookkeeping derives from this logical requirement. Banks, by issuing their own acknowledgment of debt and lending it to the economy, are at the origin of money and, at the same time, represent the pole to which money instantaneously flows back as soon as the payment it conveys has occurred. Since money is not a net asset and cannot finance any net purchase, the only apposite conclusion is that it can only 'finance' the simultaneous sales and purchases of the beneficiaries of its emission. Every purchaser must be a seller, and every seller a purchaser; this is the logical requirement imposed by the vehicular nature of bank money.

Two questions arise at this stage of the analysis: what is the logical point of injection of money, and how does money acquire its purchasing power? These questions are closely related, and so are their answers: it is through production that money acquires a purchasing power, and firms are its point of injection. This is so, because firms, as intermediaries through which produced output is given a monetary form and is distributed between its final consumers, are at the same time purchasers (of productive services) and sellers (of produced output). The monetary remuneration of productive services (human labor) and the sale of their product are the two faces of a unique reality: national production. As can easily be derived from Keynes's fundamental equations, production and consumption are the two identical terms of a unique process; or, in Schmitt's words, of a unique emission. Production is a creation of money and consumption is its necessary destruction, the unity creation-destruction being imposed by logic. The circular flow of money coincides, therefore, with the circular flow of income, and firms are the key element of both circuits. It is true that production, the payment of wages, and consumption, the final purchase of produced output, are separate events in chronological time. Yet, it is also certain that the product is sold, albeit not finally, from the moment its costs of production are paid for. This is enough to prove that firms, in their productive function, are both purchasers and sellers. They are purchasers on the labor market, and they are sellers when they cover their costs of production either by selling the product of their workers or by borrowing from income-holders, that is, by selling claims on the financial market.

The nature of bank money imposes both its circular flow and the circular flow of income, and these two circular flows establish as a logical necessity the identity between firms' sales and purchases. Because firms are at the same time sellers and purchasers, they are the logical point of injection of money. Money is issued by banks and put into circulation by firms. At the same time, it flows back to its point of emission again through the mediation of firms. Firms, considered in their productive function, are intermediaries: through them economic output is monetized (payment of wages) and demonetized (product's final purchase). The law of the monetary circuit is substantially another version of the law of exchange, and hence, unavoidably, the consequence is the same: productive firms' profits are necessarily nil. The integration of money into an economy of production implies the circular flow of money injected by banks to the benefit of firms, and the law of the circuit does not allow for any positive or negative difference between firms' sales and purchases.

Does this imply that the existence of profits is irremediably at odds with that of the monetary circular flow? Not at all, since the logical impossibility for firms' sales to exceed their purchases applies only to firms functionally defined as productive firms. What is true for productive firms is not necessarily true for firms considered as income-holders. In other words, nothing prevents firms from being simultaneously present in the circuit as points of money's injection and rejection, that is, as fundamental elements whose sales and purchases are necessarily equal, and as parts of a composite element. The identity of values and prices is verified for every element of the monetary circuit. Yet, within a composite element a difference may arise that causes a re-distribution of income between workers and firms. Whereas productive firms cannot derive any profit from money's and income's circular flows, commercial firms can benefit from a transfer of income. Indeed, '[e]very income whose source is situated within a composite element of the circuit is an income of transfer' (Schmitt 1975: 54, our translation). The primary source of income is the payment of wages, and this payment requires the intervention of firms in their productive function. Once formed, income can be transferred from its initial holders, wage-earners, to other economic agents, commercial firms included. Profits are derived from wages; they result from a transfer operated on the market for products through the sale of produced output at a price greater than its value. Any contradiction with the law of exchange is avoided by the fact that this (microeconomic) sale occurs within a composite element, and it is no hindrance to the (macroeconomic) sale-purchase carried out by productive firms in compliance with the logical identity of values and prices.

The theory of profits is complete only if it explains both their formation and their expenditure consistently with the identity of values and prices, yet allowing for prices to benefit from a degree of freedom with respect to values. This is achieved through Schmitt's quantum monetary analysis, thanks to his discovery of quantum time, which makes it possible to reconcile the logical identity, always in place in quantum time, with the numerical difference, manifesting in chronological or continuous time. Andrea Carrera's analysis does not go as far, its aim being to introduce the reader to the implications of the theory of profits over that of investment and capital formation. One of Carrera's main concerns is to show how the investment of profit affects our economies and what should be done to avoid the insurgence of economic and financial crises due to the inconsistency between the current system of monetary payments and the logical distinction between banks' monetary and financial intermediations. The investment of profit is a transaction implying a new production and, as such, it must be clearly distinguished, in theory as well as in practice, from the re-distribution of profit. Carrera's critical investigation of the main analyses of profit advocated in the past, which he develops in the first part of his book, aims at clarifying the nature of profit enough to provide the analytical tools required to address the problem of investment rigorously, in compliance with the logical laws that characterize our monetary economies. The emergence and evolution of the banking system has made the identification of these core logical principles easier, doing justice in the process to the deep insights of the great authors of the past.

Carrera's study is both historical and pertinent to the analysis of today's economic pathologies. Instead of concentrating his efforts exclusively on Schmitt's analysis, which he explicitly adopts as reference, Carrera succeeds in his endeavor to identify points of convergence between quantum macroeconomics and other heterodox approaches, mainly post-Keynesian economics. He does so by first considering the nature of money in a production economy, focusing also on the role of central banks for the orderly working of domestic payments systems. In this regard, Carrera points out the asset-liability nature of bank money, notably when the payment of wages occurs on the labor market, giving rise thereby to national output in the form of produced goods and services. This payment originates national income, a part of which can be captured by firms on the product market as profit, which has both a real and a monetary dimension since it is a part of produced output as well as of national income.

In this light, Carrera explores the classical and neoclassical theories of profit critically. He thus explains the conceptual and analytical flaws that affect in particular Marx's and Walras's theories of profit: the former cannot provide a sound theoretical explanation of firms' monetary profit, since within the economy as a whole there is not enough income for it in a Marxian framework, whilst Walras and his followers consider profit as the remuneration of capital, as if the latter were a factor of production originating income on its own – which is logically impossible, because only labor can give a new utility form to matter and energy, hence originate added value in the form of wage-units. As Carrera shows, contemporary neoclassical models suffer from the same shortcomings as regards the definition of profit and functional income distribution, since they are based on so-called microfoundations of macroeconomics. He then moves on to investigating Keynes's and post-Keynesians' analyses in this regard. Starting from the Keynes (1930a) concept of 'windfall profit', and then considering Keynes's (1936) so-called normal profit, Carrera explains that all attempts to include Keynes's ideas into a neoclassical framework are doomed to fail, owing to the conceptual and methodological flaws that affect that framework. The problems in this perspective originate in the (wrong) ideas that saving must precede investment, and that there is an equilibrium relation between saving and investment at the relevant interest rate in the market for loanable funds. To overcome these issues, Carrera presents a new macroeconomic analysis of profit, first proposed by Bernard Schmitt. In this perspective, profit is both real and monetary, and firms' investment of it gives rise to a pathological capital that actually affects the whole economic system by inducing both inflation and unemployment. This is the reason why Carrera ends his journey into the macroeconomics of profit by proposing a monetary-structural reform, to make sure that the investment of profit is entered into banks' book-keeping, respecting the nature of money, income, and capital. The result of this reform is to avoid both inflation and unemployment in our monetary economies of production.

As testified by his numerous, adequate references and quotations, Carrera is well read and his research work allows for a thought-provoking journey through the realm of macroeconomics. Academics and policy-makers will find this work challenging.

Alvaro Cencini and Sergio Rossi

Foreword and acknowledgments

It is my firm opinion that diversity should always be supported and protected, since it leads to progress in every aspect of human life. Accordingly, as concerns economics, I think that economic prosperity will be achieved as soon as men embrace pluralism in economic analysis. A number of economies have not yet fully recovered from the impact of the Global Financial Crisis of the early 21st century. Therefore, action is needed today, as always, to guarantee a prosperous economic future to all of them. Truth may well be secluded in the writings of overlooked economic thinkers like Bernard Schmitt, the author of the theory presented in this volume.

I was trained as a traditional economist. As far as economic theory is concerned, I have taken standard neoclassical courses, and I also came to study the neoclassical synthesis of John Maynard Keynes's *General Theory* as well as new Keynesian and post-Keynesian models. However, during graduate studies, I suddenly chanced upon the works of Schmitt, a heterodox economist, so to speak, and I ended up asking myself: 'What was he saying?'. I finally decided to take up the challenge of writing a personal retake of his theory – or, rather, of some features of it – because I see, in it, a way toward financial stability.

The analysis proposed in the following pages was first carried out by Schmitt (e.g., 1960, 1966 [1975], 1984, 1986, 1996a) and explained further by other authors, including in particular Cencini (e.g., 1982, 1984, 1988, 1997, 2001, 2003, 2005, 2015) and Rossi (e.g., 2001, 2003, 2005, 2006, 2007, 2009). Yet, much effort is needed to provide the theory with a strong analytical apparatus and to make it accessible to wider audiences. This volume seeks to contribute in such a direction, as a new synthesis of Schmitt's theory of profit.

Bernard Schmitt was born in Colmar, France, in 1929. After studying in Strasbourg and in Nancy, he pursued doctoral studies at the University of Paris-Sorbonne. Meanwhile, in 1953, according to Baranzini and Mirante (2018: 50), Schmitt enrolled as a research student at Trinity College, Cambridge, supervised by Prof. Sir D. H. Robertson. There he met with other scholars, including Pierangelo Garegnani, who had matriculated under the supervision of Piero Sraffa at the same time as Schmitt, and Amartya K. Sen, who received, among other awards, the Nobel Prize in 1998 and is now Lamont Professor of Economics at Harvard. While in Cambridge, Schmitt got in touch also with Maurice Dobb, Richard Kahn, Joan Robinson, and Piero Sraffa. The stormy personal and scientific relations that followed, between Mrs. Robinson and Schmitt, did not prevent her from asking him to translate into French her famous book *Exercises in Economic Analysis* (1960), which he duly did in 1963. Back in France after the research time spent in England, Schmitt received his PhD from the University of Paris in 1958. By 1960, Schmitt had laid down the foundations of his economic theory.

It was then that, on both sides of the Atlantic, the theory of economic growth was revived for the first time since the times of Adam Smith and David Ricardo. In 1956, Robert Solow (Nobel Prize winner in 1987) published his famous neoclassical model of economic growth in *The Quarterly Journal of Economics*. In the same year, Nicholas Kaldor proposed his post-Keynesian model of distribution and growth in *The Review of Economic Studies*, and in 1957, he wrote about the same topic in *The Economic Journal*. The monetary theory developed by Schmitt dates back to that time.

Economists were in the middle of the most renowned economic debates of the 20th century. Cambridge, UK, at that time was a 'battleground', as Amartya Sen defines it (1998). He is certainly right. Harsh quarrels were going on between major Keynesian and neoclassical economists. Despite much effort made by and large since then to reach full knowledge of economic phenomena, much work remains to be done by economists so as to univocally explain and avert the economic troubles that often hit, one way or another, a number of world economies. Now that the storm of the Cambridge 'battleground' has died down, the time may have come to shed light on another theoretical product of those years: Bernard Schmitt's economic theory has many ties to Keynesian economics at large; still, a theory showing that the 'premises' of monetary economies do not rely on government intervention, despite its crucial role, for instance, to fairly allocate national resources and to protect the environment.

Schmitt became professor of economics in 1965 at the University of Fribourg, Switzerland, and later at the University of Bourgogne in Dijon, France, where he worked most of his life. Starting from 1954, he carried out research activities at the *Centre National de la Recherche Scientifique* (CNRS) in Paris, where he 'found [. . .] the material and moral conditions to carry out his job' (*Acknowledgments* in Schmitt 1966, our translation). Robert Goetz-Girey no doubt played a major role in encouraging Schmitt to move his steps into academia. Moreover, Henri Guitton, Jean Marchal, Robert Mossé, Pierre Dieterlen, Bernard Ducros, Maurice Flamant, and in particular Henri Mercillon, Jacques Houssiaux, and Jean-Claude

Eicher all encouraged Schmitt to complete the 'difficult tasks of the isolated researcher' (*Acknowledgements* in Schmitt 1966, our translation). Schmitt was awarded two medals from the CNRS in 1961 and 1973.

The French economist was well known in France and, to a certain extent, in the English-speaking world. As an academic teacher, he got to know some of the most famous economists of his time, such as George Ackerlof (Nobel Prize winner in 2001), Maurice Allais (Nobel Prize recipient in 1988), and Luigi Pasinetti (a great intellectual figure from the University of Cambridge), and he founded the so-called 'Dijon School', a school of thought in the field of monetary economics. I have never personally met Schmitt, but I have worked with some of his closest colleagues and friends. Stories surround the French economist. To the eyes of some, he was a very stubborn and intolerant economist. To the eyes of others, he was an extremely clever man, fully devoted to economic research. Personal interests and sentiments, however, are not my concern here, as my focus is not on the man, but on his ideas.

Bernard Schmitt passed away in Beaune, France, in 2014. His legacy belongs to the fields of national and international economics. On the one hand, his studies of national economics concern the process of production, the emission of money, the origin of profit, and investment activities. On the other hand, his contribution to international economics concerns international payments as well as sovereign debt formation and the payment of sovereign debt interests. Schmitt's major works include: *La Formation du Pouvoir d'Achat* (1960); *Monnaie, Salaires et Profits* (1966 [1975]); *Macroeconomic Theory: A Fundamental Revision* (1972); *New Proposals for World Monetary Reform* (1973); *Théorie Unitaire de la Monnaie, Nationale et Internationale* (1975); *Inflation, Chômage et Malformations du Capital: Macroéconomie Quantique* (published in 1984 and now being translated into English on behalf of Routledge); 'The Process of Formation of Economics in Relation to Other Sciences', in Baranzini and Scazzieri's (eds) *Foundations of Economics: Structures of Inquiry and Economic Theory* (1986); 'A New Paradigm for the Determination of Money Prices', in Deleplace and Nell's (eds) *Money in Motion: The Post Keynesian and Circulation Approaches* (1996); 'Le Thèoréme de l'Intérêt' (2007); and 'The Formation of Sovereign Debt: Diagnosis and Remedy' (2014).

Over the years, a number of scholars came to know Schmitt, whose intellectual heir is, without doubt, his former student and life-long friend Alvaro Cencini, a Swiss-Italian economist. Cencini was born in Lugano, Switzerland, in 1946. After obtaining his A-Levels at the *Liceo Scientifico* in Lugano, southern Switzerland, Cencini moved to the Swiss French-speaking region, where he studied economics at the University of Fribourg. Following graduation, Cencini enrolled in a PhD program, working as Bernard Schmitt's research and teaching assistant. Cencini received his PhD in 1978. Members of his committee included Pietro Balestra, a well-known Swiss econometrician. Subsequently, Cencini applied for graduate studies at the

London School of Economics and Political Science (LSE). After admission, he was supervised by Meghnad Desai, who is now a life peer of the United Kingdom and Emeritus Professor at LSE. During the years he spent in London, Cencini wrote a thesis that granted him a second PhD title (1983).

Cencini's works include: *La Pensée de Karl Marx: Critique et Synthèse* (co-authored with Bernard Schmitt in 1977); 'The Logical Indeterminacy of Relative Prices', in Baranzini's (ed) *Advances in Economic Theory* (1982); *Time and the Macroeconomic Analysis of Income* (1984 [2013]) and *Money, Income and Time* (1988), both with a preface by Meghnad Desai; *External Debt Servicing. A Vicious Circle* (co-authored with Bernard Schmitt in 1991); *Monetary Theory. National and International* (1997); *Monetary Macroeconomics: A New Approach* (2001); *Macroeconomic Foundations of Macroeconomics* (2005); *Elementi di Macroeconomia Monetaria* (2015); *Economic and Financial Crises: A New Macroeconomic Analysis* (co-authored with Sergio Rossi in 2015); and *Quantum Macroeconomics: The Legacy of Bernard Schmitt* (co-edited with Jean-Luc Bailly and Sergio Rossi in 2017).

It is worth noting that another economist has taken over from Schmitt and Cencini: Sergio Rossi, who holds the Chair of Macroeconomics and Monetary Economics at the University of Fribourg, Switzerland. After graduating and obtaining a PhD at the University of Fribourg (1997) under the supervision of Schmitt, Rossi moved to London, and obtained a PhD in economics from University College London (UCL) in 2000, under the supervision of Victoria Chick. A well-known economist, Rossi has contributed to dozens of publications.

Rossi's bibliography includes: *Modalités d'Institution et de Fonctionnement d'une Banque Centrale Supranationale, le Cas de la Banque Centrale Européenne* (1997); *Money and Inflation: A New Macroeconomic Analysis* (2001); 'Money and Banking in a Monetary Theory of Production', in Rochon and Rossi's (eds) *Modern Theories of Money. The Nature and Role of Money in Capitalist Economies* (2003); 'Central Banking in a Monetary Theory of Production: The Economics of Payment Finality from a Circular-flow Perspective', in Fontana and Realfonzo's (eds) *The Monetary Theory of Production: Tradition and Perspectives* (2005); 'The Theory of Money Emissions', in Arestis and Sawyer's (eds) *A Handbook of Alternative Monetary Economics* (2006); *Money and Payments in Theory and Practice* (2007); *Economic and Financial Crises: A New Macroeconomic Analysis* (co-authored with Alvaro Cencini in 2015); and *Quantum Macroeconomics: The Legacy of Bernard Schmitt* (co-edited with Jean-Luc Bailly and Alvaro Cencini in 2017).

Cencini and Rossi have inspired and guided me toward a better comprehension of the theory put forward by Schmitt. Constant encouragement has come from them to develop the analysis presented in this volume, which addresses an old issue in economic theory: namely, the nature of macroeconomic profit, whose 'existence [. . .] is a puzzle that has raised serious considerations, and one that many economists have attempted to resolve' (Rochon 2009: 57).

This volume is a development of my doctoral thesis (Carrera 2016b). I presented drafts of this volume's chapters during the annual meetings of the Canadian Economic Association in 2014 and 2016, of the Eastern Economic Association in 2015, 2016, and 2017, and during the annual meeting of the European Society for the History of Economic Thought in 2018. My research was undertaken between 2012 and 2018 in Canada, Switzerland, and the United States.

This work has benefited from encounters with numerous economists I met with along the way. My gratitude goes in particular to the following scholars: Alvaro Cencini (University of Lugano), a fatherly figure over the years; Julián Sánchez González (Autonomous University of Madrid); Louis-Philippe Rochon (Laurentian University); and Sergio Rossi (University of Fribourg). I shall always feel for them the most genuine and dearest friendship and affection. I would also like to thank Luigi Pasinetti (Catholic University of Milan and Lincei Academy of Rome) for suggesting useful literature during my first steps into academic research, as well as Mauro Baranzini (University of Lugano and Lincei Academy of Rome), Ludovica Marcotti (University of Lugano), Amalia Mirante (University of Applied Sciences and Arts of Southern Switzerland), and Estrella Trincado Aznar (Complutense University of Madrid), for having been ever-present so far. I also feel indebted to many others, for their useful comments – at times concise, at times prolific, but always up to date – during my lectures, over private lengthy conversations, or following the reading of a draft of this volume. Far from being able to draw an exhaustive list, I thank Fletcher Baragar (University of Manitoba), Riccardo Bellofiore (University of Bergamo), Robert W. Dimand (Brock University), Giuseppe Fontana (Leeds University Business School), Carmine Garzia (University of Pollenzo and University of Applied Sciences and Arts of Southern Switzerland), Jonathan M. Harris (Tufts University), Yun K. Kim (University of Massachusetts Boston), Marc Lavoie (University of Ottawa), Virginie Monvoisin (Grenoble School of Management), Kari Polanyi-Levitt (McGill University), Salewa Olawoye (York University), Pierluigi Porta (University of Milan-Bicocca), Lino Sau (University of Turin), Malcolm Sawyer (Leeds University Business School), Mario Seccareccia (University of Ottawa), Andrea Terzi (Franklin University Switzerland), Leanne Ussher (University of Massachusetts Boston), and Guillaume Vallet (University of Grenoble Alpes). I would further like to express my gratitude to Simona Cain (University of Lugano), Alvaro Cencini, Niklas Damiris (Stanford University), Edouard Maciejewski (International Monetary Fund), Michael Paysden, and Carol Theal (University of Lugano) for providing their linguistic advices, and to Michael Paysden for helping me translate some early passages from Italian. I shall always be thankful to Andy Humphries, Anna Cuthbert, and their team for their professional expertise on behalf of Routledge, and to Julián Sánchez González for granting me permission to reproduce here some excerpts of my articles published in the Spanish *Cuadernos de Economía*. I also thank everyone who has encouraged my research over the years: in particular, Fabio Bosatelli (Polytechnic University of Milan), Erika Carminati (University of Bergamo), Gabriel L. Poggio (UADE, Buenos Aires), Paul Serrano (Complutense University of Madrid), and my parents.

I apologize to the reader for any errors of fact and opinion present in the text, which are purely my responsibility.

Andrea Carrera
Boston and Madrid, December 2018

Introduction

Humans have always produced goods and services of many kinds so as to satisfy a number of necessities and desires. Men and women are driven, by need as well as by intellectual curiosity and natural predisposition, to carry out specific productive activities. In the end, everybody produces so as to satisfy her/his needs either directly or through exchange. This is why people have always bartered something with something else. Teenagers clean their bedrooms so as to be allowed to go camping. Students study hard to get good grades at school. Neighbors cultivate tomatoes and potatoes so as to exchange the ones for the others. And so on. The use of money facilitates the exchange of goods and services between their producers and their final users. Money, as medium of payment, conveys goods and services from hand to hand and allows for the allocation of output in the hands of different economic agents.

World economies, though differing one from the others, all share a common trait: they all depend on the interaction between workers, firms, and banks. Workers, no matter what their skills and roles are, carry out productive activities. Some of them, driven by the entrepreneurial spirit, give birth to a number of companies that specialize in specific sectors, from telecommunications to car manufacturing, from cultivation to education, from banking services to insurance, and so on. All workers, from entrepreneurs to laborers, from teachers to bellhops, provide their services according to their skills. The ultimate reason of commercial activities is to allocate produced goods and services among workers and among companies. In fact, goods and services are needed, on the one hand, by workers to satisfy their individual needs and wishes and, on the other hand, by companies to help workers carry out productive activities.

Broadly speaking, the allocation of the national product between workers and companies is made possible thanks to the use of money. It is money, in fact that has the function of channeling goods and services from the companies where they have been produced to their final users, that is, specific individuals and specific firms. Monetary wages and monetary profits are respectively credited on the bank accounts of workers and on the accounts of companies, thanks to the intermediation of banks. When both wage-earners and companies have spent their incomes to purchase the national product, the allocation of the entire national stock of produced goods and services among wage-earners and companies is final. Being issued by banks, money always turns back to its originators.

It is rarely the case, however, that workers and companies fully dispose of their monetary incomes. In fact, a fraction of monetary wages and monetary profits is always distributed to specific individuals, such as children, housewives, shareholders, rentiers, and the elderly. Isn't it true, indeed, that fathers and mothers spend a good portion of their monetary incomes to cover the expenses of their daughters and their sons? Isn't it true, in fact, that the individuals in working age pay for the pensions of retired people? Isn't it true, also, that companies' monetary profits are partly distributed to shareholders as dividends and to the State as taxes? Such distribution of monetary incomes from the hands of workers and from the hands of companies is made either directly – from parents to their children, for instance – or through the intervention of the State – as happens, for example, when war veterans are paid public pensions. Therefore, in the end, rather than between workers and companies, national output always ends up being allocated among households and companies. Arguably, how all this works is still little known, even by the best minds in economics and banking.

This volume seeks to explain the origin and the investment of profit in productive activities, as well as the relation between profit and the amount of loans any commercial bank can grant to its clients. Yet, the road toward a full knowledge about the nature of profit is relatively long and requires a full understanding of the basic laws underlying economic activities. Nothing in fact can be said about profit and investment without a prior knowledge about production, consumption, and banking. There could be no corporate gain or profit, indeed, without goods and services, without individuals willing to purchase them, and without available income to be spent on the product market. This is why the volume starts with an investigation into the relation between production, consumption, and banking.

History shows that the production and the circulation of goods and services are always made possible by the use of money. No wages would be paid or spent, in fact, without money. Corporate gains would not be possible, nor could they be distributed or invested, without the existence of money. Money, as the medium to carry out economic transactions, is fundamental to the survival of economic activities. Yet, little is known about money. It is most likely clear to everybody, however, that money is issued and managed by banks and that banking techniques follow the rules of double-entry bookkeeping. All monetary transactions worldwide are carried out, in fact, by means of accounting entries on banks' books. It is beyond dispute that, at least since the creation of banks, any monetary payment has a bookkeeping nature. Money itself has a bookkeeping nature. Does this mean that money is nothing but a numerical tool in the balance sheets of banks? If it is true that money is nothing but a number in banks' books, what can be inferred about paper money or, which is the same, about cash? Is currency in circulation pivotal to economic activities? The volume shall seek to provide proper answers to these fundamental questions. It shall be argued, as suggested for instance by the case of Sweden, an almost cashless society, that debit and credit cards as well as electronic means of payment prove to be valid alternatives to cash.

Everyone acquainted with banking and finance is surely aware of the fact that production triggers the emission of money and the formation of a positive wage-income. Yet, many questions remain to be answered. What is the relation between real output and money? Also, what relation holds between production and consumption? What is the role played by banks with regard to money, production, and consumption? Proper answers to these economic issues can be provided as soon as one observes economic systems as they are and takes into account their history. Answers are to be found in banking practice as well as in the evolution of commercial and central banking. History shows that productive activities have been carried out thanks to the intermediation of commercial banks. This happened, for instance, in the United Kingdom, where, despite the existence of the Bank of England since the late 17th century, commercial banks alone proved to be efficient intermediaries to business activities. But this is also the case of the United States, where the Federal Reserve System started its activities as intermediary of commercial banks only in the 20th century. Therefore, another question arises at once: what is the role played, in any monetary system, by commercial and central banks? As it shall be shown, whereas the prime scope of commercial banks is to serve as intermediaries between companies and households, the prime goal of the central bank is to allow for interbank payments.

Only once full knowledge of banking, production, and consumption is achieved can a proper investigation into the origins of profit be developed. Indeed, if it is clear, on the one hand, that monetary profit, from a microeconomic perspective, is conceived as the positive excess of a company's revenues over its costs of production, it remains to be established, on the other hand, whether monetary profit, at the macroeconomic level, is positive or not existing at all. Let us ask the reader to pull out $10 coins from the pocket and give them to someone nearby. Can the reader get $12 coins back out of those $10 coins? The problem holds even with regard to national economics. Indeed, it must be explained if and how, for instance, companies sustaining overall costs of $100 trillion may get revenues above that amount and, accordingly, make a net profit. If total savings in a monetary system amount to $100 trillion, can companies get, for instance, $120 trillion in revenues, and thus make a profit of $20 trillion? Also, broadly speaking, profits being usually conceived in monetary terms, can they be reduced to a mere monetary phenomenon? The solution to the problem is not easy. What is the nature of any corporate gain? What is the nature of the overall amount of profits? Profits are made in money, and no objection can be raised against this fact. However, it is also undisputable that profits also have a real nature. Can't it be indeed that, to a certain extent, produced output ends up in the hands of companies as real profits? The volume shall seek to provide answers to all these issues.

A number of authors have spent their entire lives in search for answers to these problems. An analysis of the conceptions of profit that have been developed by economists since the advent of modern political economy in the 18th century is therefore very likely to prove rich in fruitful insights. What are the features of major economic streams since the time of Adam Smith to the present day? Are there any points of convergence between different profit theories? Have economic theorists come to a unitary theory of profit? The book is partly devoted to the search of a satisfying answer to these questions, with the aim of deriving from them a new unitary theory of profit.

Too little is taught nowadays in university classrooms about the old authors of the past who have gone down in history as classical economists. This is likely due to the fact that the classical theories of profit may appear to have no practical relevance today in terms of economic policy. Be that as it may, it must be observed that the classical school was deeply concerned with the study of profit. Intellectuals like Adam Smith, David Ricardo, and Jean-Baptiste Say, for instance, wrote extensively, among other issues, about profit. Their readers shall acknowledge that, broadly speaking, the classical authors were convinced that profit is a net, positive income, in the same manner as the wages of workers and the rents of landlords. Therefore, the volume shall include a short account of classical writings. In Chapter 2, particular reference shall be made to the economics of Karl Marx, who, in fact, made the most important attempt to explain the existence of monetary profits. However, it shall be observed that he failed in his attempt. It shall be argued that, despite its influence on a great number of communist and socialist figures and an even greater number of readers, the theory of Marx was fundamentally flawed on logical grounds. Yet, it was most probably because of political and economic interests, rather than flaws of contents, that Marx's theory was attacked by neoclassical authors, who believed in the free market and took the defense of the bourgeoisie.

The neoclassical school of economics, fathered by Léon Walras with his *Eléments d'Economie Politique Pure* in 1874, has always enjoyed great success. The neoclassical theory has since imposed itself as the principal current of mainstream economics. Current and former students in economics shall acknowledge that the neoclassical theory is widely taught in undergraduate and graduate programs. Several are, in fact, the neoclassical models and their most recent adaptations that any student is required to study in order to pass official academic examinations. Given the importance attributed to the neoclassical theory by a great number of economists, the volume includes an assessment of neoclassical analysis, from its outset to current models of growth and distribution. What was Walras's conception of profit? Was profit conceived as a net income or as nil? What contributions have been made to the theory of profit by later neoclassical authors? These are some of the questions we will be dealing with in Chapters 2 and 3.

A challenge to neoclassical economics was set in the 1930s by John Maynard Keynes, one of the most influential economists of the 20th century. A major intellectual from the University of Cambridge, Keynes worked extensively on a number of economic issues, from the reparations of World War I to the Indian currency, from international trade to the sovereign debt. The attention of Keynes was also paid to profit. Indeed, in *A Treatise on Money* (1930a,1930b), Keynes carried out a study of windfall profits. In *The General Theory of Employment, Interest and Money* (1936), instead, he developed the idea of normal, entrepreneurial profits. The volume shall inevitably cover the contributions of Keynes to the theory of profit.

An assessment of Keynesian studies since 1936 shall be subsequently made. It must be remembered that the neoclassical theory was seriously put at stake by Keynesian economists in the second half of the 20th century. Many economists who grew up between the 1950s and the 1970s remember, with a good dose of nostalgia, the intellectual zeal that characterized the economic debates of the time. Great attention was paid to the study of profit, for instance, by the greatest economists in the United Kingdom and the United States. In this context, the volume shall go through the neoclassical versions of *The General Theory* and other models that have been developed in the attempt to include Keynes's theory into the neoclassical theoretical framework. These models can be found mostly in the neoclassical synthesis and in the new Keynesian theory. Attention shall be paid then to post-Keynesian studies, including seminal and most recent post-Keynesian research work on the theory of profit. Some authors, in the wake of Keynes, argued that households' savings are a primary source of national investment. Indeed, investment has been traditionally identified with the sum of savings both from wages and from profits, or with the sum of workers' and capitalists' savings.

Now, almost three hundred years have passed since the rise of political economy and, oddly enough, a general consensus has yet to emerge on the nature of profit. Indeed, in economics, '[o]ne of the contentious issues that still needs to be resolved is the existence of profits' (Rochon 2005: 136). This explains why the volume seeks to propose new directions in the theory of profit. It is not a mere matter of definitions, but a thorough understanding of the nature of corporate gains.

It should be no surprise that banks function as intermediaries between households and companies. Indeed, banks' intermediation allows for the payment of wages and their distribution among households. Starting from this fact, the volume shall seek to explain the way in which, to a certain extent, monetary wages end up in the hands of companies as monetary profits. Still, monetary phenomena are just one side of the story. In the end, indeed, money is just a medium that, through consumption, allows for the circulation of produced output from companies to its final users. Therefore, the volume shall pose other important questions. What are the laws of output allocation? How do goods and services end up being allocated among households and companies? How do companies get real profits, consisting of goods and services at their disposal? At this point, the volume shall inevitably deal with a fundamental issue. If any, what is the ontological difference between micro- and macroeconomic profits? What relation holds between microeconomic and macroeconomic profits?

The volume shall then delve into the relation between profit and investment. The idea that profit and investment are somehow related to each other is not new in economic theory. Interestingly, economists have always thought in fact that a functional relation does hold between profit and investment, although consensus is still missing on the causality between the two. What does come first, profit or investment? Is profit the source of investment or, vice versa, is investment the spur of profit? The solution to the problem shall require an insight into retained profits. The reader shall acknowledge in fact that companies usually make gains so as to retain and invest them in new business projects. This is tantamount to saying that retained profits are spent by companies to finance the production of new products and services. Think for instance of the billions of dollars of profits made by Apple. Isn't it true that many of those billions are being invested in the development, for example, of new technologies, iPhones, and iMacs? Undoubtedly, however, despite the importance attributed to retained profits in relation to investment, the volume shall provide a full analysis of profit distribution as dividends, interests on capital, and so on.

The volume shall subsequently raise other questions. In fact, the study of profit cannot be said to be accomplished until it provides some considerations on the nature of interest rates. Economists have always held in high regard the interconnection between profit and, in particular, the interest on consumption, the interest on fixed capital, as well as the so-called natural and market interest rates. The theory presented in the following pages shall provide new causes for reflection about the existence of profits and the evolution of interest rates. The volume shall also provide insights into the growth of fixed capital. This issue strictly relates to the origin and the investment of profits over time. Is there a limit to the growth of monetary and real profits? Is there a limit to the accumulation of capital? What can be said about the growth of monetary deposits with regard to the investment of retained profits in the long-term?

Therefore, the volume shall guide the reader through the fascinating, yet challenging, twists and turns of a positive theory of profit. There is more, though. If it is true, as it is indeed, that the beauty of any positive theory lies in the internal consistency of its constructs, it is as much true that perfection is reached when the positive is matched by the normative. In this light, the true legacy of the theory presented in this volume lies in the usefulness of its outcomes in terms of economic policy. And, apparently, world economies are desperately looking for new economic norms.

At the beginning of the 21st century, the world has been hit by the Global Financial Crisis, one that has been labeled as the greatest economic turmoil since the Great Depression in the 1930s. The unbiased management of bank credit in the first years of the current century has been identified as the major cause of the crisis. A number of developed economies in North America and in Europe have experienced lots of troubles since the unfortunate financial events of 2007–8. Many of these economies have not yet fully recovered from those harsh episodes. Even worse, some observers are worried about the likelihood of a new financial crisis. What has been done so far to avoid or contain the risks of a new economic downturn? Are lending policies strong enough to ward off a new credit crisis?

Important financial regulations have been adopted globally as a reaction to the Global Financial Crisis. The US Dodd-Frank Act is a notable example of the attempts made by national legislators to protect the economy from the raving behavior of financial actors. Europe has reacted as well, for instance by fostering a fully functioning banking union and a strong supervisory framework. Yet, being under continuous political attack, national and regional regulations appear to be fragile. Likewise, things are not better at the international level. Indeed, the implementation of the set of rules known as Basel III, for example, runs into the lengthy times of bureaucracy and the suspicious eyes of political opponents.

Also, as it is certainly true that the resilience of financial regulations worldwide is threatened by the interests and the tantrum of politics, it is likely true that the weakness of such regulations lies in the lack of a macroeconomic strategy with regard to the management of credit. Regulations, from national to regional as well as global, usually set the criteria that banks are required to follow to decide whether they should grant credit to their individual clients. Of course, such criteria are more than welcome, since prudence is always wise, and so much so in the perilous post-crisis years. However, much more should likely be done by monetary authorities to manage the overall amount of bank credit. How much credit can a bank lend to the whole of its clients? What is the relation between monetary transactions, savings, and credit? Should banks be allowed to finance credit through the over-emission of money? These important issues shall be addressed in the following pages.

Given this state of affairs, the volume shall propose the outlines of new bank regulations, as sketched by the Schmitt plan for a reform of the system of national payments, as a way out of any financial troubles. The plan, developed in the 1970s and proposed publicly since the 1980s, concerns the structure of the monetary system as such, calling for a clear accounting of monetary transactions, savings, and investment levels. The plan relies neither on political nor on ideological considerations. Being outside the scope of political and particular economic interests, the plan could be easily implemented by commercial banks under the guidance of national monetary authorities.

The plan stands out for one important and powerful feature, among others, concerning profits and credit. Namely, if the plan became reality, monetary authorities would have a real-time knowledge about profit levels. These would turn out to be a strong potential indicator used by commercial banks to settle sustainable amounts of credit to their clients. By keeping record of monetary transactions, savings levels, and invested profits, banks would undertake lending activities on sound grounds. In this context, the central bank would keep its role of settling and clearing national interbank payments. The outcome of a positive theory of profit, the implementation of the plan would be, without any doubt, a milestone in the history of economics.

Chapter 1

Money, production, and profit

Households, companies, and banks mainly interact the one with the others so as to pay out wages, to transfer monetary savings, as well as to allow for consumption. Wages and corporate gains are the motor driving individuals, companies, and banks to produce, distribute, and purchase the national product. In this context, money is a required component of any economic system. Yet, economists disagree with each other about the way in which economic players interact as well as about the nature of monetary and real incomes. Thus, this chapter shall propose a study of production, consumption, and banking, in hopes of a new consensus on the basic laws underlying economic phenomena. This chapter aims to prepare the ground for a study of corporate profits. In this light, the investigation shall seek to explain the relation between money and the real economy, focusing on productive activities, on consumption, and on the role of commercial banks as intermediaries between households and companies. An inquiry shall also be made about the historical and theoretical scope of central banks, with particular regard to the Bank of England and to the Federal Reserve System. What are the laws of production, consumption, and banking? What are the functions of commercial and central banks? What is the link between households, companies, and banks?

Bank money and the real economy

Production, consumption, and commercial banks

Traditionally, economists have thought of money as the currency in circulation; that is, banknotes and coins. It comes as no surprise, then, that most theories treat money as a physical object. Even at our times, whenever thinking of money, the one-dollar bill springs to mind. However, currency in circulation is just one side of the story. After all, today's massive use of electronic means of payment shows that scriptural money is by far larger in amount than banknotes and coins. One can even go further by asserting that some economies are transitioning very quickly toward a cashless future. On this regard, for instance, Sweden is in the lead. As argued by

Wheatley (2017) in a study for the International Monetary Fund, banknotes and coins account for only 15% of payments in Sweden, a country where cash is used by less than half of commercial banks and has fallen 'by nearly 15 percent between 2007 and 2015. Even homeless sellers of Stockholm's street magazine accept mobile payments' (Wheatley 2017: 32–3). What is money, then? What relation holds between money and output? What is the relation between money, production, and consumption?

History influenced the general opinion about money. As recalled by Smith in his *Wealth of Nations* (1776 [1981]: 41), the incomes of the Saxons, in ancient times, did not consist of money, but 'in kind, that is, in victuals and provisions of all sorts'; metal money was started being used only later on, under William the Conqueror. Iron was already used by the inhabitants of Sparta to facilitate the commerce of goods, and it was Servio Tullio who first coined money in Rome, using 'a Roman pound of good copper' (Smith 1776 [1981]: 42). Also, at the time of Alexander the First, the Scots already used 'a pound of silver of the same weight and fineness with the English pound sterling' (Smith 1776 [1981]: 41). Over time, gold, silver, and paper money, for instance, have been used by the richest nations to facilitate production and trade.

Then, it is not surprising that money has usually been identified with a physical medium. Broadly speaking, economists (see, for instance, Phelps 1961; Friedman and Schwartz 1963; Brunner and Meltzer 1971; Phelps and Taylor 1977) usually refer to money as a stock whose quantity would determine the amount of money supply in circulation and under the form of demand deposits (for recent critiques of the quantitative theory of money and monetarism, see for instance Keynes 1936 [1964]; Desai 1981; Cencini 2005; Krugman 2016; Rochon and Rossi 2018; Rossi's forthcoming a, forthcoming b analyses). The conception of money as a physical medium of exchange and means of payment is so widely diffused that its status is almost that of an axiom.

Interestingly, according to some authors, money is not of a physical nature, but scriptural; that is, a number in bank books without intrinsic value. On this regard, Bernard Schmitt (1960, 1975, 1984, 1986, 1996) was followed, among others, by Alain Parguez (1975, 1996, 2001), Alain Barrère (1979, 1990a, 1990b), Alvaro Cencini (1984, 1988, 2001, 2005), and Augusto Graziani (1989, 2003). As Rossi (2007: 18) points out:

> [m]oney does not need to be reified into a precious metal in order for it to be a means of payment: it would be enough [. . .] a double-entry book by means of which [. . .] economic transactions are recorded and settled with a mere book-entry device.

According to these authors, money is of a numerical nature, with no intrinsic value. Money is 'a pure symbol, a stroke of the pen in the bank's balance sheet' (Realfonzo 1998: 43). It is on double-entry bookkeeping, which has existed since the 13th century, that this analysis of money is founded.

As odd or against the tide as it may appear, money is far from being the physical object described in most of the economic literature. Banking systems are based on scriptural money, which is issued by commercial banks, in the first stance, so as to allow for companies to pay out wages. The creation of money takes place alongside productive activities; better said, production is the *raison d'être* of money creation. Hence, production and money creation must always be understood on logical grounds: without money, output would have no monetary value; without output, there would be no reason for money to be issued.

Think of a commercial bank and name it Nantucket Bank, after one of the oldest commercial banks in America. As any commercial bank, Nantucket Bank holds assets and liabilities corresponding to the credits and debits toward its clients. Assets include loans, securities, reserves with the central bank, cash, and other items. Liabilities include deposits, borrowings, and others. As the laws of double-entry bookkeeping require, the amount of assets and the amount of liabilities on any balance sheet must always match. This means that the value of assets is always equal to the value of liabilities.

Now, it is no mystery that loans are granted on the basis of the amount of deposits held by the bank on behalf of its clients, according to the saying 'deposits make loans'. What is unknown to most people is the fact that a certain kind of loans gives rise to new deposits, according to the saying 'loans make deposits'. This kind of loan is made thanks to the activation of credit lines, or, in other words, when wages are paid. The payment of wages, in fact, does not rely on previously existing deposits. For the sake of clarity, an example may be of help.

Suppose a firm requests the bank to credit workers' accounts with wages, relying on a credit line that the firm has previously obtained and backed by securities (on this topic, see for instance Rossi 2007: 25). Workers are credited with wages amounting to $100. The bank grants credit to the firm and simultaneously registers deposits of workers for the same amount. As soon as the payment of wages is made, the stylized balance sheet of Nantucket Bank will be affected as follows (Table 1.1).

Table 1.1 The stylized balance sheet of commercial banks

Nantucket Bank (Massachusetts)			
Assets		*Liabilities*	
Loans	Δ$100	Deposits	Δ$100
Securities	$. . .	Borrowings	$. . .
Reserves with the central bank, cash, other assets	$. . .	Other liabilities	$. . .

Source: *author's elaboration from the Federal Reserve (2016a).* Δ *stands for 'increase'.*

As soon as wages are paid to them, workers are credited with an amount of bank deposits that is matched by a net credit of the bank toward the company. This event triggers, so to speak, the creation of wage-income. Resulting from the activation of a credit line, the payment of wages gives rise to an increase in the overall level of the assets and of the liabilities on the books of Nantucket Bank. Wage-income has thus formed. Workers are credited, while the firm is debited. To the bank accounts of workers corresponds a security on the financial market, namely a certificate of deposit, whose real object is the output produced and warehoused within the company. Interestingly, the terms 'output', 'product', and 'goods' also refer to services, for 'goods and services are both examples of economic goods' (Solow 2012: 271). The remuneration of workers coincides with the production costs incurred by the company, which are the objective, monetary value of real output. Identifying wages as the measure for output value is equal to defining a product-wages relation where money functions as a unit of account for wages – Keynes (1936 [1964]) used the expression 'wage-unit' to refer to the measure of output value. Keynes's (1936 [1964]: 20) words can easily be borrowed here: 'the income derived in the aggregate by all the elements in the community in a productive activity necessarily has a value exactly equal to the value of the output'.

Now, the payment of wages always confers to wage-earners as a whole the right to purchase produced output. Whenever wage-earners use their credit cards, for instance, they spend their income to purchase a product or a service. Consumption allows companies to cover the production costs they have sustained on the labor market, also known as the market for productive services. Through consumption, goods and services leave the warehouses of companies and are allocated among their final users to satisfy their needs; the flow of money that is credited on corporate bank accounts allows for a reduction in the debts of companies toward the bank. Again, an example may be of help.

Think of a territory, which we call Nantucket. It well may be an island, an estate, or simply a university classroom. Suppose that Seafarer Co. is the sole company at Nantucket. Wage-earners at Seafarer Co. produce ten tons of seafood chowder. Hence, the output produced at Seafarer Co. is made of chowder. At the beginning of January, Seafarer Co. obtains the opening of a credit line by Nantucket Bank. At the end of the month, the credit line shall be activated and wages shall be paid. For the sake of simplicity, suppose all entries in Nantucket Bank's balance sheet to be nil. Suppose also that only scriptural money is used; that is, neither coins nor banknotes exist (nonetheless, some comments on banknotes and coins shall be made further on). At Nantucket, wage-earners include all kinds of workers, without any social class distinction: for instance, workmen, employees, managers, consultants, and so on. In this sense, workers include entrepreneurs. The entrepreneur indeed should be regarded as a worker providing his services. 'It is preferable to regard labour, including, of course, the personal services of the entrepreneur and his assistants, as the sole factor of production' (Keynes 1936 [1964]: 213–14). It has to be noted that this is far from meaning that the company makes no profit. As argued later on, income is made not only of wages, but also of profit. In the real world indeed, as soon as output is sold, companies usually expect to make profits. Suppose also that, at Nantucket, for a number of reasons, some individuals do not work and receive a share of wages from wage-earners. For instance, some children receive tips by their parents to buy fresh chowder at the local market. Thus, it shall be assumed that bank deposits are constituted in favor not only of wage-earners, but of households broadly speaking.

Money is simultaneously a company's debt and a credit of workers considered as a whole, both toward the banking system (Schmitt 1966: 286–7). The remuneration of labor (nominal wages) constitutes the monetary form of global output, and, if companies' profit is zero, it confers to workers the right to purchase the whole of real product. An example may help clarifying this point. Suppose that households spend the totality of wages altogether to purchase seafood chowder. In this context, if the company does not seek to gain from the sale, the selling price of output shall be equal to production costs. Households shall purchase the totality of consumption-goods. The price of $100 being equal to production costs of $100, households dispose of the sufficient and necessary income to purchase ten tons of seafood chowder. Nothing remains unsold after the sale.

Accounting entries in Table 1.2 show this process. Entry 1 refers to the payment of wages. Seafarer Co. is debited, and households are credited by the bank. This is respectively shown in the assets and in the liabilities of the bank's book. Entry 2 concerns income expenditure. When households spend their monetary income, Seafarer Co. covers its production costs and is able to pay back its debt to the bank. As soon as all the debit-credit relationships are extinguished, as shown in entry 3, monetary income is finally spent, and households benefit from using the goods they have purchased. The asset and the liabilities in the balance sheet of Nantucket Bank decrease accordingly.

Table 1.2 Wage payment and consumption

Nantucket Bank (Massachusetts)			
Assets		*Liabilities*	
(1) Seafarer Co.	$100	Households	$100
(2) Households	$100	Seafarer Co.	$100
(3)	$0		$0

Source: *author's elaboration from Cencini and Rossi (2015).*

What is worth inferring with the help of double-entry bookkeeping is that the nature of money is twofold, for it is a numerical flow (money-as-a-flow or vehicular money) and a numerical stock (money-as-a-stock).

On the one hand, vehicular money is used as a means of payment in every single transaction. Money, as a vehicle, is instrumental to credit and to debit the accounts of income-earners. For instance, in the banking system a bookkeeping entry accounting for the payment of wages is instantaneously positive and negative, and it implies the debit-credit of every single agent. The final expenditure of wages is an operation in which money is again used, as a vehicle. In the former case, income is created, meaning that bank deposits increase; in the latter case, income is definitively spent, since the relationship credits-debits between workers and the company is definitively extinguished, meaning that bank deposits decrease accordingly. Vehicular money is also used in all other payments. Consider, for instance, what happens when individual A orders his bank to lend or transfer \$1,000 to individual B on his behalf. The outcome of the payment is as follows: a reduction of \$1,000 takes place in A's bank account and, at the same time, the same amount of income is registered in B's bank account. Money, as a vehicle, is instantaneously spent and created. One will observe that, in this example, the vehicular use of money does not change the overall deposit level; namely, the use of vehicular money does not alter income levels. Thus, to be true, when a transfer is made from agent A to agent B, it is a matter of substitution rather than distribution. The result of the payment is in fact the substitution of a certain amount of monetary income from one bank account to another.

On the other hand, money-stock, namely bank deposits, defines the unity of a stock of goods and of their monetary form, where 'real' goods are the object of every payment. Between the payment of wages and their final expenditure, a double stock does exist: namely, a stock of goods and a stock of financial securities (deposit certificates) corresponding to the amount of bank deposits. The 'causality runs from money as a flow (means of payment) – the *primum mobile* – to bank deposits (stock of wealth)' (Rossi 2003: 345). As money 'covers' the physical product, a numerical form is given to real output. An absolute or numerical value of output originates when wages are paid, since goods and services are monetized thanks to the union of money and output. Output is then demonetized with consumption, when production costs are covered by the company and its debt is paid back to the bank. As soon as the company sells the product, the company covers production costs. Assuming that no further wage payments have been made, the level of bank deposits decreases accordingly. Once national output has been deprived of its absolute or monetary value, only a subjective value-in-use is left into the real world.

It is crystal-clear, therefore, that money is essential to productive and consumption activities. It is thanks to money creation and to its integration with output that heterogeneous, physical products become homogeneous, economic products. It is thanks to money expenditure, further, that homogeneous, economic products are turned, once again, into heterogeneous, physical products. Thus, money builds a temporary bridge between production and consumption. Money matters for its being a bridge between current and future economic activities. Once wages are paid, wage-income is deposited in bank accounts in the guise of a temporary, monetary capital and, simultaneously, as a physical stock within companies. As soon as wages are finally spent, the income level decreases by the same amount. At this point, the entire society does benefit from a product with a subjective value-in-use. It turns out that, being the numerical form of goods and services, money cannot be conceived as a commodity. Neither can money and output be two separated magnitudes, for they are in fact the two faces of the same reality. In economics, money and output are then the terms of an identity that is always true independently of time. Far from being a mere truism, the relationship between demand (bank deposits) and supply (real output) must be read as an identity. What allows for the temporary existence of monetary and real deposits is money.

In this volume, banks shall be referred to as if, acting as pure intermediaries between wage-earners and companies, they neither pay wages on their own behalf nor make any gain. These assumptions are motivated by mere didactical purposes. Usually, banks not only serve as intermediaries between households and companies, but they also act as any other company remunerating their employees and seeking profits. As a matter of fact, in any developed economy, banking activities are such that the banking industry makes a huge deal of business, employing hundreds of thousands of professionals. For instance, according to the US Department of the Treasury, the 'U.S. banking system is estimated to employ almost 2.8 million Americans' (2017: 21). In 2016, through their intermediation, US banks helped companies produce a gross domestic product of almost \$18.6 trillion (World Bank 2017: 1). As of June 2017, the financial system of the United States included about 5,900 banks and 5,800 credit unions, whose assets in the previous year totaled \$21.4 trillion and \$1.3 trillion, respectively (U.S. Department of the Treasury 2017: 21). Acting as any company, banks pay out wages relying on credit lines that are activated whenever banking services are provided. Banks also make profits the same way as profits are made by companies. Yet, when they are considered as companies producing and selling services and financial products, banks do not substantially differ from any other firm, so that the analysis of their economic activity is included in that of companies in general. What interests us here is to stress the role played by banks as intermediaries, which is why we shall consider them only in this function, at the service of the economy as a whole.

Now, what can be learned from the previous observations?

Traditional economic theories state that production is an activity that takes place over time. However, this traditional conception of production gives way when money enters the scene. It can be maintained that one should think of production not only in terms of the result, the product as a new value-in-use, but also bearing in mind the role money plays in the process of production. From a physical point of view, it is certainly true that, for productive activity to be undertaken, a period of time is necessary over which raw materials and energy are transformed into goods and services. Yet, it must also be added that only when wages are paid are goods and services monetized. It is when wages are finally spent, then, that goods and services are demonetized. In this light, production and consumption are events in which income is respectively created and finally spent. Thus, consumption cannot be understood unless it is identified as a complementary part of production, and vice versa. The physical product acquires an economic nature as soon as it acquires a numerical, monetary form. When income is finally consumed or spent, the economic product leaves its place once more to a physical stock with a subjective value-in-use. In production, the physical product is first transformed into income via wages payment; through consumption, the product is 'expulsed' from its monetary form and subsists only as a physical object. Production gives rise to a net income that is spent with consumption.

Between production and consumption, a temporary capital survives, the nature of which is twofold, being monetarily deposited in the bank's books and physically warehoused in the company. Such capital, which is made of the savings of households, is temporary, since it will be spent over time on the product market by the legitimate holders or by borrowers. This credit represents the right of households over a real capital that is stocked within the company. The financial capital deposited within banks is the credit title of households on the physical stock deposited within the company (the debt of which is registered as a bank's asset). When savings are spent, the company covers production costs and thus is able to pay back its debit toward the bank. When this happens, deposits decrease accordingly.

If the product were monetized and demonetized simultaneously, income would be created and spent at the same time. However, such an assumption would be too strict to allow for the financial intermediation of banks as well as for the development of a complex and articulated economy. Indeed, thanks to the intermediation of banks, production and consumption are two separate events, yet the two faces of the same reality. Whether right or wrong, Henri Bergson is attributed to have thought that '[t]ime is a device to prevent everything from happening at once' (see Robinson 1962; Forstater 2013: 36). His words may be borrowed to assert that banks, by issuing money, prevent production and consumption from happening at once.

Figure 1.1 may be of help. The figure shows the evolution of bank deposits over a period of two months, with $100 are paid at instant 0 – let us say, December 15 – and another $100 paid at instant 1 – January 15. For the

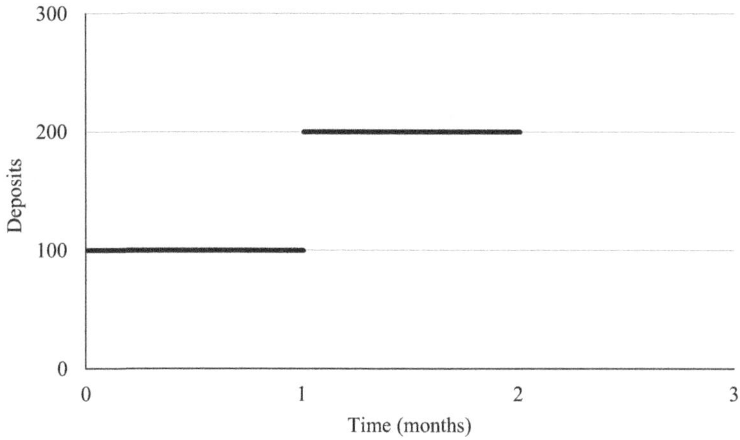

Figure 1.1 Bank deposits

sake of simplicity, suppose that wages are finally spent altogether at instant 2 – February 15. Within the time between instants 0 and 2, the amount of deposits constitutes a temporary financial capital. Bank deposits represent the temporary capital that exists between the moment in which income is created (wage payments) and the moment in which income is definitively spent. Therefore, in any given moment of time, the level of deposits depends on the total sum of previously created incomes that have not yet been spent. The income level over a given period depends on the total sum of global deposits during that time interval.

For instance, if total income amounts to $100 and households spend $70 in purchasing goods and services, firms are credited with $70 and households are debited to the same extent. The amount of bank deposits after the purchase equals $30. As a result of consumption, firms are still debited on the Assets of banks' balance sheets ($30); households are credited for the same amount on the Liabilities of the balance sheets (see Rossi 2003: 345). The remaining income of $30 will be definitively spent when the product is entirely sold by firms to households.

It is certainly true that income-earners can always exert the right over their demand deposits. As a matter of fact, they always have the right to spend the income they have been credited through production. A certain amount of time elapses, though, between the constitution of a deposit in favor of an income-earner, and the moment when she/he spends it. Meanwhile, banks legitimately lend a certain amount of income to their clients (this topic shall be examined further on in the volume). If Mr. Smith, for instance, earns $100, bank technique is such that his income can be lent to

Mrs. Marple, who is a borrower. Mrs. Marple, who spends \$100 to purchase goods and services, will be able to pay out her debt toward the bank as soon as new income forms on her bank account. In that precise instant, Mr. Smith will be able to spend \$100, too.

Now, commercial banks, acting as intermediaries between households and companies, always manage monetary transactions as well as monetary deposits. Still, new issues must be investigated at this point. Are commercial banks alone capable to manage the national monetary system in a sound manner? As regards instead the central bank, what is its role? Have commercial and central banks proven to ward off economic and financial troubles both from national economies and globally? An answer shall be provided by a short history of banking systems, since their early expansion in the 17th century to the present day.

Banks since the industrial revolution

Modern productive processes are an inheritance from the industrial revolutions started in England in the 1760s and in the United States in the 1820s. The 17th and 18th centuries were an epoch of substantial changes in the social, political, and economic life in a number of countries. The industrial revolution in England and, soon afterwards, in Northern Europe (e.g. see Zamagni-Negri's 2017 account of the economic history of Europe since 1700) took place in an era of enlightenment in many fields of knowledge. Thinkers like Smith, Condorcet, and Turgot started debating about economic issues, among which they included, for instance, free competition and, to a certain extent, the intervention of the State to prevent famines (see Rothschild 1992, 2001). The 18th century

> has been identified [. . .] with the political institutions of modern times: a new British empire in India, a new land empire in North America, and a new and more enlightened (or less benighted) Atlantic economy in the West Indies and Spanish America. It was a founding period of modern ideas in a vaster sense: of the competitive economy, of individual rights and the government of law, and of industrial or industrious transformation. It was a time when laissez-faire was new and when even the idea of the economy or of economic life [. . .] was unusual and insecure.
>
> (Rothschild 2011: 3)

> [T]hree sets of events [. . .] have been identified [. . .] as the founding moments of the modern Anglo-American world. There was the East India Company's acquisition of power over the financial administration of Bengal, Bihar, and Orissa [. . .]. There was the American Revolution [. . .] There was the construction, over the period from the decision in James Somerset's case in 1772 to the abolition of the slave trade in

> British ships in 1806, of a new and less impure British empire in the West Indies and the South Atlantic.
>
> (Rothschild 2011: 122–3)

Industrial activities and trade have also been facilitated by the development of banking as well as by the diffusion of payment instruments. Remarkable are the examples of the Italian bank Monte dei Paschi di Siena, which was founded in 1472, of the German banks Berenberg, Metzler, and Fürstlich Castell'sche, founded respectively in 1590, 1674, and 1774, as well as the examples of the Caja de Madrid and of the Bank of Spain, created in 1702 and 1782, respectively. Other forerunners were the Bank of Finland (1811), the Van Lanschot Bank in the Netherlands, the Banque Nagelmackers in Belgium (1747), the French Banque Courtois (1760) and the Banque de France (1800), as well as Landolt & Cie in Switzerland (1780) and the Bank of Ireland (1783). Some of the most important banks still in operation nowadays in the United Kingdom were founded in the 17th and 18th centuries. The United Kingdom, starting from the second half of the 18th century with its banks, its industrious people, and a unique scientific knowledge, was the ideal place for the industrial revolution to take place.

A number of commercial banks flourished alongside the industrial revolutions in Europe and in North America so as to facilitate the access of companies and households to credit. Yet, commercial banks have experienced hard times during economic and financial crises, so much so that commercial banking requires to be backed by the aid and support of central banks. To understand commercial and central banking, one has to go back as far as the 17th century in countries with the oldest central banks in the world, like Sweden and the United Kingdom. Yet, history shows that central banks were often created in relatively recent times. This is what happened, for instance, in the United States. While the United Kingdom had been provided with a central bank since 1694, the United States lacked a proper central bank until 1913. With a view to explaining the historical evolution of commercial and central banks, a short history of banks in the United Kingdom and in the United States shall be presented further on.

The old lady of Threadneedle Street

Some of the oldest commercial banks still in operation nowadays were founded in the 17th century in the United Kingdom. These include Hoare & Co. (1672), Barclays (1690), and Coutts (1692). Some of the oldest central banks in the world were created at that time. For instance, the Bank of England (BoE) was created on July 27, 1694, with the specific purpose of financing the war against France. Some of the historical events that follow in these pages can be found, for instance, in the official documents of the Bank of England (2018). The BoE was privately owned by stockholders, which included King William III and Queen Mary II, and was conceived since its earliest days to provide banking services to the government (Bank of England 2018). William Paterson, from Scotland, contributed very much to the creation of the central bank, at a time when 'the nation's finances had been in disarray and had no real system of money or credit' (Rodrigues 2009). Paterson was responsible for the 1.2 million pounds that were lent to the government by the bank's shareholders (Rodrigues 2009). The BoE, at that time and for many decades to follow, was far from developing the monetary policies that it enacts today. The BoE, at its outset, ran operations that are usually run by any commercial bank. Indeed, in 1694, under the lead of Governor John Houblon, the bank 'also started a conventional banking business, accepting deposits from the public' (Bank of England 2018). One year later, the Bank of Scotland was founded. Drummonds Bank, another notable institution, was created two decades later, in 1717.

The first financial crisis in England soon took place, in 1720. The South Sea Company, which was involved in trading with South America, managed to compete with the Bank of England in financing the British public debt (Bank of England 2018). This posed a serious threat to the central bank and caused a crash in the banking system: a number of banks asked for help from the BoE, which became a 'lender of last resort' (Rodrigues 2009). The BoE issued denominated banknotes for the first time in 1725, and in 1734, it moved from the Mercers' Hall in Cheapside to its current location on Threadneedle Street in London. Other famous banks had been founded since those times: for instance, the Royal Bank of Scotland was created in 1727, Lloyds Bank in 1765, Raphaels Bank in 1787, and State Street Corporation in 1792. Those were among the major banking institutions that contributed to financing the industrial revolution in the United Kingdom.

The Bank of England has been nicknamed the 'old lady of Threadneedle Street' since the events of 1797, when William Pitt the Younger, the Prime Minister, ordered the BoE to stop converting clients' banknotes with gold. England had recently been invaded by French soldiers, with much pain of the locals, who ran to the central bank and asked for gold in exchange for notes. 'The amount of gold held by the Bank dropped from £16 million to just £2 million' (Bank of England 2018). William Pitt, who wanted to finance the war with gold, stopped the convertibility of notes. People's discontent was depicted in a cartoon by caricaturist James Gillray, who portrayed Pitt as a man trying to get the gold off an old lady sitting on a chest of money. That year, 1797, marked the beginning of a period that lasted until 1821, over which the Bank was forced to stop converting notes with gold, as established by the Restriction Act. Meanwhile, other banks were created, including Schroders, founded in 1804, Brown, Shipley & Co., founded in 1810, and N. M. Rothschild & Sons, founded in 1811.

After the war with France, England experienced a period of crisis that lasted until approximately 1821, when the gold standard was restored in

Britain. Following the next financial crisis, in 1825–6, a number of banks went bankrupt and unemployment soared (see Neal 1998). The Bank of England reacted to the crisis by establishing some branches out of London, aiming to control the currency in circulation (Bank of England 2018).

Full powers and the exclusive responsibility to issue and control the currency in circulation in England and Wales were given to the Bank of England by the Bank Charter Act of 1844 (Bank of England 2018; Rodrigues 2009). The Act is also known as the Peel Banking Act of 1844, named after Robert Peel, who served as Prime Minister twice, during the reign of Queen Victoria. The Act also legally forced the Bank of England to back the issue of notes with gold. On October 25, 1847, however, the Bank of England was authorized by the British government to suspend the Peel Act. The BoE was allowed to issue uncovered notes, suspending the gold standard system. The government saw the suspension as a way to stop the turmoil faced by the British economy in the previous months. That year, in fact, is well known in the economic history of the United Kingdom, because the country was hit by a harvest failure that provoked economic and financial troubles. The repeal was then revoked on November 23, when the turmoil was brought under control. According to Dornbusch and Frenkel (1982), issuing fiat money, suspending *de facto* the gold standard regime, the Bank of England contributed to the restoration of normal economic and financial activities.

The British banking system was hit by the panic of 1857, which was one of the very first cases ever of commercial crisis. The turmoil had begun in the United States and had rapidly expanded to Northern Europe. The British government reacted, in particular, by suspending once more the Peel Act of 1844. During the crisis of 1857, as well observed by Hughes (1956: 194), 'domestic credit abuses and international financial manipulations brought trade and industry to grief'. Another episode of bad credit management took place a few years later, when one of the most famous banking bankruptcies of the 19th century was declared by Overend Gurney. The institution stopped its operations on May 10, 1866, having failed to receive financial help from the Bank of England. Overend Gurney failed because of bad choices in managing credit, having 'built up large piles of bad loans' (Bank of England 2018). The Peel Act of 1844 was again suspended by the British government during the crisis of 1866.

The last three decades of the 19th century were quite troubled. The United Kingdom was first hit by the crisis of 1867–9 and then by the crisis that lasted from 1873 to 1896–7. The latter crisis, which spread widely through North America and Europe, was largely due to large expansions in unsustainable investments and financial speculation. Due to its length, it is known as the Long Depression (see for instance Fels 1949; Musson 1959; Coppock 1961; Glasner 1997; Johannessen 2016).

The British banking system survived the perilous last three decades of the 19th century and, in 1914, the government, perceiving the gold standard as not beneficial to the economy, decided to suspend the regime. During World War I (1914–18), the Bank of England acted as banker of the government, by issuing War Stocks that were purchased to a great extent by the central bank itself through the bank's reserves (Bank of England 2018).

In the aftermath of the Great War, many countries faced severe economic downturns. This is the case, for instance, of Germany, the United Kingdom, and the United States (see for instance Romer 1988). In the United Kingdom, inflation started rising in 1919, followed by mass unemployment in 1920. In 1925, under the good auspices of Winston Churchill, the gold standard system was reinstated in Great Britain, provoking a reduction in exports and an increase in unemployment (National Archives 2018). In the early 1930s, the United Kingdom was hit by the Great Depression, started in the United States in October 1929 (see, for instance, Robbins 1934; Rothbard 1963; Bernanke 2009). A great fall in demand provoked a severe decrease in exports and an increase in mass unemployment. The depression led to a remarkable decision in the monetary history of the United Kingdom. In September 1931, the gold standard system was put to an end, for which reason convertibility of banknotes into gold was stopped (see for instance Eichengreen and Flandreau 1985).

During World War II, the British economy was enormously threatened by the Nazis, who, for instance, tried to destabilize the economy by introducing illegal banknotes in the country, to an extent 'that represented more than 10% of the total banknotes then in circulation in the UK' (Bank of England 2018). Luckily, the positive turn of events led to the defeat of the German regime and of the Axis powers. Governor Montagu Norman, who had ensured continuity in the operations run by the Bank of England from 1920 to 1944, played a major role, after World War II, in shaping the global financial system. For instance, '[h]e was involved in creating the *Bank for International Settlements* and the League of Nations' (Bank of England 2018).

A significant event took place in 1946, when the ownership of the Bank of England shifted from private hands to the government. This meant that, by law, the directing board of the central bank had to be appointed by the government, which, at that time, had the right to influence the policies of the bank (Bank of England 2018). The nationalization of the central bank was a first, necessary step toward the total autonomy of the central bank with respect to politics. It was so that the national bank became 'more of an instrument of government' (Rodrigues 2009). It must be observed, however, that, since 1946, the government led by Clement Attlee and the following ones never interfered with the monetary policies implemented by the Bank of England. Independence to conduct monetary policy, including the settlement of interest rates, was given to the central bank only in relatively recent times, on May 6, 1997, by the government led by Gordon Brown.

The second half of the 20th century was not exempt from economic and financial crises. One such crisis hit the United Kingdom in 1956, following the nationalization of the Suez Canal by order of Egypt's authorities. The Bank of England, together with the International Monetary Fund, successfully counteracted the speculation on the British pound that took place following the nationalization of the canal (see for instance Kunz 1991; Boughton 2000). Other famous crises, known as the energy crises, hit the United Kingdom, among others, in 1973–5 and in 1980–1. The crises were mainly due to geopolitical instabilities, caused above all by the Yom Kippur War in October 1973 and by the Islamic Revolution of 1979, which led to the fall of the Iranian Shah, Reza Pahlavi, and to the advent of the religious regime of Ruhollah Khomeini. In those years, a number of Western central banks and governments enacted a series of policy measures so as to face and abate the rise in inflation and the simultaneous economic recession, a phenomenon that has been labeled as 'stagflation' (see for instance Yergin 1991; Cooper 2011; Galpern and Keefer 2012).

In 1990 the United Kingdom joined the European Exchange Rate Mechanism, which set two price points between which the pound sterling exchange rate, as well as the exchange rates of other currencies, should have varied so as to guarantee European monetary stability. However, such a goal soon appeared to be too expensive. In 1992, the government led by John Major led the United Kingdom out of the Mechanism. Following that decision, on September 16, a Wednesday that went down in history as 'Black Wednesday', the United Kingdom was hit by a financial crash that 'was estimated to have cost HM Treasury over £3 billion' (Bank of England 2018).

Supervision on banking institutions in the United Kingdom was reinforced through the intervention of the legislature as a reaction to the Global Financial Crisis that hit the country in 2008 and 2009. As shall be observed later in the volume, the Bank of England and the British government, as well as other major central banks and legislators in the world, enacted monetary measures in the attempt to contain and erase the negative effects of the crisis on the economy.

And then there was the FED

The Federal Reserve, the system of twelve banks that together constitute the central bank of the United States, was instituted in 1913. It was born after several attempts, over more than a century, to create an institution that would aid commercial banks in guaranteeing the soundness of the monetary system and preventing economic turmoil. The monetary history of the United States is in fact full of episodes of bank failures, bank runs, and turmoil in the financial market not manageable by commercial banks alone. We shall sum up here major historical events that may help understand the factual reasons that led to the creation and development of the central bank. History also shows that the evolution of the banking system has not come to an end even at present, more than a century after the creation of the Federal

Reserve. This suggests that efforts are still needed to reach the goal of bank stability for which many bankers, economists, and politicians have striven so far. The events listed below are well known. They shall be drawn, for instance, from Mints (1965), Friedman and Schwartz (1963), Lowenstein (2016), and the Federal Reserve (2017a).

When the industrial revolution started in England, North America was facing years of political rebellion. The epicenter of the American political revolution (1765–83) was the city of Boston, where people felt oppressed by the English laws of the time. A revolution in the economic mindset started in those years under the influence of the political hostility toward the central power and in the wake of European liberal thinkers like Adam Smith and John Locke. It was at that time that laissez-faire started gaining the upper hand in the newborn United States. Following the introduction of paper money in 1775, operations were started by a growing number of commercial banks. These banks include some of the oldest banks still active at the present day, such as the Bank of New York (1784), the Manhattan Company (1799), Citibank (1812), Brown Brothers Harriman & Co. (1818), Institution for Savings (1820), Citizens Financial Group (1818), and Centreville Bank (1828).

It was following the proposal of Alexander Hamilton, Secretary of the Treasury, that an embryonic national bank was created in Philadelphia in 1791, with the goodwill of President George Washington. The Bank of Philadelphia, also known as the First Bank of the United States, was not able to prevent the famous panic of New York in 1792 and the following panics in Baltimore, Boston, New York, and Philadelphia between 1796 and 1797 (see Federal Reserve 2017a). The Bank operated for two decades, until 1811. Only five years later, in 1816, a second attempt to run a national bank was made under the goodwill of President James Madison. Even at this time the bank could not ward off the next economic depression, which took place between 1818 and 1821. The panic of 1819 led to a number of bank failures. It was so that activities of the Second Bank met the opposition of President Andrew Jackson and consequently stopped after barely ten years, in 1836.

It must be observed that the second attempt to run a central bank coincided with the American industrial revolution, which started during the 1820s. Technical innovations have surely played a major role in the development of productive activities during the industrial revolution in America. Technological progress has much improved since then, and quite often at a hectic pace. History is full of examples of this. One may think, for instance, of the relative short time that passed by between 1903, when the Wright brothers, Orville and Wilbur, piloted the first powered aircraft, and 1969, the first time of a manned mission to the Moon.

The revolution in the productive process was preceded and stimulated by the Embargo Act in 1807 and the War of 1812, which proved that the

US economy could no longer rely on the English industrial system and on English traders. A major figure of the change in the industrial system was Samuel Slater, who was named by Jackson as the 'father of the American Industrial Revolution'. Slater was the first to adopt a system of spinning mills in Rhode Island. The Lowell system, named after Francis Cabot Lowell, was adopted at Boston Manufacturing Company in Waltham, Massachusetts. The system consisted of a series of activities, from spinning to cutting, that allowed a single company to produce textile products on its own, without relying on other parties.

The origin of the industrial revolution in the United States coincides with the forty years preceding the civil war in America (Mints 1965: 125). The period between 1820 and 1860 was dominated by some of the most important economic debates of the 19th century. Surprisingly or not, the debates were enlivened mostly by non-academics.

> Nearly all the writers of importance came from New England (largely Boston), New York City, and Philadelphia, although there were several (but they were of less significance) from South Carolina. [. . .] It might be supposed that if there had been published any theoretical literature on the subject of banking in the West and South it would have been more hostile to the banks than that which we have from the large eastern cities; and yet it would be impossible to find more violent critics of the banks than Gouge and Carrol, of Philadelphia and Massachusetts, respectively. It is of some interest that monetary and banking theory had not become primarily the preserves of academic theorists. Of the more significant writers of the period, the following were largely businessmen, although a number of them were also engaged in politics to a greater or less extent: Nathan Appleton, Charles H. Carroll, Stephen Colwell, Albert Gallatin, Eleazar Lord, George Opdyke, and Samuel Hooper. Among the college teachers were John Bascom, Francis Bowen, Thomas Cooper, George Tucker, Henry Vethake, and Francis Wayland. Amasa Walker might be included within both categories. Raguet and Gouge were engaged in editorial work to a considerable extent, although the former was a businessman in his earlier life and the latter was with the Treasury for the major portion of his mature years.
>
> (Mints 1965: 175)

The Americans did not share with the English people the long-established tradition of central banking (the Bank of England was founded back in 1694). Then, it comes as no surprise that

> Americans generally were more hostile toward the banks than were the British. It was a more generally accepted doctrine in the United States that the ultimate influence of the banks is in the direction of increasing

> the quantity of circulating medium. A larger proportion of American writers recognized the fact that deposits are of equal significance (dollar for dollar) with bank notes and are created in the same manner.
>
> (Mints 1965: 176)

After doors closed at the Second Bank of the United States in 1836, three decades of free banking dominated the financial scene. This era is of specific interest because at that time, commercial bank notes and demand deposits spread across the country. A sort of interbank system was created in 1853 by means of the New York Clearinghouse, which aimed to favor the exchange of checks and to settle bank accounts. For the American economy, those were not easy times, though. A recession started in 1837, resulting into a depression that lasted for the next five years. Another recession then took place in 1857. Both downturns saw many bank failures.

Discussions about the health of the US banking system never stopped. The five decades starting from 1860 were characterized by '[a]gitation for banking reform' (Mints 1965: 198).

> At least some of the reasons which provoked and gave direction to the consideration of banking problems are not difficult to discover. Foremost among these were the panics of the period [. . .]. These panics brought out certain characteristics of the financial system which were thought to be sources of difficulty.
>
> (Mints 1965: 198)

It has to be noted that the last years of the free banking period were quite difficult, since the country was facing both economic and social rough times. Between eight hundred thousand and one million people died during the Civil War (1861–5). The National Bank Act of 1863 was a first reaction to the economic turmoil of that time. The Act regulated 'nationally chartered banks, whose circulating notes had to be backed by U.S. government securities' (Federal Reserve 2017a).

The US economy was far from being secured. Recessions and financial turmoil were typical of the last three decades of the 19th century. The recession and bank failures of 1873, for instance, gave advance notice of the depression that lasted up to 1877. Shortly after, in 1884, a renowned bank panic hit the United States. It must be observed that the problems faced by the US domestic banking system was not an isolated event. The same phenomenon was also taking place in Europe. In 1893 and 1907, two new bank panics occurred, together with the recessions of 1896 and 1901. The panics led to the interventions of J.P. Morgan (see for instance Federal Reserve 2017a on these events).

It was clear then that the monetary issue urged to be assessed by the highest political ranks. In 1908, the Aldrich-Vreeland Act passed, providing 'for emergency currency issue during crises' and 'established the national Monetary Commission' (Federal Reserve 2017a). The political debate of the next five years, whose major figures were, in particular, Senator Nelson Aldrich and President Woodrow Wilson, cleared the way for the central bank proposal of 1912 by Carter Glass and Parker H. Willis. On December 23, 1913, President Woodrow Wilson signed the Federal Reserve Act: the central bank of the United States was founded as a decentralized institution in twelve cities across the country.

The new-born Federal Reserve was set up on the eve of the political and economic events that threw the entire world into disarray over the thirty years between the beginning of World War I in 1914 and the end of World War II in 1945. The 1920s started with the economic recession of 1920–1 and ended with the terrible financial crash of October 1929. In those years, the FED started open market operations and, under the lead of New York FED chairman Benjamin Strong, the bank opened up to relations with foreign central banks, a sign that US bankers were oriented toward the internationalization of the US banking system (see Federal Reserve 2017a). A few years later, in 1933, the Glass-Steagall Act passed with the goal, among others, of protecting bank depositors. To this end, the Federal Deposit Insurance Corporation was instituted. Also, President Franklin D. Roosevelt put the gold exchange standard to an end. As a means to targeting full employment, a series of reforms were enacted up to the end of World War II. In 1935, for instance, the Federal Open Market Committee was created.

Most importantly, a new international monetary regime was established at the 1944 Bretton Woods conferences in New Hampshire. Harry Dexter White, a leading American official at the conferences, played a major role in shaping the creation and the development of international institutions such as the International Monetary Fund and the World Bank. John Maynard Keynes, as the representative of the British Treasury, had suggested the introduction of a mechanism of international settlement and clearing through which payments between countries would be made in a new currency called 'bancor'. The British initiative met the opposition of the American delegation. To the disappointment of Keynes, the new regime saw the world currencies pegged to the US dollar, which was pegged in turn to a gold ounce (see U.S. Government 1948). The harsh tones of the debate between White and Keynes are well known, so much that Steil (2013) labeled it as the 'battle of Bretton Woods'.

Despite the intense reforms that led to the creation of the post-World War II international monetary system, financial problems had not been uprooted. The Federal Reserve and the US Treasury found themselves, for instance, within inflationary and debt problems during the Korean War of 1950–3. The banking system did not stop evolving. On August 15, 1971, President Richard Nixon stopped the convertibility of the US currency to the gold ounce; the Bretton Woods system had ended. Despite new banking regulations, like the Monetary Control Act of 1980, the monetary system was not yet as strong as to avoid the energy shocks of 1973 and 1979 and, more generally, the advent of stagflation during the energy crises of the 1970s and the 1980s.

From 1979 to 2006, the Federal Reserve was led by two monetarist economists: the first was Paul Volcker, who passed the baton to Alan Greenspan in 1987. In the eyes of Greenspan, the central bank had to be a liquidity source for the entire banking system (Federal Reserve 2017a). Despite the economic expansion of the 1990s, financial authorities could not avoid a stock market bubble and a credit crunch. In the wake of the economic growth of the decade, the Gramm-Leach-Bliley Act was passed in 1999, 'overturning the Glass-Steagall Act of 1933 and allowing banks to offer a menu of financial services, including investment banking and insurance' (Federal Reserve 2017a). Greenspan's Federal Reserve increased liquidity to the banking system and lowered interest rates and lending in a number of occasions, as it happened for instance after the terrorist attacks of September 2001 in New York City.

The following events are well known. In 2018, the Federal Reserve, as well as the Bank of England, the European Central Bank, and other prestigious institutions, were still tackling the economic and financial turmoil that spread out in North America in 2007–8 and became known worldwide as the Global Financial Crisis of the late 2000s.

With regard to the objectives of the analysis developed here, it is worth observing that commercial banks alone proved to be incapable of avoiding economic and banking crises during the 19th century. Moreover, the history of the 20th century shows that even the creation of the central bank did not dispel economic and banking turmoil. This is true of many countries, including the United States. To our eyes, this suggests that banking systems still require to be perfected. In order to address the problem of how banking systems need to be reformed, it is necessary to answer a few questions concerning the relationship between commercial and central banks as well as their respective functions. If any commercial bank functions as intermediary between households and companies, what is instead the prime scope of the central bank? In particular, what is the relation between the central bank and commercial banks?

Interbank payments and the central bank

Payment settlement and clearing

Many economists of the past, especially before 1900, believed that a major role of the central bank was to provide the public with paper money (see Goodhart 1988: 5). A number of economists, including Walter Bagehot and Vera Smith, even favored a free banking system, with no central bank at all, although they agreed that abolishing the Bank of England in favor of free banking was not realistic (Goodhart 1988: 1).

Nowadays, it should be clear that central banking is needed so as to manage interbank payments. This means that the central bank serves as the intermediary of national commercial banks or, broadly speaking, of financial institutions. Indeed, national payments are never carried out directly from one commercial bank to another. Commercial banks usually hold deposits at the central bank, which is in charge of processing, settling, and clearing a number of payments on behalf of national banks, through an infrastructure that is used by the central bank itself and that is provided to national clearing houses. In the United Kingdom, for instance, 'the Bank of England has provided a way for two or more institutions to settle payments without settlement risk since the mid-19th century' (Bank of England 2018).

Thanks to the intervention of the central bank, interbank payments are made in national money. In the absence of a central institution established with the specific goal of issuing US dollars, for instance, every commercial bank would issue its own currency. The number of currencies in the country would be the same as the number of national commercial banks. Even if all banks were to name their currencies 'US dollar', in the absence of today's Federal Reserve, there would be as many currencies as the number of issuing banks.

The next example seeks to explain the matter at hand. So far, it has been assumed that Seafarer Co. is the only company in the country and Nantucket Bank (Massachusetts) is the only commercial bank. In this case, the central bank has no reason to be put in place. Think now of a second company, Apple Inc., and of a second commercial bank, Wells Fargo & Co. (California). Suppose that the two banks issue money which they both call dollar. In the absence of the central bank, the payment of households in Massachusetts, clients of Nantucket Bank, in favor of Apple Inc., client of Wells Fargo & Co., would give rise to inflation. The phenomenon is pictured in Table 1.3, which stylizes how interbank payments work in the absence of a central bank or, more specifically, in the absence of a shared mechanism of settlement and clearing.

Suppose households in Massachusetts are credited with \$100 for producing a certain amount of seafood chowder at Seafarer Co. (entry 1). Suppose also that households in California are paid \$100 for producing electronic products at Apple Inc. (entry 2). If households from Massachusetts spend their income to purchase the goods produced at Apple Inc., for instance, their bank on the East Coast makes a payment in favor of the bank in California (entry 3). The result is the constitution of both a monetary deposit of Wells Fargo & Co. at Nantucket Bank (entry 4) and a monetary deposit of Apple Inc. at Wells Fargo & Co. (entry 5). Wells Fargo & Co. has deposits amounting to \$200 at the disposal of its clients. Something is odd with the logic here. The payment made by Nantucket

Table 1.3 Interbank payments in absence of the central bank

Nantucket Bank (Massachusetts)			
Assets		*Liabilities*	
(1) Seafarer Co.	$100	Households (Mass.)	$100
(3) Households (Mass.)	$100	Wells Fargo & Co. (Calif.)	$100
(4) Seafarer Co.	$100	Wells Fargo & Co. (Calif.)	$100

Wells Fargo & Co. (California)			
Assets		*Liabilities*	
(2) Apple Inc.	$100	Households (Calif.)	$100
(5) Nantucket Bank (Mass.)	$100	Apple Inc. (Calif.)	$100

Bank on behalf of its clients in Massachusetts has given rise to an increase in the deposits at Wells Fargo & Co. The amount of money issued by Nantucket Bank has been registered as an asset of Wells Fargo & Co. At the same time, an amount of money has been issued and registered on the liabilities of the latter bank to the benefit of Apple Inc. One should expect a decrease for the same amount in the deposits at Nantucket Bank. This is not the case, though. Despite a change in their holder, from households (Massachusetts) to Wells Fargo & Co., deposits at Nantucket Bank do not decrease at all. The deposits of Nantucket Bank on the East Coast can now be lent, for instance, by the bank to its clients. Therefore, interbank payments in the absence of the central bank give rise to an over-emission of nominal money: inflation sets in.

It should be clear that, even if the payments of the clients of any given bank in favor of the clients of any other bank were of the same amount as those of the clients of the other bank in favor of the clients of the former bank, the intervention of the central bank would be required. Table 1.4 may be of help. Entries 1 and 2 refer to the wage payments in Massachusetts and in California. Households in both states are paid a total of $200, $100 by Seafarer Co. and $100 by Apple Inc. For the sake of simplicity, assume the two banks hold no deposits at the FED. Suppose the depositors of Nantucket Bank purchase products from Apple Inc. for $100 and depositors of Wells Fargo & Co. purchase seafood chowder for $100 from Seafarer Co. Also, for the sake of explanation, suppose the selling price is equal to production costs (i.e. no profit is made by the two companies). Upon the request of their clients, Nantucket Bank and Wells Fargo & Co. pay each other through the intermediation of the Federal Reserve. Entries 3 to 7 show the payment from Nantucket Bank to Wells Fargo & Co. Households in Massachusetts

Table 1.4 Interbank payments and the central bank

Nantucket Bank (Massachusetts)			
Assets		*Liabilities*	
(1) Seafarer Co.	$100	Households (Mass.)	$100
(3) Households (Mass.)	$100	Federal Reserve	$100
(4) Seafarer Co.	$100	Federal Reserve	$100
(12) Federal Reserve	$100	Seafarer Co.	$100
(13)	$0		$0

Wells Fargo & Co. (California)			
Assets		*Liabilities*	
(2) Apple Inc. (Calif.)	$100	Households (Calif.)	$100
(6) Federal Reserve	$100	Apple Inc. (Calif.)	$100
(7) Federal Reserve	$100	Households (Calif.)	$100
(8) Households (Calif.)	$100	Federal Reserve	$100
(9)	$0		$0

Federal Reserve			
Assets		*Liabilities*	
(5) Nantucket Bank (Mass.)	$100	Wells Fargo & Co. (Calif.)	$100
(10) Wells Fargo & Co.	$100	Nantucket Bank (Mass.)	$100
(11)	$0		$0

Source: Author's elaboration from Cencini and Rossi (2015).

pay Apple Inc. in California to purchase its products. Entries 8 to 13 regard the payment from Wells Fargo & Co. to Nantucket Bank. Households in California pay Seafarer Co. in Massachusetts to purchase seafood chowder. The result of the two payments is that income has been definitely spent. The balances at both commercial banks and at the Federal Reserve show that all payments have been settled and cleared.

Now, the previous is a limit case of bilateral payments. In real-world transactions, payments are managed on multilateral grounds. This means that in its daily activities, the central bank settles and clears a high volume of payments between a great number of commercial banks on behalf of their clients. Further, the previous example is based on a real-time gross settlement mechanism (RTGS). This kind of mechanism was adopted only recently by a number of central banks, including the oldest ones. For instance, as declared by the Bank of England (2018), such system of payment settlement was set up in the United Kingdom only in 1996:

> [m]ost payment systems in the UK use the Bank's RTGS system to settlement payments between their member banks and other institutions. On average day, the RTGS system settles around £500 billion between banks and other institutions – almost a third of the UK's annual gross domestic product (GDP).
>
> (Bank of England 2018)

The real-time gross settlement mechanism is just one among others currently adopted worldwide. In the United Kingdom, for instance, four are the systems of interbank payments, which are run by a number of companies: the CHAPS, the Bacs, the Faster Payment Service, and the Cheque & Credit Clearings. The Bank for International Settlements provides detailed descriptions of any payment system adopted by its member countries. Payment systems in the United Kingdom are processed, cleared, and settled as follows (Bank for International Settlements 2012b: 443–4). The CHAP works on a real-time gross basis and is managed by the CHAPS Clearing Company with an infrastructure of the central bank. The Bacs is a net settlement system that is run by Bacs Payment Schemes Ltd on a retail and deferred basis, thanks to which payments are cleared within three days. The Faster Payment Service is managed by Faster Payments Schemes Limited and settles payments on a retail, deferred basis, three times every day. The Cheque & Credit Clearings Company runs the Cheque & Credit Clearings system, settling payments in paper money. There are also other payment systems that facilitate, for instance, the withdrawal of cash from automatic teller machines and the payment via debit and credit cards. Moreover, CREST is a system that has been largely used to settle the transaction of securities since 2002 and that is managed by Euroclear UK & Ireland. Payment clearing in the United Kingdom is operated by four clearing houses – LCH.Clearnet Ltd., ICE Clear Europe Ltd., EuroCCP, and CME Clearing Europe – which deal with a variety of commodity products, credit default swaps, derivatives products, equities, fixed income, foreign exchange, futures, and options (Bank for International Settlement 2012b: 443–4).

As in the United Kingdom, the United States relies on a few mechanisms of interbank payment. Fund transfers in the United States are made through a number of payment mechanisms that work via cables, wires, or wireless. The modality and the timing of every transaction, which vary according to regulation, depend on the type of payment instrument. According to the Bank for International Settlements,

> [i]n the United States, interbank payments are processed and settled primarily through the following mechanisms: (1) cheque clearing, (2)

> ACH, (3) card networks, (4) same-day electronic funds transfer systems (Fedwire and CHIPS) and (5) the Federal Reserve's National Settlement Service (NSS). Using these mechanisms, banks exchange and settle payments directly with each other, through private sector clearing houses, through correspondents, or through the Federal Reserve.
>
> (BIS 2003: 440–1)

For the sake of explanation, a short overview shall be provided of the main payment mechanisms in the United States, drawing from the Bank for International Settlements (2003, 2012a). Retail payments are made through check clearing, ACH, and card networks. Large-value payments are processed by the Fedwire, the CHIPS, and the NSS.

Whenever checks are drawn and paid by the same financial institution, the settlement is made 'via accounting entries on the books of the paying institution' (BIS 2012a: 492). Most checks are deposited on third parties, though, for which reason checks are cleared and settled through interbank payment systems. These are made by a number of institutions. A good deal of interbank payments is processed directly by the paying and receiving parties; payments are also made through clearing houses and their networks or through the FED (BIS 2012a: 492).

The Federal Reserve processes automate clearing house transactions (ACH) to settle batch payments on a net basis. The payments are settled through the accounts of financial institutions held at the central bank.

> Wells Fargo & Company (NYSE: WFC) is the No. 1 Automated Clearing House (ACH) electronic payment originator among U.S. based financial institutions, according to NACHA – The Electronic Payments Association. In 2012, Wells Fargo originated 3.5 billion ACH payments – ranging from deposits such as payroll and Social Security to consumer payments for auto loans and insurance premiums.
>
> (www.wellsfargo.com, April 11, 2013)

The associations that manage credit cards, automated teller machines (ATM), and points of sale (POS) are responsible for communicating, authorizing, and settling interbank payments. Net payments are usually settled one or two days after the order is issued by the acquiring bank.

Large-value funds are transferred from one financial institution to another through major wire systems: the Fedwire Funds Transfer System (Fedwire) and the Clearing House Interbank Payments System (CHIPS). Whereas the Fedwire settles payments on a real-time gross basis, the CHIPS is run on a net basis.

Through the Federal Reserve National Settlement Service, payments are settled on a net basis through accounts held at the FED.

It is fundamental to observe here that, independently from the specific mechanism of clearing that is chosen, interbank payments must comply with the flow nature of bank money and avoid payments to be financed via money creation. As in the example of Table 1.4, the mechanism of inter-bank clearing must allow for payments to be financed out of the income formed through production, while money issued by commercial banks flows through the central bank and is transformed into national currency.

A cashless future?

Much has been written and said about money over the last centuries. Classical authors, for instance, thought of money as a commodity (see, for instance, Baumol and Becker 1950 on the outcome of the discussion about classical monetary theory). Yet, it is worth mentioning, without incurring into speculation, that Adam Smith was likely the first author in modern times to argue that money is 'altogether different from the goods which are circulated by means of it' (Smith 1776 [1981]: 289), for '[m]oney is neither a material to work upon, nor a tool to work with' (Smith 1776 [1981]: 295). Marx went as far as claiming that '[e]very one knows [. . .] that commodities have a common value-form which contrasts in the most striking manner with the motley natural forms of their use-values. I refer to the money-form' (Marx 1867 [1982]: 139, I).

Over the last century, at least, money has often been identified with banknotes and coins. Yet, this concept of money is challenged by technology, which is producing cashless societies – through, for instance, electronic instruments of payments. Sweden, for instance, will likely be the first country going cashless. Remarkably, the Bank of Sweden, which is the oldest central bank in the world, is guiding the country toward a no-cash future. For the sake of argument, a stylized balance sheet of central banks shall be proposed hereafter (Table 1.5). The assets of the central bank include securities and lending to depository institutions. The liabilities include banknotes and coins in circulation, commercial banks reserves, central bank reserves, and capital.

It is sure that a high number of cash payments are still made every day all over the world. The point here is that, if the central bank were to withdraw all banknotes and coins from circulation, global demand, expressed

Table 1.5 The stylized balance sheet of central banks

Federal Reserve			
Assets		*Liabilities*	
Securities held outright	. . .	Banknotes in circulation	. . .
Lending to depository institutions	. . .	Depository institutions reserves	. . .
		Capital and central bank reserves	. . .

Source: *author's elaboration from the Federal Reserve (2016b: 4).*

as total income, would remain unvaried. The same can be said in the case in which currency in circulation increased relative to checkable deposits. In our economies, where money is often identified with notes and coins, notes and coins are just a material tool used to represent nominal demand. Let us focus on this point.

Strange though it may appear, when the redemption of banknotes and coins in circulation is stopped by legal ruling, currency in circulation is not lost to the banking system. Think, for instance, of the replacement of the Italian lira with the euro. Over the last years, the Bank of Italy has redeemed Italian liras (banknotes and coins) held by those individuals who requested lira-euro exchanges before the deadline of February 28, 2012. Operations of redemption have been 'carried out by drawing on the funds the Bank of Italy had transferred to the State on 6 December 2011 – the equivalent value of all the lira currency still in circulation at the time' (Bank of Italy 2017). All the lira currency held by individuals who did not ask for redemption within the deadline of February 28, 2012, became scrap paper. Total income in the system did not decrease, though, since, by means of the Italian central bank, the purchasing power was transferred, in euros, from the holders of lira currency to the State. Indeed, the decrease in liras in circulation was matched by an increase in State bank accounts in euros.

Now, it must be observed that, even following an increase in currency in circulation, total income does not vary at all. Suppose a salary of $100 is credited on the bank accounts of households on behalf of Seafarer Co. As previously seen, Nantucket Bank enters wages on the Liabilities of its balance sheet; at the same time, the bank enters a corresponding debit of the same amount for Seafarer Co. Think now of the situation in which households withdraw a fraction of their deposits amounting to x dollars and hold them in cash. In this case, the households' gross income in the banking system – Nantucket Bank and the FED – remains unchanged. Nantucket Bank registers a reduction of x dollars in checkable deposits in the Liabilities of its own balance sheet and an equal reduction in reserves with the central bank. Meanwhile, on the Liabilities of its balance sheet, the central bank registers an increase in debit with regard to banknotes' holders (an increase in notes and coins in circulation) and a reduction in reserves with the commercial banking system. Hence, it can be seen that there is no change in global demand: income levels remain unaltered, independently of any consumer decision to maintain higher or lower levels of cash. Otherwise, the monetary base level is not affected by variations in currency in circulation, because the increase in banknotes is matched by an equal decrease in commercial banks' reserves with the central bank.

Every banking system can do without currency in circulation. From an economic viewpoint, in fact, cash levels do not impact at all on global demand. From a legal perspective, a reduction in the use of cash may help reduce illegal activities such as the ones conducted on the bootleg market. Be it as it may, the statistics of central banks often show that the number of cash transactions is decreasing over time. More than this, most transactions in terms of value are carried out through checks, debit, credit, and electronic payment instruments.

In a publication for the International Monetary Fund, Wheatley (2017: 32) observes that a number of countries are getting rid of cash: for instance, fewer and fewer banknotes are used by banks in Northern Europe, India has reduced currency in circulation by 86%, and, starting from 2020, coins will no longer be used in Korea. Electronic cards and mobile phones are substituting cash in a great number of payments: '[i]n the Netherlands, for instance, the number of card transactions surpassed cash [. . .] for the first time in 2015' (Wheatley 2017: 32). Yet, the rush to cashless banking systems is not proceeding everywhere at the same pace. Wheatley (2017: 32) acknowledges that in countries such as Austria, Germany, Japan, Singapore, and Switzerland, banknotes and coins will still abundantly be used for the future to come. The use of cash may well decline whenever new payment instruments come to the fore:

> 'Today we can say the same thing about modern communication technology as about the printing presses in the 17th century. Access to the Internet is widespread, and computers, smartphones, and tablets are household items. Thus, the conditions are ripe for launching more electronic payment forms', Cecilia Skingsley, deputy governor of Sweden's Riksbank, has said.
>
> (Wheatley 2017: 32)

Think, for instance, of the United States. In 1969 the first automated teller machine was installed by Chemical Bank in New York. The machine sort of innovated the habits of US individuals toward cash withdrawal. The diffusion of several types of payment instruments in the last decades changed those habits once more and, today, electronic means of payment are still changing consumers' payment habits. 'Recent research indicates that debit card, credit card, ACH, and check payments facilitated through the U.S. banking system amounted to over 144 billion payment transactions in 2015 with a value of almost $178 trillion' (U.S. Department of the Treasury 2017: 21).

Table 1.6 provides some statistics from the Federal Reserve of San Francisco (2016) on recent use of various payment instruments. On the one hand, data show that the number of cash transactions, despite decreasing from 2012 to 2015, were still significant in 2015, totaling about one third of all transactions. However, all cash transactions in 2015, in terms of value, represented only 9% of all payments made in the United States. In 2015, electronic means of payment were the most popular payment instrument,

Table 1.6 Payment instruments in the United States

Share of Transaction Number by Payment Instrument (%)						
	Cash	*Check*	*Credit*	*Debit*	*Electronic*	*Other*
2015	32	6	21	27	11	3
2012	40	7	17	25	7	4
Share of Value by Payment Instrument (%)						
	Cash	*Check*	*Credit*	*Debit*	*Electronic*	*Other*
2015	9	19	16	18	35	3
2012	14	19	16	18	27	5

Source: *Federal Reserve Bank of San Francisco (2016).*

followed by checks, debit instruments, and credit instruments. Also, whereas the share of value of cash transactions decreased from 2012 to 2015, the value of payments made through the other major payment instruments followed another trend. In particular, the value conveyed by checks, credit, and debit means did not change; remarkably, it did increase in the case of electronic instruments.

To sum up, we can therefore maintain that the need for the banking systems to rely on cash is not required for monetary economies to survive, whereas both factual and theoretical reasons stand up for the existence of commercial and central banks. It can be even argued that banking techniques are evolving toward perfection over time, especially thanks to informatics. For instance, the management of interbank payments conducted by the central bank – that is, the payments between all commercial banks and other institutions in the national monetary system – has substantially improved along the years. Yet, economic turmoil and bank panics are typical of modern history. Is there a way out of them? What can banks do to prevent them? As I shall argue later in the volume, the answer is strictly related to the existence of profit. Profit may turn out indeed to be of help in the way out of banking troubles. What is profit, then? Who does it accrue to? Is it globally nil or positive?

What room for profit?

So far, it has been shown that production always gives rise to a positive wage-income. Indeed, whenever goods and services are produced, wages are credited to workers as deposits in the books of commercial banks. At the same time, commercial banks balance their debt to income-earners with an equivalent credit on companies on whose behalf they pay wages. It turns out that the income formed through the payment of wages corresponds to the cost of production incurred by companies. Therefore, at this point, it should be clear that, whenever equality holds between the selling price of output and its productive costs, wage-holders shall be able to purchase the entire stock of produced goods and services. Serving as mere productive intermediaries, companies always channel goods and services from workers-producers to workers-consumers (to households, broadly speaking).

However, facts show that, seeking for their own remuneration, companies must also be conceived as income-holders. For instance, in 2016, the 500 largest corporations in the United States earned approximately $890 billion, with a 6% increase in total profits relative to the previous year (Wieczner 2017). As reported by *Fortune* (Wieczner 2017), for example, Apple gained $45.7 billion, amounting to 21% of its revenues:

> Apple still has more money on hand than it has so far figured out what to do with, to the tune of more than $250 billion in cash. Apple plans to return some $13 billion of that hoard to shareholders in the coming year in the form of dividends.

Among the top ten corporations in the country, Apple was followed by J. P. Morgan Chase, Berkshire Hathaway, Wells Fargo, Alphabet, Bank of America, Microsoft, Johnson & Johnson, Citigroup, and Altria Group.

Seeking for profits, companies usually aim to sell goods and services at a mark-up. In microeconomic terms, the profit made by a company is thus given by the excess of its monetary revenues over its monetary costs. Yet, as soon as companies are thought of as a set, things are not as easy (see Cencini and Schmitt 1977: 142–3; Cencini 2015). Indeed, once companies are conceived as a whole, the amount of income derived from the sale of produced output cannot exceed the sum of wages paid to wage-earners: no extra money can be made from the sale of output. Households' outgoings in the product market shall always correspond to the corporate costs sustained in the employment market. If, for instance, the whole of companies pays out wages to a total amount of $100 billion, wage-holders shall spend $100 billion, at the most, to purchase the whole product. Inevitably, corporate revenues shall be equal to corporate outgoings. Computed as the excess of revenues over costs, the corporate gain shall amount to $0.

As soon as companies are conceived of as a set, no positive difference is possible between corporate earnings and corporate costs. Understood as the excess of earnings over costs of production, the profit of companies, taken as a whole, shall always be nil. If it is true that profit, in microeconomic terms, is positive, the story is less straightforward as soon as companies are conceived as one single set. Does this mean that companies, taken as a whole, can make no profits? To understand the issue at hand, the reasoning must be further developed.

Suppose households at Nantucket produce ten tons of chowder, for which they are paid $100 by Seafarer Co. through the intermediation of Nantucket Bank. Suppose also that workers gratuitously produce two extra tons of chowder at the disposal of the company. In this case, profit is conceived as an excess product in terms of what is required by households for consumption. From the sale of ten tons of chowder – wage-goods – Seafarer Co. shall make $100 in revenues. Seafarer Co. shall also make a real profit of two tons of chowder – profit-goods – that shall turn out to be unsalable. The company shall seek to sell profit-goods, with no success, though. Wages being spent in the purchase of wage-goods, no monetary income shall be available in the system for the purchase of profit-goods. Should one infer that the monetary gains of the set of companies shall always be nil? The problem is not easily resolved. A journey through the history of economic thought may help clear up one's mind about the existence of profit (an argument in this direction was made by Cencini 2015).

Classical economists thought that the value of produced goods and services should be measured in the labor-time necessary to produce them. Also, the Classicals agreed that the value of output and its price cannot diverge from one another. In fact, the classical law of exchange states that goods must be exchanged in full compliance with the equality between exchanged values. Namely, if the production time of a product is one week, it shall be exchanged for those goods requiring an entire week to be produced, and vice versa. This means that, according to classical authors, the value of products, measured in labor-time, is determined within production, not through exchange. Indeed, exchange shall simply allow for the circulation of a certain number of products whose value is already known.

The equality between prices and values can also be found in neoclassical contributions. In this theoretical framework, the origin of output value is not to be found in production. It is in fact through exchange that, according to the neoclassical theory, values and prices are determined. Since Walras, neoclassical economists have always thought that the monetary prices of goods reflect a numerical ratio at which products are exchanged one for the others. Namely, 'the value of one table will be equal to the value of two chairs if the exchange ratio between tables and chairs is 1 table for 2 chairs, i.e. if the relative price of the table is 2 chairs' (Cencini 2015: 118, our translation). In the neoclassical framework, the value of produced goods is determined through exchange and coincides with relative prices. Hence, whereas classical writers think that value is determined by production, neoclassical authors believe it to be determined by (relative) exchange.

In the 20th century, Keynes carried out an important study of profits in accordance to the law of exchange (see, above all, Keynes 1930a,1930b). Labor being the sole factor of production, according to Keynes (1936), the value of total output must necessarily be measured in wage-units. One should then think of profit – and other non-wage incomes – to be but a substitution income; namely, an income that derives from wages.

Broadly speaking, the equality of values and prices has always been a law on which economists have always agreed. Yet, the law of exchange sets a great challenge: if prices are identical to values, how can one explain the existence of profits? Since the 18th century, many attempts have been made by economists worldwide to explain the origin and the nature of profit. Yet, as it shall be observed in the next two chapters, consensus has yet to emerge in this regard.

The volume shall then seek to explain the existence of profit in full compliance with the equality between prices and values. 'How can it be [. . .] that prices and values do coincide and that, nevertheless, positive profits do form?' (Cencini 2015: 118, our translation). It shall be argued that the origin of monetary and real profits can be explained once equal attention is paid to both production *and* exchange. The profits of companies, taken as a whole, are the effect of a new allocation of wages, initially paid to workers, from the hands of households to the hands of companies. Once profit has formed, it shall be argued that monetary wages included real wages and real profits. 'In these circumstances profit does not represent an increase in real wealth. Rather, the excess of price over value does not influence at all wealth formation. It represents nothing but a change in the allocation of wealth, as profits bite into wages' (Cencini and Schmitt 1977: 64, our translation). 'Income is not an *a posteriori* construct. [. . .] Being modern requires a shift from complementarity to inclusion' (Schmitt 1966: 266, our translation). The understanding of profit so conceived shall pave the way to the study of investment and to a number of considerations in terms of economic policy.

Chapter 2

Classical and neoclassical theories of profit

The beginning of modern political economy is to be traced back to the *Tableau économique* of Francois Quesnay (1758), to Adam Smith's *Inquiry into the Nature and Causes of the Wealth of Nations* (1776), and to David Ricardo's *On the Principles of Political Economy and Taxation* (1817). Prior to modern economic theories, as Deane puts it (1978: 1–2), the epochs of economic thought can be associated with classical Greek authors, medieval scholastics, and the mercantilists.

In ancient Greece,

> [w]ithout wages and interest [. . .] there could not be a theory of prices in any modern sense. Prices derive in one way or another from production costs, and production costs were not a visible function in the slave-owning household. So it remained for Aristotle to ask only whether prices were just or fair, a concern that would be central to economic thought for most of the next two thousand years.
>
> (Galbraith 1987: 13)

During the Middle Ages in Europe, the scholastics and the mercantilists developed the concept of a fair or just price or *justum pretium*, as they called it in Latin. The just price was conceived, by some, as the fair price that allows the buyer to maintain his or her status, or, by others, as the market price (on this, see, for instance, Hagenauer 1931; Schumpeter 1954 [1994]; De Roover 1958; Baldwin 1959; Deane 1978; Pasinetti 1986).

No systematic attempt to study profit was made before the 18th century (Deane 1978: 4; Pasinetti 1981; Galbraith 1987). The transition from the pre-theoretical to the theoretical level took place thanks to classical authors, who paid increasing attention to wages, profit, and capital. The industrial revolution was the phenomenon that drew the attention of economists to the study of profits and capital accumulation (see, for instance, Pasinetti 1981, 1986). In the 18th century, authors started developing some theories of value. As noted by Pasinetti (1986: 414), '[t]he approach to discussions on value changed dramatically towards the end of the eighteenth century.

From the ethical pronouncements on value, writers began to move on to *theories* of value'. Moreover,

> Over most of the modern life of economics [. . .] the theory of value and the theory of distribution [. . .] have been the ultimate concern. It is still thought that economics came of age when these two matters were tackled systematically in the latter part of the eighteenth century.
>
> (Galbraith 1987: 6)

In the 19th century, theorists 'narrowed themselves down to a choice between two quite different and alternative routes. Namely, the "objective" route of a cost-of-production and, more particularly, of a labour theory of value' (Pasinetti 1986: 414), which is to be identified with the classical school; 'and the "subjective" route of a "marginal utility" theory of value', or 'pure exchange economy' (Pasinetti 1986: 414), namely the theory that became to be known as neoclassical. What concepts of profit were proposed by the best minds of the last three centuries? Did economists share, from Adam Smith to David Ricardo, from Karl Marx to Léon Walras, a common theory of profit?

The old quest for the surplus

The first theories of profits were worked out in the 18th century, mainly through the contributions of the Physiocrats and the Classicals.

On the one hand, the Physiocrats were interested in the study of public policy 'with respect to trade and taxation; and to this end they fashioned the concept of an "economic order"' (Dobb 1973: 39–40). Accordingly, as claimed by Dobb (1973: 40), they were investigating on the 'physiology of economic society – with procedures and rules of its own to which governmental policy must be adapted if not subordinated'. The economic system of the Physiocrats was made up of three social classes: landowners; agricultural workers, the sole productive class; and artisans, who produced manufactured goods from raw materials. The latter two classes existed at subsistence level: their output continually reproduced so as to maintain 'productive consumption' over time. The sole net product was derived from nature and it was considered a surplus, a profit to be transferred to landowners, who consumed the product received from the other two classes. Quesnay (1758) represents this conception of the economy in his famous *Tableau économique*. Following a traditional reading of the *Tableau*, nature, through agricultural activity, supplies the net product necessary to restore the initial situation so that the circular process of production can start all over again.

On the other hand, the origin of the classical school, as well as the founding year of political economy, may be traced back to 1751, albeit economics, at that time, was considered to lie within the field of moral sciences. It was in 1751 that Adam Smith was appointed to a teaching position in logic at the University of Glasgow, where he also held the Chair of Moral Philosophy from 1752 to 1764. Smith sought to build an economic theory 'within the ambit of moral philosophy as a normative study of society' (Deane 1978: 13), where economic norms are related to a 'moral [. . .], a philosophical rather than a logical or mathematical discipline' (Deane 1978: 13). The classical school conceived individual interests and competition as the pillars of a 'well-ordered society' where 'each man works for others, while believing that he is working for himself' (Dobb 1973: 41). The Classicals as well as the Physiocrats were interested in normative economics, being 'philosophic system-builders concerned to establish the nature of the laws underlying the total socioeconomic order – as it was and as it ought to be' (Deane 1978: 5).

Classical authors, including Smith (see 1776), Jean-Baptiste Say (1821 [1971]), and David Ricardo (1817), conceived the society as divided into three social classes – namely laborers, capitalists, and landlords – and, accordingly, they studied the subdivision of national output into wages, profit, and rent. Therefore, 'it is not too fanciful to argue that the roots of the [. . .] theory' of profit 'may be observed in the work of certain classical economists' (Wood 1975: 10–11).

One of the first classical inquiries into the existence of profits was made by Smith in 1776 (see Meek 1954 on this regard). According to the classical thinker, '[i]n that original state of things, which precedes [. . .] the accumulation of stock, the whole produce of labour belongs to the labourer' (Smith 1776 [1981]: 82). Once it accrues to specific individuals, a stock shall be used as a means to carry out productive activities and, ultimately, to make a profit (Smith 1776 [1981]: 66). Through the exchange of produced goods, profit shall be made by those who advanced the stock.

> In exchanging the complete manufacture either for money, for labour, or for other goods, over and above what may be sufficient to pay the price of the materials, and the wages of the workmen, something must be given for the profits of the undertaker of the work who hazards his stock in this adventure.
>
> (Smith 1776 [1981]: 66)

Hence, as turns out from the *Wealth of Nations*, laborers earn wages and the capitalists earn profits. 'The revenue derived from labour is called wages. That derived from stock, by the person who manages or employs it, is called profit' (Smith 1776 [1981]: 69). Profits are conceived as the excess of revenues over the costs sustained by the capitalist. 'Though the manufacturer has his wages advanced to him by his master, he, in reality, costs him no expense, [. . .] wages being generally restored, together with a profit' (Smith 1776 [1981]: 330). Wages and profits are conceived as revenues that differ the one from the other. 'In the price of commodities [. . .] the profits of stock constitute a component part altogether different from the wages of labour, and regulated by quite different principles' (Smith 1776 [1981]: 66).

In the *Wealth of Nations*, the price of products is always made of three components: wages, rents, and profits.

> [T]he whole price of any commodity must still finally resolve itself into some one or other, or all of those three parts; as whatever part of it remains after paying the rent of the land, and the price of the whole labour employed in raising, manufacturing, and bringing it to market, must necessarily be profit to somebody.
>
> (Smith 1776 [1981]: 69)

Being made of three parts, any price allows for the remuneration of the three social classes, which live on wages, profits, and rent. 'In the price of flour or meal, we must add to the price of the corn, the profits of the miller, and the wages of his servants' (Smith 1776 [1981]: 68). Yet, compared to wages and profits, rents appear to be of less importance: '[w]ages and profit accordingly make up, upon most occasions, almost the whole of their high price' (Smith 1776 [1981]: 191).

Smith's cogent contribution met with great success at the time of its publication in 1776. Nonetheless, another Scottish author had already advanced some ideas on profit a few years before. Indeed, James Steuart was one of the very first authors to write about the concept of profit. In Book II, Chapter VIII, of his *Inquiry into the Principles of Political Economy* (1767), Steuart classified profit into three categories, which he called 'positive', 'relative', and 'compound'. Positive profit corresponds to an increase in the general wealth of society, whereas relative profit turns out to have an impact on the allocation of wealth between individuals:

> Positive profit, implies no loss to any body; it results from an augmentation of labour, industry, or ingenuity, and has the effect of swelling or augmenting the public good. [. . .] Relative profit, is what implies a loss to somebody, it marks a vibration of the balance of wealth between parties, but implies no addition to the general stock.
>
> (Steuart 1767: 206, Vol. 1)

Compound profit was conceived by Steuart as a combination of the other two, which may happen to exist both at the same time. 'The compound is easily understood; it is that species of profit [. . .] which is partly relative, and partly positive. I call it compound, because both kinds may subsist inseparably in the same transaction' (Steuart 1767: 206, Vol. 1). The work of James Steuart never attracted as much attention as the contributions of major classical political economists, such as Smith, Say, and Ricardo.

It must be observed that the division into social classes is a *fil rouge* of classical writings, where profit is usually conceived as the income of the capitalist class. Yet, profit acquires a broader sense in Jean-Baptiste Say's *Treatise on Political Economy*, first published in French in 1803 – the English translation dates back to 1821. Profits, in the *Treatise*, are conceived as the revenues of each individual as well as the revenues of each social class. On the one hand, the national revenue is made up of the total revenues made by individuals. 'The whole amount of profit derived by an individual from his land, capital, and industry, within the year, is called his annual revenue. The aggregate of the revenues of all the individuals, whereof a nation consists, is its national revenue' (Say 1821 [1971]: 318). On the other hand, the total value of the product was thought to be subdivided into three portions, or three kinds of profit, each corresponding to the income of the class that receives it (see Say 1821 [1971]: 317). Landowners receive the 'profit of land' and at times they distribute it to the 'farmer'. The capitalists, who advance or lend capital, receive their quota of income, which is called 'profit of capital'. Workers receive an income called 'profit of labour'.

Say argued that, through production, individuals make profits according to the value added by them to the product:

> in whatever class of industry a person is engaged, he subsists upon the profit he derives from the additional value, or portion of value, no matter in what ratio, which his agency attaches to the product he is at work upon. The total value of products serves in this way to pay the profits of those occupied in production.
>
> (Say 1821 [1971]: 68–9)

In individual terms, the profit of someone was conceived by Say as someone else's loss (Say 1821 [1971]: 307). In this context, profits were conceived as the difference between income and expenditure: '[t]he profits of an individual are limited to the excess of his income above his expenditure, which expenditure, indeed, forms the revenue of other persons' (Say 1821 [1971]: 318). Yet, throughout his life, Say was never able to provide a proper explanation of the laws underlying the existence of profit.

In the first decades of the 19th century, David Ricardo surged as one of the most influential classical economists. Ricardo, in the *Foreword* to his *Principles of Political Economy* (1817), argued that the object of investigation of economics is the determination of the laws governing the distribution of income. This was identified as 'the starting point common to all the economic theories of income distribution' (Pasinetti 2000: 188), from a perspective that goes beyond the physiocratic conception of the natural system, and according to which the product of nature was regarded 'as "by far" less important than those connected with the process of production' (Pasinetti 1981: 6). It should be observed that Ricardo's intellectual contributions are contained in *The Works and Correspondence of David Ricardo*, edited by Piero Sraffa in collaboration with Maurice Dobb (1951–73 [2004]), as well as in Pierluigi Porta's book from 1992. As Porta recalls (1992: x), the collection edited by Sraffa does not contain Ricardo's *Notes on Malthus's Measure of Value*, which were rediscovered in 1943, together with the *Mill-Ricardo Papers*. From the content of these papers, it emerges that Ricardo thought that goods do have an absolute value (see Porta 1992: x). Yet, failing to find it, Ricardo grew convinced of the 'impossibility of attaining a perfect measure' of value (Porta 1992: xiv).

A well-known interpretation of the Ricardian economic system is given by Pasinetti (1960). See also, among others, Davidson (1959), Barkai (1959, 1965), Samuelson (1959), Garegnani (1960 [1972]), and Casarosa (1978). However, Ricardo's many interpreters have had difficulty in concisely stating his complete system, 'and the reason lies in the peculiarity of some of the concepts he used which are not always defined in an unambiguous way' (Pasinetti 1960: 78). Ricardo has a number of merits. For instance, he largely carried out a 'differential theory of rent' (Pasinetti 2000: 189) – although it had already been proposed by James Anderson in 1777 (Pasinetti 2000: 385) – the 'principle of diminishing returns' (Pasinetti 2000: 189), and a 'subsistence theory of wages' (Deane 1978: 62). In line with other classical economists, Ricardo also sought to study the relation between wages, profits, and rents.

Global output, in Ricardo's analysis, is made of the aggregation of wages and profit. In particular, as stated by Garegnani (1960 [1972]: 9–10):

> [t]he quota constituting wages is determined when [. . .] wages are fixed at a given level [. . .]: the excess constitutes profits. [. . .] The relationship between the value of such excess and the value of the entirety of goods attributed to workers as wages determines the rate of profit.

Interestingly, rents from land are not conceived on the same conceptual level as wages and profits – a peculiarity of the Ricardian system. Rents indeed are thought as included into profits: deriving from profits, rents are an income of distribution. As argued in *An Essay on The Influence of a Low Price of Corn on the Profits of Stock*, '[i]n treating on the subject of the profits of capital, it is necessary to consider the principles which regulate the rise and fall of rent; as rent and profits [. . .] have a very intimate connexion with each other' (Ricardo 1815 [2004]: 9, Vol. 4). 'Rent [. . .] is in all cases a portion of the profits previously obtained [. . .]. It is never a new creation of revenue, but always part of a revenue already created' (Ricardo 1815 [2004]: 19, Vol. 4).

Following an intense exchange of opinions with Thomas Malthus, Robert Torrens, and Edward West, among others, Ricardo came to believe that the value of the product is made of two components. The first part of value corresponds to the labor bestowed in the product, and it is called wages. The second part of value corresponds to the value of capital, added by the capitalists and measured as accumulated labor. Indeed, in the *Note on Absolute Value and Exchangeable Value* (1823 [2004]), Ricardo argued:

> [t]hat part of the value of a commodity which is required to compensate the labourer for the labour he has bestowed upon it is called wages, the remaining part of its value is retained by the master and is called profit. It is a remuneration for the accumulated labour which it was necessary for him to advance, in order that the commodity might be produced.
>
> (Ricardo 1823 [2004]: 380, Vol. 4)

The classical concepts of profit never merged into a unitary theory, and over time, they were consigned to oblivion by the great majority of economists. In the second half of the 19th century, the theory of profit proposed by Karl Marx – the theory of surplus value – drew the attention of a great number of intellectuals.

An old impasse

In his *Capital* (1867 [1982]), Karl Marx investigated the nature of profit and the laws of its monetization. Yet, as it shall be observed hereafter, Marx was not able to explain the existence of monetary profits.

Marx rejected the idea that profit is made through exchange, as argued for instance by Adam Smith and Thomas Tooke. Indeed, in the *Capital*, the exchange of goods does not give rise to profit, but rather to the distribution of values. To support his argument, Marx provided the following example:

> A sells wine worth £40 to B, and obtains from him in exchange corn to the value of £50. A has converted his £40 into £50, has made more money out of less, and has transformed his commodities into capital. Let us examine this a little more closely. Before the exchange we had £40 of wine in the hands of A, and £50 worth of corn in those of B, a total value of £90. After the exchange we still have the same total value of £90. The value in circulation has not increased by one iota; all that has changed is its distribution between A and B.
>
> (Marx 1867 [1982]: 265, Vol. 1)

Being impossible for profit to arise from exchange, the subdivision of total income into wages and profit, a concept inherited by Marx from Ricardo, was sought out at another level. Indeed, Marx wrote: '[w]e have shown that surplus-value cannot arise from circulation [. . .]. [C]an surplus-value originate anywhere else than in circulation [. . .]?' (Marx 1867 [1982]: 268, Vol. 1).

According to Marx (1867 [1982]: 317, Vol. 1), capital and profit are strictly related the one to the other (on this, see also Garegnani 1960 [1972]). The Prussian author conceived capital as subdivided into two parts. The first part, made up of the 'means of production, i.e. the raw material, the auxiliary material and the instruments of labour', was defined as 'constant capital'. The second part was defined as 'labour power', made of 'those mental and physical capabilities existing in the physical form, the living personality, of a human being, capabilities which he sets in motion whenever he produces a use-value of any kind', and which, all together, were defined as 'variable capital' (Marx 1867 [1982]: 271, Vol. 1). To the eyes of Marx, when profit is made, capital comprises a constant part, a variable part, and profit itself. Therefore, profit would originate from capital and would feed it. Further on, we shall develop a critical assessment of the theory of surplus value, drawing on Cencini and Schmitt (1977).

What makes it impossible for profit to form through the circulation of goods is the 'law of exchange', a law shared by classical authors according to which heterogeneous products can be exchanged between each other only provided they have equal values. In particular, price and value are necessarily equal one to the other, for the price is the monetary expression of value. It is Marx himself who wrote this explicitly:

> Price, taken by itself, is nothing but the *monetary expression of value*. [. . .] Looking somewhat closer into the monetary expression of value, or what comes to the same, the conversion of value into price, you will find that it is a process by which you give to the *values* of all commodities an *independent* and *homogeneous form*.
>
> (Marx 1898 [1969]: 16, emphasis in original)

Therefore, the direct consequence of the law of exchange is that profit cannot form during the circulation of goods, since the exchange of equivalents gives rise to no monetary gain of any sort.

Given this state of things, Marx came to believe that the origin of surplus value lies in the productive process. 'The value of a commodity is expressed in its price before it enters into circulation, and it is therefore a pre-condition of circulation, not its result' (Marx 1867 [1982]: 260, Vol. 1).

In this context, human labor is conceived as the sole source of value. Wages correspond to a share of total output value, the remaining part being equal to monetary profit. Indeed, according to a 'conventional view' (on this, see Wood 1975: 11–12), both Ricardo and Marx, among others, conceived profit as a residual between output per capita and the subsistence wage. (On this, see, for instance, Robinson 1942; Kaldor 1956). This interpretation of the *Capital*, however, is not the only one to be found in economic literature; in this regard see, for instance, Wood 1975). Marx attempted to explain such division of the product into wage-goods and profit-goods, or monetary wages and monetary profit, by introducing a particular commodity: labor power.

Labor power was identified as a particular commodity sold by each worker in exchange for monetary wages. By spending wages, then, workers shall purchase subsistence goods they have themselves produced. Wages measure the value of those goods or revenue that shall be purchased by workers for their subsistence. Money is 'in the hands of the worker as the money form of his wage, [. . .] i.e. as the money form of the revenue that he receives from the [. . .] sale of his labour-power' (Marx 1867 [1982]: 515, Vol. 2).

Further, workers produce a stock of goods – profit-goods – that is gratuitously appropriated by the capitalists. Therefore, surplus value or profit was conceived by Marx as the 'difference between total labor and labor absorbed by wages' (Cencini and Schmitt 1977: 20, our translation). Since real wages represent that part of the total product that ends up in the hands of workers and allows for their subsistence, real profit is that part of the total product that ends up in the hands of the capitalists. '[T]his appropriation is permitted by the particular nature of the labor-power commodity' (Cencini and Schmitt 1977: 19, our translation).

In the *Capital*, real profit forms during the productive process, whereas its monetary realization must somehow take place through the circulation of goods. Yet, Marx acknowledged that surplus value cannot form from the sale of profit-goods. The wage-fund, the capital used to pay out wages, is recovered by the capitalists once wage-income is spent by workers in the purchase of wage-goods. It follows that, since capital reproduces and maintains at a constant level, profit-goods are unsalable. Indeed, in this reproductive process, there is no way for monetary profit to form out of the expenditure of wages. 'Thus the question is not: where does surplus-value come from? But rather: where does the money come from which it is turned into?' (Marx 1867 [1982]: 404, Vol. 2). Although Marx made some further attempts to understand the nature of monetary profit, the problem was left unsolved.

From approximately the 1870s onwards, Léon Walras's general equilibrium theory came to the fore as an alternative to classical economic theories. Walras's theory marked the beginning of what, at the present time, is known as mainstream or orthodox economics. According to Pasinetti (1981: 12), the success of the neoclassical theory is likely to be due to the combination of two features of that time, namely Marx's *Capital* and the 'widespread social unrest' in Europe. On the one hand, Marx's vision of the capitalistic system as a transitory phase from the Middle Ages to a future socialist system had distanced economic theory from the Classical theory, which had 'accepted the society in which they lived as part of the order of Nature' (Pasinetti 1981: 12). On the other hand, '[i]t is worth recalling that the whole of Europe had just been under the impact of shivering revolutionary waves', such as the formation of the first Socialist International in 1864, and 'the first communist revolutionary attempt ever to be made (the Paris Commune, March–May 1871)' (Pasinetti 1981: 13). These two features were likely to be perceived by the bourgeoisie as a threat to the capitalist system, and hence to the existence of the bourgeoisie itself. It should also be noted that, laying socio-political reasons aside, the success of the neoclassical theory was due to the failure of classical authors to carry out a convincing theory of value. At the end of the 19th century, the neoclassical theory seemed to be a breath of fresh air in economic ideas.

Profit at the outset of the neoclassical theory

There is a fundamental difference between classical and neoclassical theories: classical authors generally considered labor to be the only factor of production and, broadly speaking, to be excluded from the product market; in the neoclassical theory, labor is one among many other productive inputs, and it becomes a good like any other. From 1874 onwards, indeed, labor is no longer thought to be the sole factor of production, and, as well as other productive factors, it is given a price. All productive factors, including labor, are thereby conceived as if they were commodities. Thus, Walras undertook a fusion between the product market and the market for productive inputs. This means that, in the neoclassical theory, there is no causal relationship between labor and products. Money – the 'numéraire' – is also conceived as a commodity to be exchanged in the same way as any other product. Also, a fusion does occur between production and exchange. In the classical theory, production precedes exchange, for the value of output is thought to be created within the productive phase. In the neoclassical theory, the prices of productive factors as well as product prices are made to depend on the interaction between supply and demand during the exchange phase (Schmitt 1986: 107).

The neoclassical theory is based on the concept of economic equilibrium, within which price determination takes place. Following Walras (1874 [1965]: 225), the hypotheses underlying equilibrium in exchange are as follows: the demand for and the supply of production factors ('productive services') are equal, their price being stationary; and the demand for goods equals the supply of goods, their price being stationary. A third characteristic concerns instead equilibrium in production: the selling price of goods and the costs of productive factors are equal. Walras viewed equilibria as 'ideal' states, both because, in his opinion, the selling price of a product is never equal to its production cost, and because the supply and demand of factors and products are never equal.

With respect to his predecessors from the classical school, Walras introduced something of an innovation into his profit analysis: first and foremost, profit has a tendency to disappear. Let us consider the concept of equilibrium and its implications with regard to profit. Walras believed that the 'normal' state of things is to be found in equilibrium, a situation 'towards which things spontaneously tend under a regime of free competition in exchange and in production' (Walras 1874 [1965]: 224). In this theoretical economic state,

> if the selling price of a product exceeds the cost of the productive services for certain firms and a profit results, entrepreneurs will flow towards this branch of production or expand their output, so that the quantity of the product [on the market] will increase, its price will fall, and the difference between price and cost will be reduced.
>
> (Walras 1874 [1965]: 225)

A search for maximum benefits drives the producer-seller to sell goods to the buyer-consumer. Yet general economic equilibrium theory does not allow for the existence of profit. In fact, the hypothesis that underlies the neoclassical model of general equilibrium, and according to which companies operate in conditions of perfect competition, implies that selling prices are equal to production costs: since there is no positive margin between the selling price and the cost of production, it is impossible for profit to form (see, for instance, Ullmo 1969: 8–9).

Walras's theory had an enormous influence on the generations of economists succeeding him. Marshall was an example of this. Despite differences in interests, the technique used by neoclassical authors in all periods differs in no fundamental way from that employed by Walras and, earlier still, by Cournot: the technique of differential calculus applied to economics (see Hicks 1934: 338). One of the most important hypotheses that usually underlies the neoclassical models is to assume that an economy operates in a state of perfect competition. According to Walras, if the equilibrium is perfectly competitive, profit disappears. The entrepreneur is remunerated for managing the productive process. Marshall (1920 [1961]: 138–9) identified such remuneration as the reward of the organization (see Hicks 1934: 338).

Over the 20th century, Walrasian price theory was extended to various fields of application. Among the most eminent formalizations of economic equilibrium theory, applied to utility theory, are those of Mosak (1944), Arrow and Debreu (1954), and Debreu (1959) (see also Pasinetti 1986 and Mas-Colell, Whinston, and Green 1995). These are known as pure exchange, or pure preference models, employed in the framework of the subjective theory of value to represent a pure exchange economy, in which price determination takes place during the exchange phase. Other economists, including Pasinetti (1981, 1986), prefer to call it a pure utility or pure preference economy, since it is a single individual's search for maximum utility or satisfaction that motivates the exchange. Such an optimization problem is set in every microeconomic test to establish the minimum expenditure necessary to buy a basket of goods that will provide an individual with a given level of satisfaction or utility.

It is worth mentioning that, once the model is solved, it would appear that relative prices are determined. Whereas '[t]o determine also the absolute level of prices, one should at this point go on to introduce money' (Pasinetti 1986: 418). However, this issue is likely to deserve further study. Some authors argue that, in the neoclassical theory, the general level of prices, so-called absolute or monetary prices, is indeterminate – in other words, the total value of production remains indeterminate – and that relative prices cannot be determined, either (see, for instance, Schmitt 1984, 1996a; Cencini 1982, 2001, 2015; Schmitt and De Gottardi 2003).

Profit and interest: a comment

The existence of profit allows companies to pay interest to capital owners (see e.g. Ullmo 1969: 28). According to Adam Smith, interest is that part of profit necessary to remunerate the owner of capital.

> The revenue or profit arising from stock naturally divides itself into two parts; that which pays the interest, and which belongs to the owner of the stock, and that surplus part which is over and above what is necessary for paying the interest.
>
> (Smith 1776 [1981]: 657)

Generally speaking, all economists share the idea that interest is the remuneration of the owner of the capital. Such a remuneration is legitimated by the fact that society benefits from the increase in physical production that is enabled by the use of capital. However, some questions remain controversial.

First, although it is a common belief that profit and interest are bounded together, economists disagree with regard to the nature of this relationship. Obstacles arise as soon as a definition of profit is attempted. In fact, without finding a shared answer, economic theory puts the question as to whether profit belongs to the capitalist, understood as the owner of the mediums provided to run the company's activities; to the entrepreneur, understood as the figure managing business activities or providing the funds and mediums to run them; or to the company, an abstract entity. It is, in fact, very difficult to clarify this matter, notwithstanding the contributions of notable researchers into interest, among whom are Smith, Ricardo, Walras, Wicksell, Böhm-Bawerk, Myrdal, Ohlin, and Keynes. In order to explain the role of the capitalist, the entrepreneur, and the company, the nature of the income made by each of them must be investigated. That is, it might be of high importance to establish whether their incomes are newly created, i.e. production incomes, or whether they are derived or distributed incomes, i.e. of substitution. In other words, it might be necessary to investigate *how* profit forms in the hands of companies, entrepreneurs, and capitalists. Such an investigation is an old and controversial one in economic theory.

According to classical authors, or at least according to the English classical school, it is considered an established fact that profit is positive. So far as classical economists are concerned, the existence of a positive profit allows interest to be paid to the capitalist-entrepreneur-company. It is thereby company profit that allows the payment of interest to the capitalist. Walras believed that the classical reasoning in this regard is mistaken.

> The theory of interest, especially that of the English School, [. . .] fails to distinguish between the figure of the capitalist and the figure of the entrepreneur. [. . .] That is why the term profit, as they use it, signifies simultaneously interest on capital and profit of enterprise.
>
> (Walras 1874 [1965]: 423)

According to the neoclassical theory, a distinction needs to be drawn between the capitalist, understood as the individual who receives interest on capital, and the entrepreneur-company. To the eyes of Walras, interest is the profit of the capitalist. 'Profits in the sense of interest charges on capital is defined as "a remuneration for the abstinence of the capitalist who has saved the capital"' (Walras 1874 [1965]: 423). From this viewpoint, the role of the entrepreneur coincides with that of the company and should be distinguished from that of the capitalist. Walras maintained that the surplus profit of the entrepreneur-company system is null, since the profit of one individual corresponds to the loss of another.

> So far as profit is concerned, in the sense of profit of enterprise [. . .], the English School fails to see that it is the correlative of possible loss, that it is subject to risk, that it depends upon exceptional and not upon normal circumstances, and that theoretically it ought to be left to one side.
>
> (Walras 1874 [1965]: 423)

Walras's reasoning has been applied to the neoclassical theory of production and growth, according to which the 'cost' of capital coincides with the profit-interest of the capitalist. In this theoretical environment, entrepreneur-company's profit is considered nil.

Thus, classical and neoclassical theories do not draw a net distinction between the roles of the capitalist, of the entrepreneur, and of the company. In point of fact, even minimal reasoning and observation of our daily reality should be enough to raise doubts regarding the classical and neoclassical theories of profit and interest. It is by no means rare for the entrepreneur to be a company manager who receives a wage-income, or a company shareholder who receives dividends. It is true, of course, that dividends originate in profit. But such profit does not belong directly to the entrepreneur.

Generally speaking, entrepreneurs benefit only when some measure of profit is distributed to them through the payment of dividends. It is therefore reasonable to suppose that the figures of the entrepreneur and of the company should be conceptually differentiated one from the other. At first sight, the entrepreneur's income would appear to belong to the production income category, inasmuch as it is wage-income; on the other hand, recipients of dividends, including the entrepreneur, receive an income that is most probably a substitution income, since it derives from profit. What has been noted for the entrepreneur applies equally to the capitalist, who might well be either a manager or simply a company shareholder. The interest received by the capitalist may well derive from profit, being thus a distributed income as well as dividends. However, the origin of profit as company income is still to be explained. By failing in this, classical and neoclassical theories alike fail to satisfy the need to explain the nature of incomes accruing to the entrepreneur, to the capitalist, and to the company.

Profit and contemporary neoclassical models

Contemporary neoclassical theory unfolds around at least two lines of research: the theory of economic growth and the theory of output fluctuations. Both areas of research have been developed upon the neoclassical theory of distribution; that is, upon hypotheses concerning the subdivision of output into different income categories. For full studies of contemporary neoclassical economics see, for instance, Solow (2000), Romer (2001), and Mankiw (2015), from which we draw some causes for reflection in the analysis that follows. It shall be noted that the assumptions of neoclassical models have not backed out of criticism in the past. As profit is concerned, no significant progress has been made in neoclassical models since the end of the 19th century.

Economic growth and output fluctuations

Economic growth pertains to one of the most important and fascinating areas of economic theory since the 1950s. Classical authors had already sought to study those conditions that would allow output to grow over time. Yet, from the end of the 19th century through the first half of the 20th century, economic analysis developed on the basis of static or short-run considerations. The neoclassical theory of general economic equilibrium and Keynes's research represent the most important examples of this tendency. The focus of neoclassical authors during the early days was the determination of relative prices by means of equation-based systems. The early versions of the theory of marginal utility and marginal productivity also left no space for considerations of a dynamic type. As it shall be observed further on in the volume, Keynes's work was frequently criticized by modern authors of economic growth, inasmuch as Keynes studied employment trends in the short-run, rather than analyzing its evolution in the mid- to long-term.

Harrod's and Domar's studies of economic activity over the long-run (see Harrod 1939, 1948; Domar 1946) were, instead, a starting point for two different lines of thinking: the neoclassical theory of distribution and growth – including the neoclassical interpretations of Keynes's *General Theory* (1936) – and the post-Keynesian theory of distribution and growth. The neoclassical theory of distribution evolved to satisfy formal requirements, so as to facilitate the study of production functions (analogous with utility functions) through mathematical analysis. The subdivision of income into wages and profit, an idea inherited from classical times by neoclassical economists, is dictated essentially by formal requirements taken for granted: the term 'profit' has even fallen into disuse in traditional economic theory; in its place, neoclassical economists favor the use of the word 'interest'.

Nowadays, research on income distribution is often carried out on econometric, rather than on theoretical, grounds. Also, it must be observed that income distribution and growth is the object of study of welfare economists. As Mishan (1981: 3) puts it, welfare theory 'can be defined as the study of criteria for ranking alternative economic situations on the scale of better or worse', and it 'implies "ought" propositions that derive ultimately from the ethics of society', its purposes being, for instance, those of reaching 'high employment levels', guaranteeing 'the free movement of goods and factors', and pursuing 'economic and social stability'. Since the times of Edgeworth and Pareto, and particularly over the last forty years, welfare economics has greatly improved. Notable contributions in the field have in fact tried to enhance the discourse by adding the human factor. Examples of such improvements are Sen (1970, 1971) on the 'impossibility of a Paretian liberal', Peacock and Rowley's 1972 article against Pareto optimality, Sen's 1977 'Rational Fools', and Hirschman's 1984 work on 'human endowments' and 'tensions'. See also, for instance, Atkinson (1975, 1980, 2011, 2015), Sen (1992, 1994, 1997), Cohen, Piketty, and Saint-Paul (2002), Atkinson and Piketty (2010), and Galbraith (2012, 2014). Interestingly, empirical research has been carried out so as to understand increasing inequality and decreasing growth rates in a number of countries and regions (see, for instance, Gordon's 2016 account of the US economy).

Neoclassical growth theory is therefore more recent than Walrasian price theory and the theories of marginal utility and marginal productivity. The entire theory of growth was developed with the aim of studying long-run trends in national output, isolating short-run fluctuations from such trends. Therefore, the kernel of modern neoclassical theory is the growth of potential output. The reasons why economists distinguish between short-run phenomena and long-run trends are also important. According to mainstream economics, short-run output fluctuations are thought to be determined by aggregate demand, which also affects the price of output in the long-term.

Output and prices in the short-run are thought to depend on aggregate supply. On the one hand, aggregate demand shifts, for instance, following changes in the money supply, in government spending, in taxes, in net exports, and in the economic expectations of consumers and companies; on the other hand, aggregate supply is thought to be affected, for example, by changes in the price of productive factors, in supply shocks, and in government and fiscal regulations (see e.g. Mishkin 2016).

The features of the neoclassical model were developed with the aim of solving the Ramsey (1928) problem. 'The first problem I propose to tackle is this: how much of its income should a nation save?' (Ramsey 1928: 543). Ramsey's model represented a theoretical economy managed by an immortal planner who maximizes utility over an infinite period of time, given a particular technology. A large number of companies faithfully follow the plan of a single planner. There are two well-known versions of Ramsey's problem: the version described above, i.e. with a centralized or planned economy, and the version with a decentralized economy, in which companies act freely in perfect competition. Be that as it may, in both cases the economy follows an equilibrium path.

Growth models may be divided in various categories, each one delineated by an elevated level of related research. The main groups of models are the following.

The *Solow growth model* (1955–6), or basic neoclassical model of growth. One of the main features of this model is technical progress, which is considered as exogenous to the economic system. Individuals' choices and the behavior do not affect the stock of capital in the hands of companies (see also Swan 1956).

Infinite-horizon and overlapping-generations models

See, for instance, Allais (1947), Cass (1965), Koopmans (1965), Diamond (1965), Modigliani (1966), and Blanchard and Fischer (1989). These models usually assume the existence of a representative household, a representative firm, and a social planner. The stock of capital is endogenously determined by utility functions. This means that households, seeking to maximize their utility, shall determine the quantity of savings to be supplied to companies.

New growth theory

One of the main features of new growth theory is the inclusion of human capital and technical knowledge. 'There are two kinds of capital, [. . .] in the system: physical capital that is accumulated and utilized in production under a familiar neoclassical technology, and human capital that enhances the productivity of both labor and physical capital, and that is accumulated'

(Lucas 1988: 39). Another important feature is that technological progress is taken as endogenous. See, for instance, Romer (1986) and Lucas (1988) See also Vercelli (1991).

Money and growth

Generally, little is said concerning money in neoclassical models of growth. Neoclassical models are based on the concept of commodity-money. The literature is full of examples of this tendency. For instance, Lucas (1988: 6) states: 'I will [. . .] be abstracting from all monetary matters, treating all exchange as though it involved goods-for-goods'. However, a small number of neoclassical authors must be acknowledged as having included money in their models (for an in-depth view, see, for instance, Tobin 1955, 1965; Orphanides and Solow 1990).

If, on the one hand, economists pay great attention to the concept of economic growth, on the other hand, research into the short-run has in no sense been abandoned. It is in fact true that, particularly from the 1980s onwards, the so-called fluctuation theory has achieved great success. The theory of output fluctuations subdivides into two lines of research, though sharing the same methodology. On the one hand, real-business-cycle theory is based on the idea that output levels vary cyclically, following real shocks. On the other hand, new Keynesian theory represents the most significant attempt to formalize Keynes's *General Theory* and, therefore, to study the possibility that output fluctuations are the result of nominal (monetary) shocks. Although the basic hypotheses are diametrically opposed, both theories resort to the use of so-called models of general economic equilibrium, these being of a stochastic and dynamic type (DSGE models). The use of such models in studying output fluctuations has been criticized by many non-mainstream authors, but – and this is not without significance – these models have also met the opposition of notable neoclassical authors. For example, Solow's criticism of DSGE models (2010: 12) is well known:

> I do not think that the currently popular DSGE models pass the smell test. They take it for granted that the whole economy can be thought about as if it were a single, consistent person or dynasty carrying out a rationally designed, long-run plan, occasionally disturbed by unexpected shocks, but adapting to them in a rational, consistent way [. . .]. The protagonists of this idea make a claim to respectability by asserting that it is founded on what we know about microeconomic behavior, but I think that this claim is generally phony. The advocates no doubt believe what they say, but they seem to have stopped sniffing or to have lost their sense of smell altogether.
>
> (Solow 2010: 12)

As noted by David Romer (2001: 174), the subdivision into the two types of fluctuation theories is an 'oversimplification', because it omits the possibility that '*real non-Walrasian* theories' exist. According to the American author, under the hypothesis that nominal shocks have no effect on output fluctuation, output variations might potentially be explained by taking a distance ('departures') from the traditional Walrasian model. Among aspects to be considered, he includes 'imperfect competition, externalities, asymmetric information', and so on. Interesting is his opinion (Romer 2001: 174) that there are many more ways of approaching macroeconomics than those that exist at present.

While the neoclassical theory of growth sets out to study the long-run evolution of output, the neoclassical theory of the medium-run is based on the idea that output fluctuates regularly, following cycles with high and low points that alternate with each other over very brief intervals of time. More specifically, real-business-cycle (RBC) theory studies year-to-year increases and decreases in employment and output (see, for instance, Long and Plosser 1983). The analysis undertaken focuses exclusively on real economic activity: in this theoretical context, money in no way influences the real economy – in other words, the hypothesis is that economic disturbances are exclusively of a real type. Fluctuation models are an elaborated version of Ramsey's model, given that they include shocks and disturbances inserted into a long-run context of growth. It should be noted that all RBC models are no more than a single version, among many, of the basic Walrasian model, for these are based on the concept of equilibrium between labor supply and labor demand: employment levels are made to depend upon households' utility or satisfaction, which is a function of consumption and other variables, among which is leisure time. It should also be mentioned that fluctuation models exist in two forms: one with an analytical solution and a version that, on the contrary, gives no analytical solution. See, for instance, Kydland and Prescott (1982), Hansen (1985), Christiano and Eichenbaum (1992), and Baxter and King (1993).

Suffice to mention here some of the main features of neoclassical models. Although, in the neoclassical theory, production is made to depend on an unspecified number of inputs, the factors considered are usually reduced to two or three: 'the factors of production are the inputs used to produce goods and services. Labor, land, and capital are the three most important factors of production' (Mankiw 2015: 374). Labor is understood as the number of individuals engaged in a given productive activity or the number of working hours. Capital is meant as the machines used in this same activity. It should be said that the theory is confined to the limited case in which a homogeneous commodity is produced, being destined for sale and accumulation. Namely, labor and capital serve to produce a single typology of good that is partly consumed by purchasers and partly used as capital. Moreover, labor is taken as exogenous, while capital depreciates. It is useful to note that '[t]here is no special connection between the neoclassical model of growth and the determination of factor prices. The usual practice is to appeal to the same view of factor pricing that characterizes static neoclassical equilibrium theory' (Solow 2000: 378). This means that 'factor' prices, i.e. unitary wages and unitary interest (profit), are made to depend upon a certain number of equations and a number of unknowns inserted into a mathematical system, as is the case when determining the relative prices of goods. We previously noted that, according to some authors (see Cencini 1982, 2001, 2015; Schmitt 1984, 1996a; Schmitt and De Gottardi 2003), in the neoclassical theory, the relative prices of goods and services cannot be determined, since the system of equations proves to be over-determined. Analogy therefore leads one to conclude that, were this the case, the prices of productive factors could not be determined, either. However, hereafter it shall be assumed that factor prices are determinable, so as to go on in the investigation.

Labor is supplied by households and, just as if it were a commodity, it is given a price; i.e. the wage rate. One should ask, however, whether wages may truly be considered the 'price' of labor, as if labor were a commodity. Households consume output with the aim of maximizing their utility or satisfaction. In itself, the concept of utility is abstract, and its measurement cannot be made objectively. Yet, for the last few decades, growth theorists have introduced inter-temporal utility functions into their models (see Cass 1965; Koopmans 1965). 'The social welfare to be maximized is [. . .] represented by the total of the discounted utility of consumption per capita, where a general concave utility index is employed' (Cass 1965: 233). Furthermore, households purchase goods subject to a budget constraint. It is assumed that disposable income is fully spent on the basis of well-defined preferences. On the other hand, company investment is finalized with the aim of maximizing profit, according to the technology available on the market. Profit or benefit, in this theoretical context, corresponds to the difference between earnings and costs (defined via functions with their own properties). Remarkably, 'the assumption of profit maximization by firms can be replaced by some other systematic criterion of behavior' (Solow 2000: 352), a criterion chosen arbitrarily. Moreover, traditional neoclassical models assume there is a regime of perfect competition for labor and goods, in which companies are price-takers. The observation that large interest groups in the real world are instead price-makers has led neoclassical theoreticians to a new formulation of the basic model, thus assuming imperfect competition (e.g. see Romer 1990).

The reigning mathematical tool in the neoclassical theory of growth is the production function. Its features, always true for the most widely used production function, the Cobb-Douglas (1928) production function, are highly restrictive. After all, 'it should be made clear that we do not claim to have actually solved the law of production' (Cobb and Douglas 1928: 164). The concept of returns to scale is well known and underlies the entire basic neoclassical model. Namely, the assumption is that the physical product or output varies by a multiplicative factor t whenever each productive input is multiplied by such factor t. Moreover, it is assumed that the sum of the distributive quotas is always equal to the unit: if one quota diminishes, then the other increases, and vice versa, in such a way that equality is always respected and, therefore, one productive factor may be substituted for another (see, for instance, Sylos Labini's 1995 inquiry on the Cobb-Douglas exponents). The hypothesis of diminishing returns to scale of individual factors is also important. It in fact allows for productive inputs to be aggregated, as if they were a unitary and homogeneous productive factor. However, it defies understanding to imagine how factors such as labor and capital may possibly be aggregated *as if* they formed a single homogeneous physical factor. Therefore, the concept of returns to scale of individual factors appears to belong exclusively to a world that, according to Solow, does not correspond to the real one. One should consider the '[n]eoclassical growth model as being a story about an imaginary economy that has only one produced good that can be consumed directly or stockpiled for use as a capital good' (Solow 2000: 351).

The neoclassical theory of production is based on a mathematical model whose aim is to minimize production costs, these being subject to an output constraint (see, for instance, Mas-Colell, Whinston, and Green 1995). Dealing with the problem of optimization would allow a solution in equilibrium to be reached for the consumer. The final goal is in fact to derive an equilibrium cost function that provides the minimum production cost, given the prices of productive factors (usually, labor and capital). It should be observed that the neoclassical problem of optimization in the productive context was developed in perfect symmetry with the neoclassical theory of utility. In fact, the study of individual utility involves an exercise in optimization in which a consumer spending constraint must be minimized given a given utility function.

In both growth models and RBC models, output is subdivided into two parts: one that is consumed and one that is accumulated and used as capital. So it is that the part not destined for consumption is invested. Otherwise said, investment always amounts to the sum of households' savings. As Solow (2000: 356) states, the neoclassical theory assumes that consumption and investment take place on the basis of 'mechanical rules' or 'mechanical optimization procedures', in such a way that the sums for consumption and investment 'add up to total output'. This is a delicate matter: if the distribution and the allocation of income are not sufficiently investigated, it is likely that neoclassical models do not explain either the existence of profit or its relation with investment.

The neoclassical theory of distribution

The neoclassical theory of distribution is often an object of debate, as happened, for instance, in 2000, when Nobel Prize winner Robert Solow and

Keynesian economist Luigi Pasinetti produced two articles concerning the neoclassical theory of growth and distribution, on the one hand, and its critique, on the other hand. Hereafter, a short assessment shall follow of the neoclassical theory of distribution, drawing on the exposition made by Pasinetti. As it shall be observed, this theory has met serious criticism over the last century.

Although the problem of income distribution was already tackled during classical times, it remains a controversial subject. The established marginal principle in the neoclassical theory goes back to the Ricardian principle of diminishing returns from land, which neoclassical authors extend to those elements that can be defined as productive 'inputs' or 'factors'. Therefore, from the neoclassical viewpoint, an extension of the principle of diminishing returns to all presumed productive factors, such as labor and capital, renders the principle of diminishing returns from land a particular case within a wider theory. There is an enormous, fundamental difference between classical and neoclassical approaches: while classical authors believe that the value of goods and services derives exclusively from labor, neoclassical economists limit labor to being one among a few productive factors, together with land and capital. From Walras onwards, labor and, then, capital, were inserted into the theory of production in the same way in which Ricardo considered land.

The difference between the two approaches is substantial: although both are based on a physical concept of inputs and output, the causal relationship changes according to the theory under study. There is a clear symmetry between productive factors in the neoclassical theory – impossible, instead, in Ricardo's theory – since they are placed on the same conceptual level. Translated into mathematical terms, symmetry is evident in the production function, developed initially by Wicksell (1901 [1934]). The properties of this function are well known, as are productive function typologies. What matters in terms of the discourse here is the way in which income is distributed within this theoretical environment. The first neoclassical models were based on the idea that physical production depends on quantities of land and on the 'quantity' of labor employed in the productive activity. Given a unitary income from land, r, and the unitary 'price' of labor, w, a typical budgetary constraint for this model was: $Y = rT + wL$, where Y stands for output, T for land, and L for labor. Output is thus distributed to landlords and laborers in a complementary manner. Unitary wages and unitary income from land therefore complement each other. This means that, for the neoclassical theory, rents and wages are two incomes placed on the same conceptual level: indeed, were labor to be absent, rents could still exist. The way in which unitary income from land and unitary wages are determined remains unspecified – as previously observed, their determination is entrusted to an explanation analogous to that used in explaining relative prices.

There is even more: the hypotheses that the function is homogeneous and linear means that output distribution among the 'social classes' (laborers and landlords in the example) in no way depends on the class that receives the residual income – i.e. the class that undertakes productive activity. The introduction of the two hypotheses allows for the equality $Y = (\partial Y/\partial T)\,T + (\partial Y/\partial L)\,L$. In the absence of any asymmetry, unitary rent is made equal to the marginal product from land, and unitary wages are made equal to the marginal product from labor. 'The temptation that naturally comes is to assume that F is precisely a function of this type, so as to make equality satisfied and coincidental with' the equation $Y = rT + wL$ (Pasinetti 2000: 391). There is no logical-factual motivation justifying the use of this type of production function. Yet, merely formal considerations have induced generations of neoclassical economists to adopt the production function.

In order to create a production function that may be studied using mathematical analysis, other properties are attributed to this function. The hypotheses that the first derivatives of the function are positive and the second derivatives are negative guarantee that the function is convex. 'It turns out to imply constant return to scale and diminishing returns to the variation of the proportions between the two factors of production (a process which can be interpreted as a phenomenon of substitution between the two factors)' (Pasinetti 2000: 391).

> Whoever be the entrepreneur (who maximizes his own earnings), and whatever be the initial endowment of the production factors, a market with free competition will lead to such factors prices (i.e. to a wage rate and to a unit rent) which not only maximize the product, but also distribute to each factor of production precisely its physical marginal product, without leaving any (positive or negative) residual to anyone.
>
> (Pasinetti 2000: 391)

The reasoning behind land and labor factors may be extended to the case in which production is a function of an n number of factors. While developing their models, neoclassical authors from the last few decades have assumed that production is a function of just two factors: labor and capital. The introduction of capital, K, into the production function is interesting for this inquiry, since it has led to the introduction of profit into the neoclassical theory of growth. More particularly, profit or interest is identified with the part of income destined to the owners of capital. If households received no wages, profit would still exist. The basic relationship thus becomes the following, analogous to what has been previously stated about the income from land:

$$Y = (\partial Y / \partial L)L + (\partial Y / \partial K)K$$

where the marginal product of labor is equal to the wage rate, and the marginal product of capital is equal to the profit rate, π:

$$Y = wL + \pi K$$

The majority of neoclassical models of growth are based on this distribution theory. Yet, this theory has often been the object of criticism, in particular following the works of Wicksell more than a century ago.

> The Swedish economist Knut Wicksell (1901) [. . .] realized that [. . .] the marginal product of capital always turns out to be smaller than the rate of profits, because the variation of capital leads to changes in its price, *i.e.* to changes of the (current) unit in terms of which capital itself is measured. This divergence of the marginal product of capital from the rate of profits came to be known as the *Wicksell effect*. [. . .] [I]n a subsequent discussion with Dr Åkerman, Wicksell (1923) did confirm his previous finding of a divergence between the rate of profits and the marginal product of capital, but at the same time also realized, to his surprise, that not always did the divergence occur in the same direction. It could in certain cases – as he had always thought – be negative (the Wicksell effect), but it could also in other cases turn out to be positive, generating a Wicksell effect in reverse.
>
> (Pasinetti 2000: 404)

Criticism of the neoclassical theory became animated soon after Wicksell's findings. John Maynard Keynes's theory came to the fore in the 1930s as an alternative to neoclassical economics. The following chapter is devoted to the analysis of profit that was carried out by Keynes in two of his most influential volumes: *A Treatise on Money* (1930a [1971]) and *The General Theory of Employment, Interest and Money* (1936 [1964]).

Chapter 3

Keynes and Keynesian theories of profit

Due to his activities at the British Treasury and at the University of Cambridge, John Maynard Keynes became one of the leading economists of the 20th century. The first part of this chapter aims to highlight the major features of the theory of profit developed by the British economist. Although his concept of profit evolved over his professional life, Keynes always conceived profit as the motor driving productive activities. '[F]or enterprise to be active, [. . .] [t]here must be an expectation of profit; and it must be possible for enterprises to obtain command of sufficient resources to put their projects into execution' (1930b [1971]: 133). Profit is one of the central themes of Keynes's scientific research. As shall be observed in the second part of the chapter, the contributions of Keynes gave rise to different economic traditions since 1936. Interestingly enough, still at present, economic theory lacks a general consensus on the nature of profit.

Before starting our assessment of profits in *A Treatise on Money* and in *The General Theory of Employment, Interest and Money*, the most influential books written by Keynes, it must be observed that in *A Tract on Monetary Reform*, published in 1923, years before *A Treatise*, Keynes was already concerned with the problem of profit. In particular, it is worth noting that in the *Tract* (1923), Keynes analyzes profit by sub-dividing the society of his time into social classes. In *A Treatise*, and then in *The General Theory*, Keynes was somewhat vague in this respect. One might argue, controversially enough, that Keynes was more prone to provide his readers with an analysis of incomes rather than of social classes.

The *Treatise* was published in 1930, and *The General Theory* dates back to 1936. In *A Treatise*, Keynes wrote about 'normal' and 'windfall' profits. Normal profits, which correspond to the remuneration of the entrepreneur, are included into income, whereas windfall profits are excluded from it. Windfall profits, the central theme of *A Treatise*, are barely mentioned in *The General Theory*, where special attention is paid instead to normal profits.

A number of scholars have written about Keynes's contributions and legacy: notable examples are, for instance, Moggridge (1971–83, 1992),

Eatwell and Milgate (1983, 2011), Skidelsky (2003, 2009), Pasinetti (2007), and Davenport-Hines (2015). At present time, one among the major experts in Keynes's works is Robert W. Dimand. A former doctoral scholar of Nobel Prize recipient James Tobin, Dimand wrote extensively, in particular, on the making of Keynes's theory, focusing on the years between 1930, when *A Treatise* was published, and 1936, the publication year of *The General Theory*. See, for instance, Dimand's 1988 book (based on Dimand 1983), in which the author deals, among other topics, with the concepts of profit and quasi-rents. Keynes's analysis of quasi-rents was surely influenced by Marshall's theory and is a stepping-off point when studying Keynes's works. Nevertheless, in the following assessment, they shall be left aside, consistently with the aim of exclusively dealing with the concept of profit.

At first, they were windfalls

In *A Treatise* (1930a [1971]), Keynes used at least three expressions to refer to the concept of income: 'the community's money income', 'the earnings of the factors of production', and 'the cost of production'. In that book, income is made up of wages, the 'normal remuneration of entrepreneurs', 'interest on capital', and '[r]egular monopoly gains, rents and the like' (1930a [1971]: 111). Suppose interest, gains, rents, and the like to be null. This supposition is dictated by sole reasons of exposition. Interest, gains, and the like, though fascinating topics, are in fact beyond the scope of this chapter.

The concept of profit, in *A Treatise*, is strictly tied to the definition of income. In 1930, indeed, Keynes wrote about two kinds of profit. The 'normal remuneration of entrepreneurs' corresponds to the type of profit defined as 'normal', and it is included in the definition of income. Windfall profit, instead, is excluded from it. It must be observed that the very existence of profit, with particular reference to windfalls, is a controversial issue that creates much confusion for the reader of *A Treatise*. This topic is intimately linked to output price levels, a matter of great interest to Keynes in 1930. In fact, as Kahn (1984: 65) mentioned, Keynes was more concerned with price levels rather than with output and employment levels. Indeed, Keynes himself, in the memorandum of a letter to Ralph Hawtrey (November 28, 1930), wrote that in *A Treatise* he was 'primarily concerned with what governs *prices*' (quoted in Kahn, 1984: 108).

Although Keynes dealt with this topic in *A Treatise*, the concept of windfalls can be understood from the reading of a document to be found in Keynes's collected writings, edited by Donald Moggridge (1971–89). Such a document casts some light on the matter. On November 21, 1929, the Committee on Finance and Industry met for the first time. Also known as the Macmillan Committee, named after its chairman Hugh Pattison Macmillan, it was designated by the British government so as to find out the causes of the economic and financial crisis of the late 1930s (for instance, see Stamp 1931; Moggridge 1992). Between November 1929 and the end of May 1931, the Committee met one hundred times. Keynes was among the most active members of the Committee, together with Reginald McKenna, Theodore E. Gregory, Robert H. Brand, and Ernest Bevin. The proceedings of these meetings echo Keynes's ideas in his *Treatise on Money*, published for the first time in October 1930 (see Moggridge, 1971–89: 38, Vol. 20). In fact, as emerges from the transcripts of the Committee meetings, chaired by the Rt Hon. Lord Macmillan (see Moggridge 1971–89: 38–93, Vol. 20), Keynes had a very precise two-fold conception of profit at that time.

The first category of profit corresponds to the remuneration of entrepreneurs. The other category of profit was defined, instead, as 'windfall'; it was considered of inflationary origin and was excluded from income. Keynes is quite clear: national income is equal to the sum of total wages, inclusive of the normal profits of entrepreneurs, and exclusive of windfall profits. Keynes wrote:

> I should explain that I use 'wages' in a very wide sense, to cover what economists call 'remuneration of the factors of production'. Whether it is business men's efforts, or capital, or whatever it is, the 'remuneration of the factors of production' is very often convenient, though not quite accurate, to cover by the term 'wages'. [. . .] Including profits [. . .]; in the sense of the normal reward that a business man receives – not including windfalls.
>
> (Keynes in Moggridge, 1971–89: 45, Vol. 20)

To explain his theory of windfall profits, Keynes used an example he had developed together with the members of the Cambridge Circus. Importantly, the members of the Circus were Keynes's closest friends: Richard F. Kahn, James Meade, Austin Robinson, Joan Robinson, and Piero Sraffa. The group advised Keynes in the years following the publication of *A Treatise*, when Keynes began to develop his General Theory. This example is also to be found in Chapter 12 of *A Treatise* ('A further elucidation of the distinction between savings and investment'). Keynes hypothesized the existence of a society that owns banana plantations, on which it works. The members of this society consume bananas and save part of their income: family savings are used to finance the production cost of new investment in extending the plantations. Thus, there is equality between savings and investment, inasmuch as society's savings correspond exactly to the cost of new investment. Subsequently, Keynes supposed that individuals save more than before, and that, for various reasons, investment levels do not increase accordingly. Keynes believed that, given that bananas rot quickly, entrepreneurs shall sell them at a lower price, since, it should be remembered, savings have increased. The reduction in the price of bananas shall be proportional to the increase in savings. Because the price of bananas has fallen and wages remain unchanged, '[w]hat will happen is that you have just as many bananas consumed as before, but the entrepreneurs will lose an amount equal to the new savings of those people who have saved' (Keynes in Moggridge, 1971–89: 77, Vol. 20). Due to the increase in savings, individuals have obtained the same quantity of bananas as before, at a lower price. Therefore, the wealth of the society has not increased. 'The continuance of this will cause entrepreneurs to [. . .] reduce wages, and if they cannot reduce wages they will try to protect themselves by putting their employees out of work' (Keynes in Moggridge, 1971–89: 77, Vol. 20). To deal with this problem, Keynes believed that the use of savings in new investments can restore the equilibrium of savings and investment. '[T]here is no cure for the reduction of wages and unemployment, except universal starvation, the cartel, the calling off of the thrift campaign for these or other reasons, or the finding of some new outlet for investment' (Keynes in Moggridge, 1971–89: 78, Vol. 20). Moreover, bank intervention can lead to an excess of investment over savings. This could cause inflation and the birth of windfall profits. If banks are successful in their purpose, for example, through variations in the bank rate,

> you have an inflation. If people are able to borrow more [than] the equivalent of saving, prices rise above costs of production and the *entrepreneur* makes windfall profits and the extra investment that is created becomes the property of the *entrepreneur*. Owing to the rise of prices the consumer finds his money income worth less than he anticipated, the profiteer makes the profit and the extra quantity of goods represented by the extra investment [. . .] belongs to the profiteer.
>
> (Keynes in Moggridge, 1971–89: 80, Vol. 20)

Keynes wrote more on this in Chapter 16 of *A Treatise* ('A classification of the causes of a disequilibrium of purchasing power'), in which he once more turned his attention to the 'parable' of banana plantations. There he wrote that in the 'state of equilibrium in which the price level corresponds to the cost of production, profits are zero'. In that case, it consequently emerges that 'the cost of investment is equal to that of saving' (Keynes 1930a [1971]: 231).

Keynes wrote that 'profits [. . .] having once come into existence become [. . .] the mainspring of change in the existing economic system' (1930a [1971]: 126). Yet, possibly the most important aspect of *A Treatise* is the careful attention Keynes paid to a particular category of profit that can be defined pathological. In fact, according to Keynes, windfall profits must be nil if the economy is to be in equilibrium. In Chapter 11 ('The conditions of equilibrium') Keynes kept writing about windfall profits and economic equilibrium, a concept inherited by Keynes from his neoclassical mentors (the influence of Alfred Marshall and Arthur C. Pigou on Keynes as an economist cannot be denied, at least until 1930, the year in which *A Treatise* was published). In fact, in the following passage from *A Treatise*, Keynes wrote:

> since the profits (Q) are the difference between the value of current output and E, its cost of production, we have Q = I–S so that entrepreneurs make a profit or a loss according as the money value of current investment exceeds or falls short of current savings. Thus we have profits = value of output – cost of production = value of investment – savings; profits being the balancing figure not only between cost of production and value of output, but also between savings and the value of net investment, both in terms of money. [. . .] Now equilibrium requires that [. . .] Q should all be zero.
>
> (1930a [1971]: 136)

Therefore, as Keynes himself stated, a prerequisite for a monetary economy to be in equilibrium is that '*aggregate* profits are zero' (1930a [1971]: 137). Whenever windfall profits are positive, there will be a disequilibrium caused by the excess of investment over savings: the 'disparity between investment and saving sets up a disequilibrium in the rate of profit' (Keynes 1930a [1971]: 138). 'We may have a rise or fall of [. . .] the total profits above or below zero, due to an inequality between saving and the value of investment. We shall call this *profit inflation* (or *deflation*)' (Keynes 1930a [1971]: 140).

Following a famous passage in *A Treatise*, windfall profits are repeatedly renewed over time. The excerpt contains the examples of the 'widow's cruse', in the case of profits, or the 'Danaid's jar', in the case of losses. As explained by Kahn (1984: 106), the widow's cruse refers to the widow whose tears can never be depleted, in the Holy Bible, I Kings XVII, and, among the members of the Circus, it was firstly discussed by Austin Robinson (1977: 34). The 'Danaid's jar' refers instead to ancient Greece. As Kahn (1984: 106) puts it, '[i]n Greek legend, Argos, founded by Danaus, suffered every summer from a drought. In the lower world the fifty daughters of Danaus (the Danaids) had to carry water in broken vases'. Keynes wrote:

> If entrepreneurs choose to spend a portion of their profits on consumption [. . .], the effect is to increase the profit on the sale of liquid consumption goods by an amount exactly equal to the amount of profits which have been thus expended. [. . .] Thus profits, as a source of capital increment for entrepreneurs, are a widow's cruse which remains undepleted however much of them may be devoted to riotous living.
>
> (1930a [1971]: 125)

According to Keynes, windfall profits are spent infinite times and yet constantly restored. Profits spent in the purchase of consumer-goods appear to replenish company deposits to an equal amount. This would take place time and time again. The deeper reason behind this phenomenon is a controversial subject in economic theory. The most famous criticism of this passage of *A Treatise* originates from the Cambridge Circus. As Kahn recalls (1984: 106), '[t]he most important issue discussed by the Circus was what Austin Robinson called the '"widow's cruse" fallacy' and the "Danaid jar" fallacy'. The main criticism concerned Keynes's hypothesis that the level of consumption-goods was fixed. As Kahn recalls (1984: 107), Keynes never explained why he had chosen a fixed level of consumption-goods and, above all, he never explained how it might be possible to subdivide the total output, O, 'between R, the sales of consumption-goods, and C, the output of capital-goods plus the increment of working capital and stocks' (Kahn 1984: 107). The influence of the Circus was enormous and can be felt, for instance, in Keynes's new research into the determinants of output levels, an interest already evident in his Harris Foundation lectures in June 1931 (see Kahn 1984: 110; Moggridge 1973: 79, Vol. 20). In this context, Keynes showed a reduced interest in the determination of price levels, which, instead, had been an important line of inquiry in *A Treatise.*

Also, it has to be noted that Keynes's ideas were highly criticized by Friedrich Hayek. In particular, Hayek (e.g., 1931, 1932) stirred a heated debate with Keynes (1931) about the ideas that permeate *A Treatise*. Referring to windfall profits, Hayek was harsh. Indeed, he described windfalls as 'a stumbling-block to most readers' (Hayek 1931: 273), while adding: 'I have no fundamental objection to this somewhat irritating distinction' (Hayek 1931: 273). One of the main critiques the Austrian economist advanced against Keynes regarded profit. Hayek in fact did not agree with Keynes's explanation of profit:

> I cannot agree with his explanation of why profits arise, nor with his implication that only changes in 'total profits' in his sense can lead to an expansion or curtailment of output. For profits in his view are considered as a 'purely monetary phenomenon' [. . .]. The cause of the emergence of those profits [. . .] is [. . .] simply and solely spontaneous changes in the quantity and direction of the flow of money.
>
> (Hayek 1931: 273)

To the eyes of Hayek, the theory of investment developed in *A Treatise* laid on weak foundations:

> I pass now to the central and most obscure theme of the book, the description and explanation of the processes of investment. It seems to me that most of the difficulties which arise here are a consequence of the peculiar method of approach adopted by Mr. Keynes, who, from the outset, analyses complex dynamic processes without laying the

> necessary foundations by adequate static analysis of the fundamental process.
>
> (Hayek 1931: 277–8).

Moved by the passionate debates about his 1930 work, Keynes himself rejected the theory of profit and investment as developed in *A Treatise* and started formulating a new one. It took six years for Keynes to be able to publish another book, in 1936. Keynes's new purpose was

> to deal with difficult questions of theory, and only in the second place with the applications of this theory to practice. For if orthodox economics is at fault, the error is to be found not in the superstructure [. . .], but in a lack of clearness and of generality in the premises.
>
> (1936: v)

The importance of profit expectations

The year after the publication of *A Treatise*, Keynes defended his long-established idea that windfall profits are not included into national income (see, for instance, his article published by *Economica* in November 1931). However, to judge from his correspondence and published articles between 1931 and 1932 (see Moggridge, 1971–89, Vols. 13–14), Keynes soon began to reconsider his position.

Starting from 1932, Keynes changed the title of his lectures at King's College, Cambridge, to 'A monetary theory of production', marking the beginning of a new phase in his professional life. From 1932 onwards, new ideas sprang to his mind, particularly as regards employment levels. Keynes used the title of his lessons in an article in honor of Arthur Spiethoff, as well as in the early drafts of his new book. The book was published in 1936 by Macmillan as *The General Theory of Employment, Interest and Money* (see, for instance, Moggridge 1992; Fontana and Realfonzo 2005; Carrera and Rossi 2015). Keynes's *General Theory* was conceived with the explicit purpose of laying down the basis for a critical theory of classical works. With the term *classical*, Keynes (1936 [1964]: 3) intended not only authors such as David Ricardo and James Mill, but also the generations of economists following on from Walras, Jevons, and Menger: namely neoclassical economists including Alfred Marshall, Francis Y. Edgeworth, and Arthur C. Pigou. *The General Theory* arose as an alternative to classical and neoclassical economics, aiming to investigate the concept of 'output as a whole' (Keynes 1936 [1964]: vi). Despite being the object of numerous critiques over the years following publication, the book enjoyed worldwide success, especially among young scholars, and influenced entire generations of economists (see Pasinetti 2007 on this point).

Keynes's ultimate goal was to explain what Dimand (1986: 441) identifies as the 'weaknesses' of *A Treatise on Money*: namely, 'the lack of a functional dependence of saving on income, and the emphasis on realized windfall profits or losses rather than on the expected yields of investments' (Dimand 1986: 441). In fact, the inducement to invest, one of the fundamental messages of *The General Theory*, comes from expected returns. In any case, it remains true that without *A Treatise*, *The General Theory* would have been a different book (Dimand 1986: 441).

Thus, there is an important difference between the analysis of income developed in *A Treatise* and that dealt with in *The General Theory*. Keynes sought to develop an analysis of profit that was potentially clearer to the reader, compared to that proposed in *A Treatise*. Surprisingly enough, Keynes's theory of profits is far simpler and shorter in *The General Theory* than in *A Treatise*. In his 1936 book, Keynes's longest arguments on profits are included in Chapters 6 and 12. These chapters are respectively related to income, saving and investment, and to the inducement to invest.

The type of profit studied by Keynes in *The General Theory* is not the inflationary type to which he had dedicated *A Treatise*. In *The General Theory*, Keynes focused on the study of a single type of profit, which is included into income. However, one must also observe that the term profit is never found in the contents of *The General Theory*. Rather than to profit, Keynes's attention, broadly speaking, is paid to definitions, consumption, investment, and the relationship between money-wages and prices. These are the key-concepts of the general theory that Keynes was trying to develop. Moreover, while the determination of the price level was a major scope of *A Treatise*, the determination of output levels became the central theme of *The General Theory* (see Kahn 1984: 65).

In *The General Theory* (see Keynes 1936 [1964]: 213–14; 1936 [1964]: Chapter IV), Keynes argued that labor, including the services of the entrepreneur, is the sole macroeconomic factor of production. 'Factor cost and the entrepreneur's profit make up [. . .] *total income*' (Keynes 1936 [1964]: 23). Factor cost consists of the remuneration of workers employed in productive activities. Profit is defined in Chapter 3 ('The principle of Effective Demand') of *The General Theory* as the income of the entrepreneur. Thus, according to the traditional reading of *The General Theory*, total income is given by the sum of wages and profit. This is in line with Kalecki's accounting equation (see, for instance, Kalecki 1951; Roncaglia 2005).

Profit maximization plays a key role in productive activity. 'The entrepreneur's profit thus defined is, as it should be, the quantity which he endeavours to maximise when he is deciding what amount of employment to offer' (Keynes 1936 [1964]: 23–4). Employment levels and income are driven, according to Keynes, by the profits entrepreneurs expect to realize from a certain productive activity. 'As I [. . .] think, [. . .] employment (and consequently [. . .] output and real income) is fixed by the entrepreneur under the motive of seeking to maximise his present and prospective profits' (Keynes 1936 [1964]: 77–8).

According to the analysis developed by Keynes in his 1936 book, the desire to maximize profit is the motor driving the entrepreneur to manage productive activity. The accumulation of capital, which leads to an increase in the value of capital-goods, is deeply rooted in profit expectations. 'We have dealt so far with that part of the change in the value of the capital equipment at the end of the period as compared with its value at the beginning which is due to the [. . .] entrepreneur in seeking to maximise his profit' (Keynes 1936 [1964]: 56). All changes in capital levels are driven by profit expectations, which depend on the current profit rate: if profits are expected to change in the future, investment in capital-goods will vary accordingly. Therefore, profit drives investment activities, which are vital to avert involuntary unemployment (see, for instance, Bradley 2003). Now, if it is true that profit and investment are functionally related, a few considerations should be made concerning capital in *The General Theory*.

In the first place, in his reasoning, Keynes introduced the possibility that the entrepreneur must deal with a change, either positive or negative, in the value of machinery, independently of his own wishes.

> [T]here may, in addition, be an *involuntary* loss (or gain) in the value of his capital equipment, occurring for reasons beyond his control and irrespective of his current decisions, on account of (e.g.) a change in market values, wastage by obsolescence or the mere passage of time, or destruction by catastrophe such as war or earthquake.
>
> (Keynes 1936 [1964]: 56)

In the second place, Keynes avoided giving a clear definition of the nature of consumer-goods and investment-goods. Kahn (1984: 71) noted this problem. Keynes's decision not to define consumer-goods and investment-goods in relationship to wages and profit dates back to 1932 already, or even earlier. This statement can be supported, for instance, by a letter from Joan Robinson to Keynes, dated May 1932 (see Moggridge 1971–89: 47, Vol. 29):

> I quite agree that there is no reason to divide goods in[to] capital and consumption and say that their elasticities are likely to be different, but at the same time you are unnecessarily tying your hands by adopting a method which forces you to assume that the elasticities are related in one particular way.

When Keynes passed away in 1946, a number of economists were still seeking to clarify the issues left unclear or unsolved by *The General Theory*. On the basis of Keynes's 1936 book, entire generations of economists started developing several inquiries on profit and investment. There have been numerous studies of income distribution and growth since 1936. Some authors conceived *The General Theory* as part of a more general theory. For instance, Lange's (1938) study of the so-called liquidity preference points 'out how both the traditional and Mr. Keynes's theory are but special cases of a more general theory' (12). As explained by Hamouda (1993: 200), referring to Hicks's 1937 model, '[a]t first Hicks thought he could reduce *The General Theory* to a special case model of what he believed to be his own general theory, which encompassed all other theories including the classical one'; see also Wood and Woods on this (1989: 210). On what was defined by Joan Robinson as the problem of 'the generalization of the General Theory', see Robinson (1953, 1956).

Although it is reductive to attempt to catalog, one way or another, the works that can be defined as 'Keynesian', developments from the 1930s onwards may be subdivided into two broad lines of research: neoclassical interpretations of *The General Theory*, and post-Keynesian models. The first stream of thought is neoclassical in tone, based on the concept of economic equilibrium. Post-Keynesian authors, on the other hand, criticize the neoclassical framework and advocate a reappraisal of Keynes's contributions based on his attempt to work out a monetary theory of production. As for the approach privileged by Keynesian economists at large, it may be summarized by their claim that, within every economic system, nominal disturbances do exist to which wages and prices fail to adjust quickly. This causes fluctuations in output and employment. That is, a phenomenon would exist that is called 'incomplete – or sluggish – nominal adjustment'. In the following pages, we propose an analysis of profit following both the 'orthodox' and the post-Keynesian lines of research. The first line of thought is based on the Walrasian concept of economic equilibrium. In this particular theoretical context, profit is identified with interest. Post-Keynesian economists, as previously done by Keynes and classical authors, conceive profit, together with wages, as a part of the domestic product.

'Orthodox' versions of *The General Theory*

The neoclassical interpretations of *The General Theory* include several lines of research. In this regard, see, for instance, the famous assessments made by Modigliani and Papademos (1990), and by Romer (2001). Given a full range of Keynesian models with a neoclassical lineage, the most successful of these belong to the so-called neoclassical synthesis and to new Keynesian theories. A short description of these lines of research is given hereafter.

The neoclassical synthesis

As stated by Blanchard (1991: 504), '[t]he term "neoclassical synthesis" appears to have been coined by Paul Samuelson to denote the consensus view of macroeconomics which emerged in the mid-1950s in the United States'. Major attempts to formalize *The General Theory* within the so-called neoclassical synthesis were made by European and North American scholars such as Harrod (1937), Hicks (1937), Meade (1937), Lange (1938), Modigliani (1944), Samuelson (1948), Hansen (1949, 1953), and Leijonhufvud (1967), who are often labeled as 'neo-Keynesian' economists. Although there are differences between them, the neoclassical synthesis and pure neoclassical theory (see Mankiw 1990: 1654, 1659) share common elements (see Coddington 1976: 1265; Blinder 1988: 280). The former is, in fact, a variant of Walras's theory of general economic equilibrium. The most influential outcome of the neoclassical synthesis is the IS-LM model (Hicks 1937), which is present in two versions: one based on a closed economy and one based on an open economy. The authors of the neoclassical synthesis usually assume price rigidity – prices as given and constant – and an almost total rigidity of wages, with the aim of studying aggregate demand. The assumption is that trends in demand influence the productive choices made by companies. Along the years, the fundamental hypotheses of neo-Keynesian models have been modified. For example, such alternative models are based on different hypotheses concerning the behavior of prices and wages, as well as on forms of imperfect market: 'different combinations of wage rigidity, price rigidity, and non-Walrasian features of the labor and goods markets yield different implications about the effect of shifts in aggregate demand on output, unemployment, the real wage, and the markup' (Romer 2001: 218).

It is worth noting that all the models of the neoclassical synthesis, as well as the alternatives – which refer back to the former – are based on a physical concept of money, as if it were a commodity. An example is Modigliani, who, in the text co-authored with Papademos (Modigliani and Papademos 1990: 400), based his analysis '[o]n the assumption that money is a quantity which can be uniquely defined'. Yet, a fundamental difference between the pure neoclassical theory and the neoclassical synthesis should be noted. Although both theories share a physical conception of money, the authors of the neoclassical synthesis, contrary to pure neoclassical economists, believe in the 'monetary transmission mechanism'. Namely, they believe that the real side of the economy may be influenced by monetary shocks through certain specific mechanisms (Modigliani and Papademos 1990: 400). Therefore, they seek to develop monetary policies aimed at controlling nominal income. Such policies are made to depend 'on behavioral and institutional characteristics of the economy as well as upon the stochastic nature of the environment' (Modigliani and Papademos 1990: 401). It must be observed that the neoclassical synthesis is not the only theoretical framework based on the hypothesis that monetary shocks have non-neutral effects on the real economy. For this reason, Modigliani and Papademos (1990) undertake 'a review of four basic stochastic models relating the quantity of money to nominal income. These include classical, Keynesian and monetarist models, and a representative post-Keynesian aggregate demand and supply paradigm incorporating the effects of expectations and price dynamics' (401).

It is interesting to note that some of the authors of the neoclassical synthesis have themselves advanced criticisms of this theory. Famously, Hicks, during the mature phase of his life, distanced himself from his own 1937 Walrasian representation of *The General Theory* (see Hicks 1975, 1980–1; Pasinetti 2007: 44). Equally notable is the fact that Modigliani, during the final years of his life, was working on a new formalization of Keynes's research (see Pasinetti 2005: 29). It is, in fact, interesting to note that Modigliani and Papademos (1990: 463) propose a model in which income is expressed in terms far from being neoclassical (an assessment of this model is given in Graziani 2003: 74). In this context, profit regains the centrality it held in classical texts and in Keynes's *General Theory*. In fact, output, Y, would be given by the total for wages, W, and profit, P:

$$Y = W + P$$

As is known, this equation was not invented by the authors of the neoclassical synthesis. Its origin may be traced back to the works of the Classicals, and it was Kaldor (1956), as it shall be noted, who used such an equality, transposing into symbols the definition of income given by Keynes (1936 [1964]). Hereafter, the study shall continue with the second group of Keynesian models sharing a neoclassical lineage.

New Keynesian and other models

The following three categories of models are based on the idea that wages and prices do not fully, or immediately, adjust to monetary shocks. In other words, wages are sticky, especially in models less similar to the basic Walrasian model, and in which it is assumed, for instance, that goods and labor markets are imperfect. Furthermore, variations in the real side of the economy are due to monetary disturbances. Following Romer (2001), these lines of research have been carried out by Phelps (1968) and Lucas (1972), by the authors of so-called 'staggered adjustment models' (see, for instance, Akerlof 1969; Phelps and Taylor 1977; Taylor 1979; Caplin and Spulber 1987), and by new Keynesian authors (see, for instance, Rotemberg 1982; Akerlof and Yellen 1985; Parkin 1986; Blanchard and Galì 2007).

New Keynesian models work under the hypothesis that supposed nominal frictions or imperfections are able to cause output and employment to fluctuate in cycles close to each other. To a certain extent, these models are analogous to real-business-cycle (RBC) models. To be more specific, so as to study short-run output fluctuations, new Keynesian theory adopts the same analytical techniques as those employed by RBC theory, namely, dynamic stochastic general equilibrium (DSGE) models. This line of research is based on the IS-LM model typical in the neoclassical synthesis. 'New

Keynesian macroeconomics has pushed the idea that traditional IS-LM analysis remains the best way to think about the determination of aggregate demand' (King 1993: 80). Despite internal criticisms (see King 1993), new Keynesian economists generally focus on the development of the IS-LM model within DSGE models that are used by central banks with the aim of enacting national bank policies. For instance, Blanchard and Quah (1989) elaborated, amongst others, equations for the IS and LM curves, thereby solving a problem of dynamic optimization. These three lines of research afford no significant new contribution to the neoclassical theory of profit. As shall be observed in the last part of the chapter, profit was instead a central theme of post-Keynesian economics.

Post-Keynesian theories

Post-Keynesian literature is rich and deals with many lines of inquiry. Some of the most well-written seminal works and expositions of post-Keynesian theories include Kaldor (1956, 1966), Pasinetti (1962, 1973, 1981), Harcourt (1969, 1972), Baranzini and Harcourt (1994), Harcourt and Kriesler (2013), and Baranzini and Mirante (2013). These texts will be our main references in the pages that follow. Out of curiosity, it has to be noted that Pasinetti's 1973 paper was the Spanish translation of a lecture held by the author himself at the University of Barcelona in the same year. The paper is overshadowed by many other well-known articles and volumes written by the then Cambridge-based economist. Yet, the historical circumstances of that scholarly piece are worth mentioning. At that time, Spain was a military dictatorship led by *el caudillo*, General Francisco Franco. The paper, with its Anglo-Saxon progressive contents, testifies to the interest of some Spanish scholars in the works of Keynes.

As well stated by Pasinetti (1973: 223–4), classical research was the starting point for the so-called Cambridge theory of growth. Domar's famous article, published in *Econometrica* in 1946, was an important contribution in this direction. Domar (1946) returned to Ricardo's studies, adding new hypotheses concerning the population growth rate (a constant rate of population growth, rather than a Malthusian-like behavior), technological progress (an increase in income per capita even when progress is technically neutral), and Keynes's theory of the effective demand (Pasinetti 1973). Domar (1946: 138) defined aggregate real production, or the 'productive capacity of an economy (or an asset)', as 'its total output when all productive factors are fully employed'. He also assumed the economy to be in equilibrium 'when its productive capacity P equals its national income Y' (Domar 1946: 138). Another hypothesis concerned income and productive capacity, which were assumed to grow at the same rate (see also Pasinetti 1973: 225). Domar (1946) identified what he called 'the state of dynamic equilibrium', according to which the growth rate of net investment, g, was given by the relation between the marginal propensity to save, s, and the quotient of capital over product, k.

Domar's contribution represents a breaking point, initiated by Keynes, between the Cambridge theories and the classical tradition. Following lines laid down by Keynes, Domar realized that, by focusing attention on the 'size of the labor force', understood as 'man-hours worked', as well as on the productive capacity of labor, economic theory was 'incomplete', being unable to explain the functioning of modern economic systems and, above all, the underlying reasons for mass unemployment. According to Domar, the factors driving demand were often overlooked and remained unexplained: 'since an increase in labor force or in its productivity only raises productive capacity and does not by itself generate income [. . .], the demand side of the equation is missing' (Domar 1946: 138).

At the same time as Domar, Harrod (see, for instance, 1939, 1948) sought to contribute to the research on full employment, attempting to extend Keynes's analysis (and that of Domar) to the long-term (see Pasinetti 1973: 225–6; King 2009: 59–60). Harrod developed the concept of the 'natural rate of growth', given by the sum of the population growth rate and the growth rate of productivity. If the natural rate of growth, g_n, is equal to the growth rate of net investment, g, the employment level is considered to be of full employment. The outcome of this research line was the so-called Harrod-Domar equation, $g_n = s/k$. As Pasinetti noted (1973: 226), the Harrod-Domar equation presents a problem of practical importance, namely, the 'knife-edge' problem: if g_n, s, and k are *constant*, the path of balanced growth will be narrow. The model proposed by Kaldor in 1956 aimed at overcoming the 'knife-edge' issue. Other studies along the lines of Harrod and Domar were undertaken by Kaldor and, later, by Pasinetti. They enjoyed an enormous success at the time. The development of the neo-Pasinetti theorem (see Kaldor 1966) represents the culmination of Kaldor's and Pasinetti's joint research.

A number of seminal and more recent post-Keynesian studies shall be investigated further here. Despite hundreds of studies that have been carried out since the publication of Keynes's *General Theory*, Kaldor's and Pasinetti's theories of profit are, at present, still among the most influential outcomes of post-Keynesian research.

Kaldor: profit as a type of income

The most notable of the early works developed in the wake of Keynes is Nicholas Kaldor's 1956 paper on 'alternative theories of distribution', where he investigated the relation between profit, output, wages, and the saving rates out of wages, s_w, and out of profits, s_p. His intention was to improve economic analysis, which was based on what he was later to define the '[c]osy world of Harrod, Domar and Solow, where there is only a single saving propensity applicable to the economy – where in other words, $sY = s_w Y$' (Kaldor 1966: 311). The model at hand took several years to develop, albeit some features of Kaldor's famous 1956 article were already to be found in a text which was authored by him in 1951 (see King 2009: 62). In this article, Kaldor proposed an economic model which drew on Keynes's definition of *total income*. Starting from Keynes's (1936 [1964]: 23) definition of total income as the sum of the 'factor cost' and profit, Kaldor (1956) analytically defined national output, Y, as the sum of wages, W, and profit, P (namely, $Y = P + W$). Further, investment, I, and savings, S, were supposed to be equal ($I = S$).

Kaldor believed that entrepreneurs' savings were to be added to those of households and that their combined sum determined the amount of investment. It was Keynes who had advanced the hypothesis that investment was determined by the total for households' savings and savings from profits. Therefore, being that investment was defined as the sum of saving from wages and saving from profit, Kaldor developed the following equation of investment:

$$I = s_p P + s_w (Y - P) = (s_p - s_w) P + s_w Y$$

Observe that 'the wage-category comprises not only manual labour but salaries as well, and Profits the income of property owners generally, and not only of entrepreneurs' (Kaldor 1956: 95).

It is worth stressing the fundamental restriction in Kaldor's model: that is, the saving rate of wages is lower or equal to the saving rate of profits and their value less than one, zero and one included ($0 \leq s_w \leq s_p \leq 1$). Kaldor justified this restriction by stating that 'if $s_p < s_w$, a fall in prices would cause a fall in demand and thus generate a further fall in prices, and equally, a rise in prices would be cumulative' (1956: 95).

Assuming the rate of saving, s, to be a variable rather than a constant, with the classical hypothesis that saving from wages is null, Kaldor's investment equation, substituted in the Harrod-Domar equation, gives rise to:

$$\frac{P}{K} = (\frac{1}{s_c}) g_n$$

This became famous as the 'Cambridge equation' (see Pasinetti 1962, 1973). The result achieved by Kaldor consisted of determining, in the context of the 'Cambridge profit rate theory', the relation between profit (or, better, the percentage of profit with respect to income) and the exogenous magnitudes s_c, k, and g_n:

> it is wages, hence, according to Kaldor (and not profits, as argued by Ricardo), to be determined as a residual. [. . .] According to him, it is profits, not wages, to be determined by exogenous forces, and it is workers,

> not capitalists, to receive what is left. [. . .] The requisites of effective demand prevent capitalists from 'appropriating of all the surplus'.
> (Pasinetti 1973: 227–8, our translation)

The problem Kaldor returned to in the 1950s was not new in the history of contemporary economic thought (see, for instance, Dobb 1929, 1930a, 1930b [1971], Kalecki 1939 [1990], 1942; Robinson 1956; Hansson 1987, quoted in King 2009: 63). Kaldor, in fact, sought to formalize the idea that the distribution of income in the form of profit could 'provide the necessary increase in saving' to finance investment (King 2009: 63). In the late 1960s, Kaldor had attempted to reconcile the problem of income distribution with that of economic growth.

Pasinetti: profits as accruing to the capital's owners

Kaldor's 1956 paper became the focus of critical attention in the 1960s. Assuming that workers earn labor and property incomes, Pasinetti's 1962 model achieved the same results as Kaldor's (1956), therein stating that, independently of workers' propensity to save, the share of profit is determined by the propensity to save of the capitalists.

Pasinetti (1962: 270) rewrote the equation of investment, which he identified as 'the equilibrium condition', as:

$$I = s_w(W + P_w) + s_c P_c = s_w Y + (s_c - s_w)P_c$$

with Y being 'net income' (Pasinetti 1962: 268), I being 'the amount of investment necessary to cope with population growth and technical progress' (Pasinetti 1962: 268), and 'where P_c and P_w stand for profits which accrue to the capitalists and profits which accrue to the workers', and where s_c and s_w are the propensities to save of capitalists and workers, respectively (Pasinetti 1962: 270). The relevance of Pasinetti's research (1962) in the context of post-Keynesian theory is due to the fact that the profit rate appears to be determined as explained by the 'Cambridge equation', even when the propensity to save of workers is positive in the long-term. Thus, the results achieved by Kaldor would appear to be confirmed by Pasinetti's study, according to which, independently of workers' rates of saving, '[w]hereas capitalists are in the system, it is their propensity to save (and theirs only) the one relevant to determine the profit rate in the long run' (Pasinetti 1973: 230, our translation). On this subject, see, for instance, Harcourt (1969, 1972) and Baranzini and Harcourt (1994).

Pasinetti's outcome has been widely studied, as it showed that, under the hypotheses of the model, profit rate equilibrium does not depend on workers' behavior, even when saving rates of wages and profits are positive. Equilibrium profit rate would in fact be determined by capitalists' behavior – i.e. by their rate of saving – and by the economy growth rate (see, for instance,

Baranzini and Mirante 2013: 289). With Pasinetti's research as a starting point, an important debate arose that resulted in an article by Kaldor in 1966, containing the so-called Kaldor-Pasinetti theorem or neo-Pasinetti theorem.

There were numerous reactions to Pasinetti (1962) and Kaldor (1966). On the neoclassical front, notable scholars such as James Meade, Franco Modigliani, Paul Samuelson, and Robert Solow were skeptical of post-Keynesian research. As Pasinetti explains (1973: 228–9), the relationship $k = s/g_n$ was deemed valid by both parties. However, the quotient capital product, k, was viewed as a *variable*, not a constant, and k was conceived by neoclassical economists as an *inverse monotonic* function of the profit rate. It has to be noted that the conclusion of the so-called 'dual-theorem' (see Samuelson and Modigliani 1966a) is opposite to that of Pasinetti and Kaldor: under the hypothesis that the economy is on the steady growth path – being, therefore, in long-run equilibrium – the output capital ratio would be determined by the saving rate of workers – the only saving class in the system – together with the growth rate. See Meade (1963, 1966a, 1966b); Samuelson-Modigliani (1966a, 1966b); Pasinetti (1989); and Baranzini and Mirante (2013).

Discussions flared up in Cambridge, England, and in Cambridge, Massachusetts.

A controversy in capital theory

Three two-Cambridge controversies were sparked off by notable economists during the 1950s and 1960s (see, for instance, Baranzini and Mirante 2018). In particular, however, the debates are almost forgotten. The debates mainly took place over a period of approximately fifteen years, starting from 1953. The bone of contention was a two-sector production model with heterogeneous capital and fixed-coefficients. For a summary account of the controversy, see, for instance, Ferguson (1969), Kregel (1971), Harcourt (1972), Bliss (1975), Compaijen (1981), and Birner (2002). See also, for instance: Robinson (1953), Champernowne (1953–4), Robinson (1956), Samuelson (1962), Levhari (1965), Hicks (1965), Pasinetti (1966), Meade (1966a, b), Bruno, Burmeister, and Shesinski (1966), Garegnani (1966), Samuelson (1966), Samuelson and Modigliani (1966a, b), Brown (1969), Garegnani (1970), Ferguson and Allen (1970), Gallaway and Shukla (1974), Baranzini (1975), Sato (1976), Garegnani (1976), Burmeister (1980), Samuelson (1991), Miyazaki (1991), Baranzini (1991a), and Kurz and Salvadori (1995).

A major outcome of the two-Cambridge debates shows that the neoclassical production model stands up only in the case in which a single capital-good is produced. A case that appears highly restrictive, when brought to the test of reality. Indeed, in real life, large varieties of heterogeneous capital-goods are produced and accumulated by companies. Another outcome worth mentioning is that it is not logical to treat capital, measured in terms of value, and labor (as well as land and other factors of production), measured in physical terms, as symmetrical inputs of the production function.

In particular, Robinson (1953) noted a special case involving the so-called 'reswitching' of techniques, in marked contrast to the neoclassical assertion that production never switches back to old, less profitable, techniques. Furthermore, she also noted the possibility of 'capital reversing' – 'no inverse monotonic relation between quantity of capital [. . .] and rate of profits' (Pasinetti 2000: 406) – and this, too, was in marked contrast to the tenets of the neoclassical theory. 'But she did not draw the conclusion from this that the phenomena could better be dealt with in the framework of a dynamic theory' (Birner 2002: 23). At that time, the entire profession – from neoclassical to Keynesian economists, broadly speaking – contrarily to the classical authors, did not devote their attention to an in-depth study of economic change. This was to happen later, when the focus shifted to the theory of economic growth. 'Robinson was not the only author who failed to break out of a static framework and pursue a process-oriented line of analysis further; everyone else did so' (Birner 2002: 23). At that time, economic models were comparative-static and 'not suited for analyzing processes, [. . .] dynamic phenomena' (Birner 2002: 23). Concerning the triumph of static analysis, it is sufficient here to remember an observation made by Hicks: '[t]he more precise capital theory became, the more static it became; the study of equilibrium conditions only resulted in the study of stationary conditions' (1965: 47, in Birner 2002: 22).

A few observations by Birner (2002: 22) about the capital controversy in particular are worth mentioning here. The debate was characterized by static types of considerations, which may have pushed the controversy in one direction rather than another. Present-day economists would probably have studied the issue from a dynamic viewpoint. However, these are only suppositions, albeit suppositions of a certain importance. According to Solow (see Birner 2002: 24), Bliss was the first to mention explicitly that the question of dynamic processes was rarely investigated in the theoretical debates of the time. Despite sharing his opinion, it seems that Joan Robinson, for instance, never gave much importance to the question (see Birner 2002: 24). The fact is that, at least until the 1950s, economic theory was characterized by numerous static analyses. Until that time, economists had not dealt with economic changes. Early models that explicitly allowed for variation rates in economic magnitudes began to be more widely used thanks to the success of certain models of economic growth (among which is that of Solow 1955–6, 1956). It is unsurprising that economic models of the first half of the 20th century were based on static theoretical frameworks rather than dynamic processes. In fact, both the economic equilibrium system proposed by Walras and Keynes's theory of the short-term (1936 [1964]), which were the most influential economic theories of the period, did not allow for changes in productive factors over time. Keynes's 1936 theory, for instance, 'does not deal with the causes and consequences of changes in the capital stock' (Birner 2002: 22). With the aim of extending Keynes's analysis to the long-term, Joan Robinson (1953, 1956) undertook lengthy research into capital accumulation. 'Joan Robinson [. . .] made it her explicit goal to develop a theory of the long run which was to embed or encompass the short-run *General Theory* of Keynes' (Birner 2002: 22). However, her analysis remained tied to static considerations and was never completed with dynamic considerations.

Hundreds of studies followed what has gone down in history as Kaldor and Pasinetti's, or the post-Keynesian, theory of growth and distribution in the 1960s. Yet, a number of theoretical post-Keynesian questions are still required to be answered. A brief list of these shall be given hereafter.

Alternative lines of research

A number of post-Keynesian research lines have been developed over the years. These shall be assessed briefly in the following pages, drawing on Baranzini and Mirante (2013: 291–2) and on Rochon (2009). As it shall be observed, research is still in progress and feeds discussion.

A line of research concerns the monetary sector. Money, a constituent part of modern economic systems, is often absent from post-Keynesian models. Bank money, especially, is a controversial subject (see, for instance, Graziani 1983, 1989, 1996, 2003; Lavoie 1996, 2003, 2006a, 2006b, 2013; Palley 1996; Wray 1996, 2013; Seccareccia 1996, 2003, 2005; Terzi 2002; Kelton and Nell 2003; Bellofiore 2005; Fontana and Realfonzo 2005; Fontana 2006; Mosler 2010). Surprisingly, input-output theory, carried out by a number of post-Keynesian economists, is based entirely on a physical conception of production and consumption, completely ignoring the existence of bank money. Sraffa (1960), a major expert of Ricardian economic thought, is perhaps the most well-known exponent of this tendency. Carrying out his analysis of productive activities, he proposed a theoretical world in which all economic magnitudes, including wages, are physical. Wages are measured in a theoretical 'standard commodity' and are therefore real in nature. Regarding this, Sraffa wrote (1960: §31):

> In the Standard system the circumstances of the wage being paid in Standard commodity seems to draw its special significance from the fact that the residue left over for profits will itself be a quantity of Standard commodity and therefore similar in composition to the means of production.

Therefore, in input-output analysis, even profit has an exclusively real nature. This should not be so; the monetary aspect of profit is beyond dispute and a satisfactory analysis of its nature must explain both its real and its monetary components. An analysis of this kind requires the prior understanding of the nature of bank money. Indeed, given its importance in daily activities, bank money should always be conceived as an essential object of economic research. This is not always the case, which justifies the claim that post-Keynesian economists should seek to converge toward a common point of view on the nature and the role of money.

The economic models developed since the 1950s by post-Keynesian economists, including Kaldor and Pasinetti among others, often hypothesize the existence of social classes. Over time, researchers have carried out three lines of inquiry in this regard (Baranzini and Mirante 2013). The first one regards the introduction of other presumed socioeconomic classes in post-Keynesian models, besides those of workers and capitalists originally proposed in the first, seminal contributions. The second one concerns the study of the 'long-term distribution of wealth and of the income share of the socioeconomic classes' (Baranzini 1991b: 56). The third line of research proposes 'overlapping generation models', so as to study the intergenerational transmission of wealth among social classes (Baranzini and Mirante 2013). In economic theory, the distinction between social classes has been used time and time again by a number of scholars. For instance, famous is the classical division of society into workers, capitalists, and landowners. Post-Keynesian economists, among others, have often developed long-term models in which one class (the class of laborers) consumes and another accumulates capital (the class of capitalists). A division into classes or sectors of society favors the simplification and functioning of the steady-state models developed in particular through the 1960s and the 1970s, in which variables must grow at the same rate; such distinctions can also prove useful in explaining economic parameters (see Baranzini 2001: 224, 226–7). However, nowadays, does it make sense to think about 'the formation, persistence, and dispersion of socio-economic classes at large' (quoting Baranzini 2001: 228)?

The concept of socioeconomic classes has often been the object of debate and controversy. On this theme, one may consider, for instance, the debate between Kaldor and Pasinetti. Pasinetti (1962) based his analysis on two classes – workers and capitalists – as well as on political implications – for instance, '[t]he case of a socialist system' (Pasinetti 1962: 277). Earlier, Kaldor (1956), following Keynes, had preferred to base his own analysis on the existence of different typologies of income, independently of the social roles of income-holders. This question is very well known. In a letter addressed to Mauro Baranzini, Nicholas Kaldor expressed his reservations with regard to abandoning a typology-based study of income in favor of a differentiation of incomes based on social classes. '[Y]ou seem to ignore the main criticism I made against Pasinetti, i.e. that he is thinking of "workers" and "capitalists" as persons and not of profits and wages as types of income' (Baranzini and Mirante 2013: 290). It is, perhaps, over-simplistic to suppose the existence, for instance, of two whole classes that live respectively on dividends and wages alone. Above all, it still remains to be proven, both at the theoretical and empirical levels, that certain elements contribute to a net division of society into social classes (see Baranzini 2001: 229 for a summary of such elements).

A further line of research concerns the so-called microeconomic foundations of economics (Baranzini and Mirante 2013). Indeed, a number of economists have advanced the hypothesis that macroeconomic phenomena can be conceived as the aggregation of individual choices. A number of post-Keynesian researchers have thus followed the idea, neoclassical in tendency, that macroeconomics has microfoundations. Within post-Keynesian economics, '[t]he first principle of micro-foundations [. . .] is that macroeconomics refers to the aggregation of the outcomes of individual action, and thus should not be logically inconsistent with the analysis of individual behaviour' (Dow 1996: 98). However, an alternative line of inquiry deserves equal consideration, according to which macroeconomics has macroeconomic foundations, as sustained by many scholars from the Cambridge post-Keynesian school in the United Kingdom. Further, researchers introduced 'a differentiated interest rate on wealth' in post-Keynesian models (Baranzini and Mirante 2013). Yet there is no generally shared post-Keynesian theory of interest, but, rather, different opinions as to it. A strong theory of interest is needed. For instance, new research should be carried out on the distinction, introduced by Wicksell, between the natural interest rate and the market interest rate (1901 [1934], 1912 [1997], 1923). Research in this direction should also explain the relation between interests and profits. Many researchers have also investigated the role of the 'public sector' (see Baranzini and Mirante 2013 on this). It still remains unclear whether public intervention has the effect of creating new wealth, rather than simply redistributing it. A great deal has yet to be done to clarify this matter.

Notable scholars have tried to conciliate different Keynesian contributions. For instance, Palley's 1996 work is a well-known attempt to conciliate the research carried out by James Tobin (1956, 1963, 1965, 1969, 1971, 1972, 1974, 1975, 1976, 1980, 1982, 1993), by Nicholas Kaldor (1956, 1960, 1970, 1982), by Paul Davidson (1965, 1972, 1982, 1991, 1992), and by Hyman Minsky (1957, 1964, 1975, 1977, 1982, 1993) in England and in North America. As far as profit is concerned, Rochon (2009) points out five different lines of inquiry made by a number of economists to explain the monetization of profit, including, for instance, the contributions of Robinson (1956), Lavoie (1987), Moore (1988), Parguez (1996), Seccareccia (1996), Renaud (2000), Rossi (2001), Nell (2002, 2004), Gnos (2003), Graziani (2003), Zazzaro (2003), Zezza (2003), Rochon (2005), and Febrero (2008).

First, monetary profits may form following the 'external injection of money, such as through the existence of the state and fiscal policy, or through the existence of a foreign sector' (Rochon 2009: 62). A second solution may consist in 'borrowing the profits that firms will be making in advance of the production process and injecting them into circulation' (Rochon 2009: 62). Third, as observed by Rochon (2009: 63), some authors (see, for instance, Smithin 1997; Gnos 2003) have developed some models where production and consumption are carried out over a number of periods. The last two solutions concern the existence of instrumental capital. Indeed, Febrero (2008) and Lavoie (1987) (see Rochon 2009: 64 on this), resorting to the 'linearization of production', hypothesize the division of the investment-goods sector into subsectors. Also, Edward Nell (1996) has suggested a further solution:

> that only wages in the investment-goods sector need to be financed by bank credit. [. . .] Nell (2002) assumes that firms in the consumption-goods sector need not borrow to finance their production needs: they begin production and pay their income on consumption goods. Moreover, firms within the investment-goods sector extend credit to inter-sector firms. Through increases in velocity and inter-sector credit, M can be turned into M', so that all sectors realize profits in monetary terms.
> (Rochon 2009: 65)

Also, recently, Cottin-Euziol and Rochon (2013) have proposed a model in which investment is financed and reimbursed over many periods.

All these lines of inquiry deserve further investigation. For instance, '[a]s Nell (2002: 520) argues cogently, "it is necessary to show how the system can work without reliance on outside assistance"' (Rochon 2009: 66). Accordingly, an attempt should be made to explain the existence of profits in the absence of public authorities and the foreign sector. Also, the origins of profits should likely be traced out without resorting to banks' loans to the firms. Indeed, profits should be supposed to be made exclusively from the sale of goods and services. Finally, the existence of profits should likely be studied by assuming, at least at the outset, the absence of investment-goods in the economy. In fact, for instance, profits are often made with the aim of remunerating stakeholders rather than of accumulating capital-goods (see Baragar and Chernomas 2013 on this). Most importantly, if investment is somehow related to profit, it may be that causality runs from profit to investment, not vice versa, the existence of profit being the precondition to investment.

Be that as it may, economists acknowledge a relation between profit and investment. For instance, in her *Essays in the Theory of Economic Growth* (1962), Joan Robinson argued that profit and investment are *mutually* influenced. According to her, indeed, profit would be functional to the investment level, as also argued by Kalecki; investment would in turn be source of profit. 'The first question to be discussed is the relation between the rate of profit *caused* by the rate of accumulation and the rate of accumulation which that rate of profit will *induce*' (Robinson 1962: 48). Adrian Wood (1975; see also Wood 1978) equally maintained that profit is required if companies are to accumulate investment-goods. As it shall emerge from the next chapter, the existence of profit is indeed at the origin of fixed capital. Monetary profit likely determines investment, not the other way around.

Chapter 4

New directions in the theory of profit

Having ascertained that wages accrue to households broadly speaking, in this chapter we shall investigate how profits accrue to companies and the linkage between profits and investment. At least at the outset, we shall assume the existence, in the economy, of a single company and of a single financial institution, a commercial bank. We shall assume that the commercial bank acts as pure intermediary between households and the company. The analysis, rather than on social classes, shall be based on income typologies: wages, profit, dividends, taxes, and interests. Wages shall be supposed to be spent in the purchase of a single stock of goods and services. Exogenous money shall not be included as a source of profit. Therefore, we shall not allow for the existence of the foreign sector. Also, collecting taxes on wages and on profit, the public sector shall play a mere distributive role. Further, it shall be assumed that companies have no access to bank lending so as to finance investment, which shall uniquely be financed by profits. The chapter shall also investigate the relation between profit and interest, as well as the growth of bank deposits in the long-term.

Wages and profit allocation

We shall resume the example proposed in Chapter 1 so as to introduce profit into the analysis. Suppose that households' accounts at Nantucket Bank are credited with \$100 for producing ten tons of chowder at Seafarer Co. The value of chowder is thus \$100. Wages constitute households' credit and the debit of Seafarer Co. toward Nantucket Bank, which pays wages whenever asked for by the company. The bank acts as an intermediary between Seafarer Co. and households: on the one hand, being the company registered on the asset side of the bank's balance sheet, the product is financially deposited within the bank; on the other hand, the bank liability represents a credit in favor of households whose object is the product. Supposing chowder is sold at its production cost (i.e. if nominal wages are \$100, the price of one ton is \$10), when households spend wages to buy seafood chowder, the credit-debit relationship no longer exists. In fact, households get the product (chowder) at the very instant they spend wages; at the same time, the company pays back its debit toward Nantucket Bank. No profit has been made. However, things do change as soon as we relax the hypothesis of a selling price equal to the cost of production.

We shall consider here the case in which chowder (ten tons) is sold at a price higher than its production cost. Suppose, for instance, that nominal wages are $100 and that each ton is sold at $12.50, meaning that the selling price of total output is $125. The company will never get $125, since total income amounts to just $100. By spending their entire salary of $100, households cannot purchase the entire tonnage of chowder, but just a share of it.

Given wages, W_1, and the selling price, p, it follows that: the rate of sold output, $\alpha = W_1/p$, is 0.8; the value of sold output, αW_1, amounts to $80; the rate of profit, $\pi = 1\text{-}\alpha$, is 0.2; and profit, $P_1 = \pi\ W_1$, amounts to $20.

Table 4.1 may help clarify. Households are paid $100 (entry 1). Subsequently (entry 2), households spend $100 to purchase eight tons, valued at $80; the remaining part, two tons, valued at $20, is still stocked within Seafarer Co. The company sells a share of output and stocks the remaining part. A real income or profit accrues to the company. Further, $100 is credited on Seafarer Co.'s deposit: $80 covers the cost of production of eight tons of chowder; the remaining $20 constitutes the company's monetary profit.

Macroeconomic profit is not given by the numerical excess of the overall price level over total costs of production, as mainly thought since classical times. The previous reasoning shows, for instance, that profit amounts to $20, not to $25, as one would think at first sight.

Having covered production costs amounting to $80, the company's debt toward the bank shall be extinguished to the same extent. At this point, Seafarer Co. faces some alternatives.

(1) The stock of goods stored at Seafarer Co. (valued at $20) may turn out to be unsalable. Output may be unfit for sale, for instance, because of manufacturing defects. Output could also be deteriorated by flood, fire, earthquake, etc. In such a scenario, Seafarer Co. pays the $20 back

Table 4.1 Wages and profit

Nantucket Bank (Massachusetts)			
Assets		*Liabilities*	
(1) Seafarer Co.	$100	Households	$100
(2) Households	$100	Seafarer Co.	$80 + $20

Source: *author's elaboration from Cencini and Rossi (2015).*

to the bank, and in this way it extinguishes the debt toward the bank. Production costs have been fully covered, and the stock is thus finally purchased by the company. This case is shown in Table 4.2. Entry 1 refers to the payment of wages. Entry 2 regards households' expenditure (bank's assets), which leads to the expenditure of $80 income and the transfer of $20 to the company as profit (banks' liabilities). The company buys the stock of goods which is still warehoused by paying back its debt toward the bank, as results from entry 3.

(2) The company distributes profit back to households. This may happen for several reasons. For instance, shareholders may get dividends; Seafarer Co. may also join charity campaigns and donate its gain; profit may also be taxed by the fiscal authority and be distributed to the population. An example may be of help. Suppose Seafarer Co. distributes $5 of its profit to shareholders. Once profit has been distributed (for example, to shareholders, or in charity, or through the intervention of the fiscal authority), the bank accounts of the various beneficiaries are credited. Meanwhile, the company's bank account decreases to the same extent. The picture switches from the one represented in entry 1 (Table 4.3) to the one pictured in entry 2. Households (shareholders) are the ultimate beneficiaries of profit distribution. Following the distribution of profit, no

Table 4.2 Profit and unsalable output

Nantucket Bank (Massachusetts)			
Assets		*Liabilities*	
(1) Seafarer Co.	$100	Households	$100
(2) Households	$100	Seafarer Co.	$80 + $20
(3)	$0		$0

Source: *author's elaboration from Cencini and Rossi (2015).*

Table 4.3 Dividends, taxes, and interests

Nantucket Bank (Massachusetts)			
Assets		*Liabilities*	
(1) Seafarer Co. (output)	$20	Seafarer Co.	$20
(2) Seafarer Co.	$20	Seafarer Co. Households	$15 $5
(3) Households	$5	Seafarer Co.	$5
(4) Seafarer Co. (output)	$15	Seafarer Co.	$15

Source: *author's elaboration from Cencini and Rossi (2015).*

alteration occurs in deposit levels. At this point, as described in entry 3, households purchase a $5 stock of goods from Seafarer Co. (for the sake of simplicity, suppose at a price equal to the production cost, $5). The final situation is shown in the last row of Table 4.3 (entry 4): the company's debt toward the bank is equal to $15 (entered as a bank asset); the monetary profit of Seafarer Co. amounts to $15 (entered as a bank liability). A stock of goods valued at $15 is still to be sold by Seafarer Co.

(3) Seafarer Co. has made a monetary profit of $20 and expects to cover the costs of production of the goods still warehoused by selling them to households. In this case, as represented in Table 4.4, monetary profit is recorded on the bank account of Seafarer Co. (the liabilities in entry 3). Once both production *and* exchange are studied as part of a single, coherent framework, profit can be said to be both physical *and* monetary. Profit, at the macroeconomic level, turns out to be positive. In particular, it is a substitution income that forms thanks to the transfer of a fraction of wages to the hands of companies.

At this time, households' income is zero, though. Therefore, how are production costs covered by the company? As it shall be observed, the answer to this question is strictly connected to the investment of profit in the production of fixed capital.

Macroeconomic foundations of macroeconomics

Before studying investment, a few remarks are worth making. So far, we have studied the existence of profit over a short time period and by considering a single company. However, the analysis is not limited to such a case and may be applied to all real-world examples in which several companies interact among themselves. Rather than attempting to describe all of them – an impossible task – some examples might serve to comprehend the matter. Despite the simplicity of the following examples, infinite, more complex

Table 4.4 A way to investment

Nantucket Bank (Massachusetts)			
Assets		*Liabilities*	
(1) Seafarer Co.	$100	Households	$100
(2) Households	$100	Seafarer Co.	$80 + $20
(3) Seafarer Co. (output)	$20	Seafarer Co.	$20

Source: *author's elaboration from Cencini and Rossi (2015).*

examples could be studied as desired. Nevertheless, the reasoning remains the same in all scenarios. Its lesson is therefore universal. This highlights the fact that the analysis in question, valid in the case of a single company, also holds true for a multi-company scenario, and, above all, it includes the entire set of companies existing in the same monetary system: in this context, therefore, the object of inquiry for the political economist is the economic system taken as a whole.

Let us suppose an economy where a number of companies do exist, each company specializing in a specific productive activity. Companies specialize in food (Wal-Mart Stores Inc.), clothing (American Eagle Outfitters Inc.), real estate (Trulia), automobiles (Ford Motor Company), services (Citibank), and other sectors (see Table 4.5).

Supposing that, for instance, Wal-Mart Stores Inc. sets a selling price of $100 million, if households spend all their income in the purchase of food, Wal-Mart makes a profit of $20 million. In fact, the food company's earnings amount to $100 million, while its wage-costs total $80 million. All other companies, instead, have faced overall costs for $20 million, but have made no gain. Still, an observation shall be made. As soon as Wal-Mart's profit is distributed to shareholders, for instance, it can be spent in purchasing the goods produced by the other companies. If clothes, houses, cars, and services are sold at their production cost, shareholders will purchase the whole produced stock. Thus, all companies will entirely cover their production costs.

From a macroeconomic viewpoint, total wages amount to $100 million, which is the production cost of all companies, *taken as a whole*. Namely, if we were to consider all companies as individual branches of a unique representative firm, that firm would sustain productive costs of $100 million. The profit made by the food company is also arrived at by setting a selling price of $125 million over production costs of $100 million. A proportion may help to understand the previous example, where a company (Wal-Mart

Table 4.5 Wages in a multi-company economy (in millions of dollars)

	Wages
Wal-Mart Stores Inc.	80
American Eagle Outfitters Inc.	5
Trulia	10
Ford Motor Company	2
Citibank	1.6
Other	1.4
Total	100

Stores Inc.) makes a profit and all the others cover their production costs without making any gain:

> Productive costs of the firm making a profit: Selling price set by the firm making a profit = Productive costs of the representative firm: Selling price set by the representative firm

In the case under study,

$$\$80\text{ Mio.} : \$100\text{ Mio.} = \$100\text{ Mio.} : \$x\text{Mio.}$$

Hence, the selling price set by the representative firm would be $125 million.

Another example might help make things clearer. Suppose that households spend the totality of their wages. Suppose also that companies sell a percentage of output and stock the remaining part, meaning that all companies make profits. Further, the rates of profit differ the one from the others. This case is summed up in Table 4.6. By using the data in the first two columns, total profit can be calculated as the sum of each company's profits. When needed, numbers are rounded down.

Given global wages and companies' incomes, the profit rate of the economy, π, approximately amounts to 0.19 (more precisely, to 0.193). If we were to conceive companies altogether (Wal-Mart Stores Inc., American Eagle Outfitters Inc., Trulia, Ford Motor Company, Citibank, and the others) as belonging to one single group or as a single firm, the macroeconomic or selling price of the whole product would amount to $123,915,737.30, as given by the following formula: $p = \frac{\Sigma W}{1-\pi}$. *Caeteris paribus*, the higher

Table 4.6 Wages, prices, and profit in a multi-company economy (in millions of dollars)

	Wages	*Selling price*	*Sold product (share)*	*Sold product (value)*	*Rate of profit*	*Profit*
Wal-Mart Stores Inc.	5	6	0.83	4.15	0.17	0.85
American Eagle Outfitters Inc.	12	18.5	0.65	7.8	0.35	4.20
Trulia	50	58	0.86	43	0.14	7
Ford Motor Company	4	6	0.67	2.68	0.33	1.32
Citibank	3	4.5	0.67	2.01	0.33	0.99
Other	26	32	0.81	21.06	0.19	4.94
Total	100			80.7		19.3

the price of the domestic product with regard to its cost of production, the higher the profit, both in real and in monetary terms.

The examples proposed so far show that, whenever profit arises in the economy, a stock of goods is in the hands of one or more companies. The existence of monetary profit always indicates that the costs of production incurred by one or more companies have not yet been covered entirely.

To sum up,

> macroeconomic magnitudes [. . .] are not obtained by aggregation; they are *sets* in the mathematical sense. Each product, however 'small', is a set; the product of every individual is macroeconomic, the sum of products gives a macroeconomic result quite simply because each product is already a macroeconomic magnitude. This means that the product is the result of a *net* creation [. . .]. Each product thus increases the wealth of *society as a whole*, even if it appears in the possession of a single individual.
>
> (Schmitt 1986: 129)

Each product, taken alone, constitutes the macroeconomic foundations of macroeconomics (see Cencini 2005). All products, taken together, constitute the aggregation of macroeconomic magnitudes. One then realizes that the payment of wages allows for the creation of a real and monetary income that is a mathematical set: however small or big, this set is macroeconomic in nature, for it is a net product that modifies the overall income level in a given national economy. The macroeconomic nature of all sets is given not by their aggregation, but by the fact that each of them is a macroeconomic entity.

Wages and invested profit

When it arises in the hands of companies, profit can either be distributed to third parties or invested in the production of instrumental-goods. Humans, as well as other animal species, make use of raw materials in order to manufacture a certain number of utensils and machine tools that are functional to daily activities; interestingly, it must be observed that the human kind is the only, or among the very few, species that *produce* tools *to produce* other tools (Georgescu-Roegen 1986: 247–8). Large-scale production would not be possible without the aid of instrumental capital: 'machines to make machines to make machines', as Schumpeter put it (Georgescu-Roegen 1986: 247–8).

Hereafter, we shall suppose that, when it is distributed, profit accrues to households at large (shareholders, tax recipients, etc.). We shall also suppose that, when it is invested, profit finances the production of fishing rods, to be used by Seafarer Co. in future productive activities. Namely, so as to make investment effective, Seafarer Co. spends profit to pay wages, which are credited on the bank accounts of households (strictly speaking, on the accounts of workers). We shall call s_w the saving rate from wages in January and s_p the saving rate from profit. Their numerical values shall be given arbitrarily. At first, we shall consider saving rates respectively equal to zero and to one. Then, we shall introduce the hypothesis of saving rates between zero and one.

We shall look here at the case in which households spend their income (wages) entirely (i.e. the saving rate from wages is null) and in which profit is entirely invested (i.e. the saving rate from profit is equal to unity). Households spend all their income to purchase chowder, and Seafarer Co. invests all the profit in a production of fishing rods. The accounting entries relative to this case are registered in Table 4.7. As shown in entry 1, wages are paid, on January 20, resulting from the activation of a credit line. Wages, w_t, are \$100 and the selling price, p, is \$125. Households purchase 80% of the product (eight tons of chowder), worth \$80, and the remaining 20% (two tons of chowder), worth \$20, is left stocked within the company (entry 2). Accordingly, the value of output can be written as:

$$Y_1 = W_1\alpha + P_1$$

In other words, January's income equals the sum of real wages, $W_1\alpha$ (eight tons worth \$80) and real profit, P_1 (two tons worth \$20). On the one hand, the company's debt toward the bank is extinguished to the extent of \$80; on the other hand, profit is physically stocked at Seafarer Co. and monetarily entered into the accounting books of Nantucket Bank (entry 3).

On February 20, Seafarer Co. invests profit: workers produce fishing rods and are paid accordingly (entry 4). Profit investment gives rise to a stock of instrumental-goods worth \$20. It follows that the value of consumption-goods and instrumental-goods, Y_2, is equal to the value of chowder produced in January (\$100) and the value of fishing rods produced in February

Table 4.7 Investment or distribution (1)

Nantucket Bank (Massachusetts)

Assets		*Liabilities*	
(1) Seafarer Co. (output)	\$100	Households	\$100
(2) Households	\$100	Seafarer Co.	\$80 + \$20
(3) Seafarer Co. (output)	\$20	Seafarer Co.	\$20
(4) Seafarer Co. (investment)	\$20	Households	\$20
(5) Households	\$20	Seafarer Co.	\$20
(6)	\$0		\$0

($20), namely the sum of wages paid on January 20 and wages paid on February 20:

$$Y_2 = (1+\pi)W_1$$

It turns out that the value of total output is equal to nominal wages paid on January 20, W_1, multiplied by $(1+\pi)$, where π is the rate of profit.

We shall suppose that households spend February wages in the consumption of the two tons of chowder that remained stocked at the end of January (entry 5). If we suppose for the sake of simplicity a selling price equal to the value of production of chowder (that is, a price of $20), income is fully spent and bank deposits thus turn out to be null (entry 6).

It has to be noted that no distinction is made by the bank between profit investment and profit distribution. If the saving rate from profit were zero, Seafarer Co. would distribute all its profit to households (including, for instance, shareholders, tax recipients, and rentiers). Nantucket Bank would register the same accounting entries shown in Table 4.7. Once profit arises in the company's bank account (entries 2 and 3), Seafarer Co. will distribute it to households as dividends, taxes, and interests (entry 4). In turn, households will spend distributed profit on purchasing two tons of chowder (entry 5), thus leading to a decrease in bank deposits (entry 6). In this case, no fishing rods have been produced, but just ten tons of chowder. Thus, no distinction appears, in bank books, between income distribution (the distribution of profit) and the creation of new value (as resulting from profit investment). This does not imply at all that the two cases, re-distribution and investment, are identical and have to be analyzed in the same way. The apparent 'neutrality' of bank's entries only means that a thorough analysis of the two cases has to be developed further, in particular by distinguishing between the re-distribution of the income formed in a given period and the investment of profit in a period subsequent to that of its formation.

Table 4.8 shows the flows of wages and profits between the company and households, strictly complying with the assumption that the bank functions as a mere intermediary agent between households and firms, and that, therefore it makes no gain. The wages paid in January represent a company's

Table 4.8 Investment or distribution (2)

	Firm	*Households*	Σ	*Example*
Wages (January)	$-W_1$	$+W_1$	0	$100
Consumption (January)	$+W_1$	$-W_1$	0	$80 + $20
Investment or distribution (February)	$-P_1$	$+P_1$	0	$20
Consumption (February)	$+P_1$	$-P_1$	0	$20
Σ	0	0		

outflow and households' income. When households spend wages in the purchase of chowder, the company registers a monetary income and households register an operation opposite in kind. The payment of February wages is registered exactly as for the payment of January wages, since it is a new outflow for the company and an income for households. Transactions concerning February consumption (which we assume takes place at cost price) are registered as for January consumption.

As noted by Godley and Lavoie (2007: 6), a 'cardinal principle' must be applied in the study of flows, namely that 'all rows and all columns sum to zero, thus ensuring, in the catch phrase, that "everything comes from somewhere and everything goes somewhere"'. Accordingly, Table 4.8 shows that the total sum for company's and households' transactions (the columns) and the sum for reciprocal individual payments (the rows) are equal to zero. The economy's total income has been finally spent, and there is no debit-credit relationship between the company and households. As noted earlier, it is important to observe that the transactions registered in Table 4.8, relative to profit investment, are the same as those which would be registered if profit were entirely distributed to households. This means that an analysis of monetary flows allows for no distinction to be observed between activities related to income distribution and activities related to income creation, such as investment. Monetary transactions appear to take place in an orderly way. In fact, for both profit distribution and its investment, the sum of the data in the columns and that for the lines are null. Yet, monetary flows alone do not show that profit investment, compared to profit distribution, gives rise to a stock of goods in the hands of companies (fishing rods, in the example), and, therefore, to a net value.

The case of a null saving rate from wages and of a saving rate from profit equal to unity, as the one described earlier, was also contemplated, for instance, by Kalecki in 1935. A question arises immediately: what can be said of consumption and of investment when the saving rates from wages and from profit are respectively other than zero and unity? This topic was also the object, for instance, of Kaldor's investigation in his 1956 formalization of Keynes's 1936 *General Theory*. It should be noted that, usually, wages are not spent all together on a specific date, but a little at a time. This does not affect the previous conclusions, which remain unaltered. Indeed, supposing a given ratio wages/price, once the totality of income has been spent, a profit of $20 will have arisen. The introduction, in the theoretical discourse, of households' saving complicates the matter, although the final outcome remains unchanged. Hicks's words in his *Capital and Growth* might be borrowed here:

> I do not mean to imply that 'saving out of wages' is practically unimportant. But the complications which it introduces are not matters

> of principle; they obscure our vision if we insist on taking them into account all the time.
>
> (Hicks 1965: 146)

The same holds true for saving out of profit. Indeed, assuming that profit is partly distributed and partly invested complicates understanding without adding any matter of principle. The distribution of profit has always a microeconomic nature, because it allows for the allocation of a stock of goods and services among certain individuals (for instance, shareholders, tax recipients, and rentiers), without changing the overall value of the output initially produced. Investment, on the contrary, is macroeconomic in nature, because it corresponds to the creation of a net income, that is, the focus of the theory analyzed in these pages.

Still, the study of savings from wages and from profit might help understand better the theory at hand. Hence, the analysis shall not be relegated to the case of a saving rate from wages equal to zero and a saving rate from profit equal to one. We shall ask what happens when wages are spent only partially in January, giving rise to a profit that is partly invested in a production of fishing rods. In this analysis we shall introduce the hypothesis that at, the end of February, bank deposits are entirely spent on purchasing the chowder left unsold in January. We shall also introduce the hypothesis that a share of profit is distributed to households as dividends, taxes, and interests.

Suppose that $s_w = 0.5$ and $s_p = 0.5$. Wages are not entirely spent in January (i.e. the saving rate from wages is positive, but lower than one). Profit is partially invested and partially distributed (i.e. the saving rate from profit is positive, but lower than one). This is the most complex case among those to be studied. Therefore, formulas and conclusions on this case hold true also for all the others. Table 4.9 shows the relative bank entries. Assume that wages amount to \$100 and that the selling price is \$125 (entry 1). If s_w is equal to 0.5, workers spend \$50 (their saving, S_w, is also equal to \$50). Therefore, they purchase 50/125 of wages, *i.e.* chowder worth \$40, but priced \$50. Seafarer Co. gains a profit of \$10. The company's debt toward the bank is extinguished to an extent of \$40. This information is shown in entries 2 and 3. If $s_p = 0.5$ (to wit, 50% of profit), the company pays new wages for the production of fishing rods; households' accounts increase accordingly (entry 4). The remaining \$5 (50% of profit) are distributed as dividends, taxes, and interests (entry 5). The company's debt and households' accounts each amount to \$60 (entry 6). Supposing a selling price equal to the cost of production, if, at the end of the second period, households spend the totality of their income, they purchase chowder valued \$60 (entry 7). Income has been finally spent and the company's debt has been fully extinguished (entry 8).

Table 4.9 Investment and distribution (1)

Nantucket Bank (Massachusetts)			
Assets		*Liabilities*	
(1) Seafarer Co. (output)	\$100	Households	\$100
(2) Households	\$50	Seafarer Co.	\$40 + \$10
(3) Seafarer Co. (output)	\$60	Seafarer Co.	\$10
		Households	\$50
(4) Seafarer Co. (investment)	\$5	Households	\$5
(5) Seafarer Co. (distribution)	\$5	Households	\$5
(6) Seafarer Co.	\$60	Households	\$60
(7) Households	\$60	Seafarer Co.	\$60
(8)	\$0		\$0

Table 4.10 Investment and distribution (2)

	Firm	*Households*	*Σ*	*Example*
Wages (January)	$-W_1$	$+W_1$	0	\$100
Consumption (January)	$+c_w W_1$	$-c_w W_1$	0	\$40 + \$10
Investment (February)	$-s_p PI$	$+s_p PI$	0	\$5
Dividends (February)	$-c_p P_1$	$+c_p P_1$	0	\$5
Consumption (February)	$+(s_p PI + c_p P_{1+} s_w W_1)$	$-(s_p PI + c_p P_{1+} s_w W_1)$	0	\$60
Σ	0	0		

It has to be noted, once more, that no distinction is currently made by the banking system between profit investment (entry 4) and profit distribution (entry 5). Yet, while the former entry regards the creation of a stock of instrumental-goods, the latter does not. The structure of the banking system is such that distributed incomes and production-based incomes are treated as if they belonged to the same payment typology. Table 4.10 shows monetary transactions related to the case studied so far. As with Table 4.8, Table 4.10 shows that the sum for monetary transactions in the columns and those on the rows are also null. The analysis of monetary flows does not reveal the nature of payments, either in the case of profit distribution or in the case of investment.

Value of total output

We shall investigate here the composition of income when households spend only a fraction of wages paid at the beginning of January. We shall also study the value of total output when investment is effective. Finally, some conclusions shall be drawn.

Consider the case where the saving rate of January wages is positive. We compute output value at the end of January as the value of sold and unsold goods. January income is given as the sum of the following values:

(a) The value of sold chowder ($40 in the example).
(b) The value of unsold chowder which could have been sold if workers had spent the totality of wages ($40 in the example).
(c) Realized profit ($10 in our example). It is not known yet whether this profit will be invested or not in the production of instrumental-goods.
(d) Unrealized profit ($10 in the example). Had workers not saved, this profit would have been realized by the company, together with (c).

The sum of values (a) to (d) is given as follows:

$$Y_1 = c_w \alpha W_1 + s_w \alpha W_1 + c_w \pi W_1 + s_w \pi W_1$$

The sum of (b) and (c) is households' saving out of wages ($50). Observe also that (a) + (b) equals αW_1, that is, real wages, the value of chowder that could have been sold if the totality of wages paid on January 20 had been spent by workers ($80). Observe also that (c) + (d) is equal to πW_1, that is, profit that could have been made if workers had spent the totality of wages paid on January 20 ($20). (c) + (d) is also equal to the value of chowder that would remain unsold if all wages were spent (namely, to the value of real profit). Notice also that (b) + (c) + (d) is the value of chowder warehoused in January, UWG_1 ($60):

$$UWG_1 = s_w W_1 + P_1$$

Recall that (a) is the value of chowder sold in January, $C_1 + S_{w1} + P_1$, while (b) + (d) is saving out of wages in January, S_{w1}, and (c) is profit formed, P_1, that *can be invested* in the production of fishing rods:

$$Y_1 = C_1 + S_{w1} + P_1$$

Assuming that one half percent of profit is invested in producing instrumental-goods (fishing rods), we compute output value at the end of February as the sum of wages paid in January and February. In other words, the value of total output is equal to the value of chowder produced in January plus the value of fishing rods produced in February. We obtain that total output is:

$$Y_{total} = W_1(1 + s_p c_w \pi)$$

The expenditure of nominal wages worth $50 (out of total wages worth $100) has generated a profit of $10. In January, households have purchased chowder valued at \$40. Fifty percent of the profit (\$5) has then been invested in the production of instrumental-goods and the other 50% (\$5) has been distributed as dividends, taxes, and interests. Remaining bank deposits have then been finally spent by households on purchasing chowder.

To sum up, the value of total output is given as:

$$Y_{total} = W_1 + s_p P_1$$

being investment equal to invested profit

$$I = S = s_p P_1$$

As Keynes (1936 [1964]: 18) wrote:

> From the time of Say and Ricardo the classical economists have taught that supply creates its own demand; – meaning by this in some significant, but not clearly defined, sense that the whole of the costs of production must necessarily be spent in the aggregate, directly or indirectly, on purchasing the product.

This applies to the monetary theory developed here, whatever value the saving rates from wages and from profit may have.

The consequences on the theory of capital accumulation are far-reaching. According to Smith (1776), accumulation consists of the accumulation of a capital that is necessary for production of consumption-goods to be carried out. From the viewpoint of the theory of profit developed here, instead, the existence of capital does not precede, at least in logical terms, the productive process. We must observe that the *sine qua non* condition of fixed capital formation is the investment of part of the income formed by the production of consumption-goods.

A final consideration is in order. In an economy where profit has been invested in the production of instrumental-goods, and wage-goods have been entirely sold, income is equal to the value of wage-goods plus the value of instrumental capital, that is, *invested* profit:

$$Y_{total} = W_1 + s_p P_1$$

which is tantamount to asserting that the value of output is identical to the value of consumption plus the value of investment.

In this respect, new light is thrown on Keynes's 'truisms' resulting 'from the equality between aggregate Income (Y) [. . .] and aggregate Disbursement (D) which is the sum of Consumption-expenditure (C) and Investment (I)' (1933 [1979]: 68–9): income arisen with the production of consumption-goods and instrumental-goods is necessarily equal to the income spent by households and companies to purchase such goods. The value of total output can be defined as the value of consumption-goods plus the value of instrumental-goods, namely the sum of wages paid for the production of consumption-goods and *invested* profit.

Profit and interest

Hereafter, we shall investigate the relation between profit and interest. Specifically, by the term interest, we shall mean interest on consumption loans and interest on fixed capital. We shall also comment on the relation between natural and market interest rates. Interest has largely been the object of inquiry of a great number of economists. Keynes, for instance, in 1930, made 'the rate of interest and its relation to saving and investing the central problem of monetary theory' (Hayek 1931: 270). It was true then, as it is true at present, that the reason for the existence of interest lies in saving and in investment.

Interest on consumption loans

Interest on consumption loans (*Leihzins*, as Eugen Böhm-Bawerk called it) is an income whose existence alters the way in which national income is shared among households, although its total sum remains unchanged. We shall understand better this concept through the following example.

Suppose that Andy receives wages for \$80 and that Anna receives wages for \$20:

Andy's \$80 + Anna's \$20 = \$100

If a part of Andy's deposits, corresponding to \$10, is lent to Anna, Andy's deposits decrease by \$10, from \$80 to \$70; on the other hand, Anna's deposits increase by \$10, from \$20 to \$30:

Andy's \$70 + Anna's \$30 = \$100

The total sum of deposits remains unchanged and corresponds, both before and after lending, to \$100. For simplicity, suppose that the income deposited in the bank accounts of Andy and Anna is not spent.

The following month, Andy receives further wages worth \$80 and Anna receives wages worth \$20:

Andy's \$80 + Anna's \$20 = \$100

If Anna repays \$10 to Andy, plus interest, suppose of \$2, Andy's deposits increase by \$12 and Anna's deposits decrease by \$12. The total sum for deposits remains unchanged. Supposing the new income not be spent, the total for bank deposits amounts to a temporary capital (bank deposits) of \$200. Andy and Anna are therefore free to dispose of a total income of \$200.

Andy has received wages of $160, and has also received an interest of $2, deriving from Anna's wages:

$$\$(80-10)+\$(80+10+2)=\$162$$

On the other hand, Anna has received wages for a total of $40, $2 of which corresponds to the interest paid to Andy.

$$\$(20+10)+\$(20-10-2)=\$38$$

Obviously, the example given is for didactic purposes. In reality, borrowers spend their own income, together with the short-term loan received, to purchase goods and services. The previous example appears more plausible once we assume that Anna spends almost immediately her wage-income and the loan initially granted ($20 + $10, respectively). For a certain period, Andy waives the expenditure of $10 of his initial income ($80). Andy shall be able to spend the $10 at a later date, once the debit-credit has been extinguished. Once he has received the interest of $2, Andy will also be able to spend this interest on the purchase of further goods and services.

Any consumption loan does not generate new income, since it exclusively modifies the sharing-out-of-income among individuals. The entire income is definitively spent, sooner or later. Interest on consumption loans has no linkages with investment and is to be distinguished from interest paid on fixed, or instrumental, capital.

Following Wicksell, Böhm-Bawerk had already contemplated the existence of a difference between interest on consumption and interest on fixed capital. '[I]nterest on pure consumption loans [. . .] is no part of the large social income categories: wages, rents and (with respect to the whole economy, as derived from [. . .] production) interest' (Wicksell 1912 [1997]: 23–4). We shall therefore make a few observations concerning the relationship between interest and fixed capital.

Interest on fixed capital

Besides the interest on consumption loans, another type of interest deserves attention: the interest paid to the owners of capital (Böhm-Bawerk used to call it *Urzins*). Interest on capital is an income distributed to the owners of fixed capital. The analysis undertaken so far has shown that capital is a means of production. That is, capital increases the physical production of labor but is not a productive factor of value in the same way as labor. Fixed capital has its own value, inasmuch as it is a product of labor, yet it does not directly create economic value.

As with profit, interest may also correspond to a portion of the wages intercepted by companies. Above, a numerical example was proposed, in which households spent their entire income of $100, thereby giving rise to a profit of \$20. In that example, other incomes, including interest and revenue, were supposed to be null. If we now assume that interest must be paid to capitalists, we immediately note that, as long as the *Urzins* is positive, the macroeconomic price of wage-goods should be initially greater than their value. That is, their price should be inclusive of the price of interest-goods. In fact, the general rule holds, according to which the price of wage-goods is inclusive of *all* other, non-wage, goods, such as profit-goods, dividend-goods, interest-goods, etc. Indeed, nominal wages initially paid include the value of consumption-goods and the value of all other goods, such as profit-goods, dividend-goods, interest-goods, etc. Schmitt (1984) argued that interest on fixed capital, contrary to interest on consumption loans, is therefore a macroeconomic type of interest, with features of its own.

Natural and market interest rates

Keynes must be included among those scholars who preeminently investigated the nature of natural and market interest rates (especially in his *A Treatise on Money*). Another economist is worth mentioning, though. In fact, ideas of great interest can be found in the writings of Johan Wicksell.

Wicksell defined the natural interest rate as 'the rate of interest which would be determined by supply and demand if no use were made of money and all lending were effected in the form of real capital goods' (1898 [1965]: 102). The monetary, or market, interest rate is, instead, the interest rate fixed for credit transactions between individual savers and companies. If the two rates diverge, then the level of production and its price will vary until natural and market interest rates coincide. To explain this adjustment of the two interest rates, Wicksell resorted to the concept of equilibrium.

It has been previously noted that interest is the compensation paid to the capitalists for having undertaken investment activity. Therefore, the interest rate is defined as the ratio of interest over fixed capital. According to an interesting intuition (to be found in Schmitt 1996: 38), if full employment were achieved, and monetary anomalies entirely disposed of, interest rate or natural interest rate would equal what has been called Euler's number, e – as a percentage – the mathematical constant discovered by the Swiss mathematician Jacob Bernoulli, an expert in interest theory. Interest on loans, which is called instead market interest, is influenced by the central bank. According to Schmitt, the market interest rate would depend on the natural interest rate even though the level of the latter would line up with that of the former. In fact, in order to be granted a consumption loan, borrowers must offer a market interest rate that is higher than, or equal to, the natural interest rate. Were this not the case, investment activity would always be more advantageous than lending activity.

Even though Wicksell considered it as an equilibrium variable, the natural rate of interest can be considered as the rate determined in any given economy between interest and capital or, since interest is derived from profit, between profit and capital. In other words, it is licit to interpret Wicksell's natural rate of interest as the rate of profit. Quite interestingly, a correlation between the market interest rate and the natural interest rate would appear to be confirmed through the observation of modern monetary economies. Market interest rates are increasingly lower, due to the intervention of the central bank in favor of industrial activity (and to the detriment of financial activities). Following central bank intervention, the market rate usually tends to fall short of the natural interest rate. However, the natural interest rate (the profit rate) is increasingly lower, for the profit–accumulated capital ratio decreases over time. The very reason of this tendency of the ratio to decrease is that profits can never be greater than wages. The decrease in the market interest rate follows, as an attempt by the central bank to limit the damages to the real economy by the tendency of the profit rate to decrease. Traditional theories does not convincingly explain this tendency to decrease toward the usual lowest limit (zero).

Profit and capital growth

Economic activities are influenced both by the ability of income-earners (households and companies) to purchase the macroeconomic product (demand), and by the effective availability of the product (supply). Indeed, it can be argued that there is a symmetrical relationship between supply and demand. Such a symmetry should be evident by a simple look at bank books: produced output is the object of the debt incurred by firms to banks and is entered on the assets side of banks' balance sheets; the debt incurred by companies as a consequence of the payment of wages is always and necessarily matched by the deposits, entered on the liabilities side, resulting from the loan granted by wage-earners to banks. Demand and supply turn out then to be the two terms of an identity (see, for instance, Cencini 2005, 2015; Cencini and Rossi 2015).

Hereafter, we shall analyze the payment of wages over infinite periods. Assuming constant saving rates out of wages and out of profits, we shall seek to find the price of domestic output, as divided into consumption- (or wage-) and instrumental-goods, produced over infinite periods of time.

Suppose that wages are always fully spent in the purchase of consumption-goods, and profit is always fully invested in the production of capital-goods. Households' expenditure of \$100 wages in the purchase of consumption-goods at a price of \$125 gives rise to a monetary profit of \$20 and to corresponding physical goods temporarily stocked in the company. Profit is then fully invested by the company. Following the production of investment-goods, households are credited with new wages. Assuming, for the sake of simplicity, a constant price/value ratio, the \$20 stock is sold then at a price of \$25. A stock worth \$4 is still left unsold, and company's bank deposits are still credited with \$4. Supposing that a new production of investment-goods takes place, households are credited with \$4. Repeating the reasoning infinite times, wage payment takes place over infinite periods of time. Wages shall follow a decreasing trend approaching zero (see Table 4.11).

Table 4.11 The infinite horizon

T	0	1	2	3	...	∞
W_t	100	20	4	0.8	...	→0

The process follows a geometrical progression. In particular, total investment over the infinite horizon has a value amounting to \$25. Wages follow an exponential decay. In particular, wages follow a trend expressed by $W_t = W_0 e^{-\lambda t}$, where t = 0, 1, 2, 3, . . ., +∞. In our study case, $\lambda = 1.6094$. For instance, $\$4 = \$100e^{-2\lambda}$; $\lambda = (\ln 25)/2 = 1.6094$. Total output value over the infinite horizon (\$125) is: $Y_{total} = \sum_{n=0}^{\infty} W_0 q^n = W_0 \frac{1-q^n}{1-q}$, where $q = e^{-\lambda} = \pi$, where π is the rate of profit. The initial price of consumption-goods (\$125) includes the value of consumption-goods and the value of capital-goods produced over the infinite horizon.

So far we have dealt with one single payment of wages, starting from which an infinite number of other wage payments has followed (through profit investment over infinite time-periods). In real-world economies, the creation of a net wage-income takes place every accounting period (the month, for instance), thanks to the credit lines granted by the banking system to firms. In fact, it is thanks to credit lines that companies, without disposing of previous funds, pay wages to their employees. This amounts to saying that a process of income distribution and investment starts every time an initial payment of wages is made. Table 4.12 might help understand this issue.

Consider ten time-periods (from $t = 0$ to $t = 9$), supposing that each time-period is equal to the solar month. Every month, thanks to banking intermediation, \$100 wages are paid for the production of consumption-goods. We also suppose that the profit rate is constant and equal to 0.2, and that profit is always fully invested in several productions of fixed capital. This means that, besides the payment of wages for the production of consumption-goods, every month further wage payments also take place for the production of capital-goods. The overall process leads to a monthly increase in the deposits level (as shown in the last row or, equally, in the last column, of Table 4.12): in particular, deposits approach the upward limit of \$125.

For the sake of clarity, observe also Figure 4.1, which shows the deposits levels over ten time-periods. At the beginning ($t = 0$), the first payment of wages gives rise to deposits amounting to \$100 (nominal wages measure a physical stock of consumption-goods). The following month, wages for \$100 are paid for a new production of consumption-goods. Meanwhile, \$20 are paid for the production of capital-goods. The total deposits level equals \$120. A similar reasoning can be extended to an infinite number of

Table 4.12 Deposits growth (per month, in dollars): an upward limit

0	*1*	*2*	*3*	*4*	*5*	*6*	*7*	*8*	*9*	
100	20	4	0.8	0.16	0.032	0.0064	0.00128	0.000256	0.0000512	**124.9999872**
0	100	20	4	0.8	0.16	0.032	0.0064	0.00128	0.000256	**124.999936**
0	0	100	20	4	0.8	0.16	0.032	0.0064	0.00128	**124.99968**
0	0	0	100	20	4	0.8	0.16	0.032	0.0064	**124.9984**
0	0	0	0	100	20	4	0.8	0.16	0.032	**124.992**
0	0	0	0	0	100	20	4	0.8	0.16	**124.96**
0	0	0	0	0	0	100	20	4	0.8	**124.8**
0	0	0	0	0	0	0	100	20	4	**124**
0	0	0	0	0	0	0	0	100	20	**120**
0	0	0	0	0	0	0	0	0	100	**100**
100	**120**	**124**	**124.8**	**124.96**	**124.992**	**124.9984**	**124.99968**	**124.999936**	**124.9999872**	

Notes: Months (0 to 9) are shown in the first row. Deposits, expressed in dollars, are shown in the other rows. Bold numbers are the sums of deposits over time.

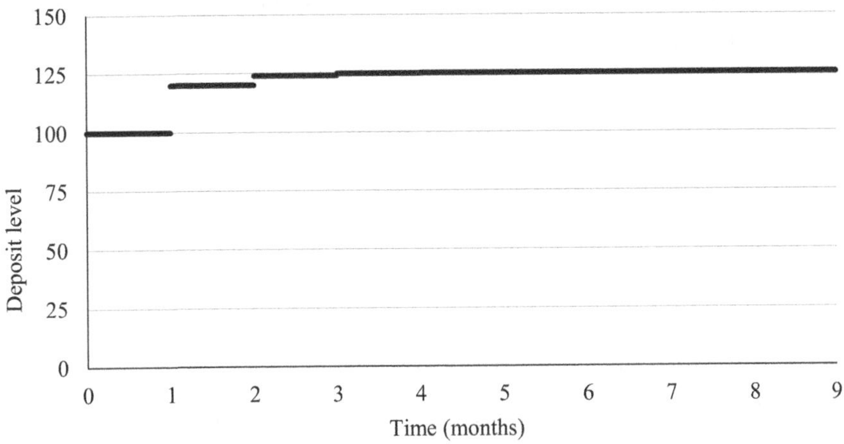

Figure 4.1 Deposits growth (per month, in dollars): an upward limit

time-periods. It is of particular interest, indeed, that, after the first three to four months, the deposits level approaches the upward limit already.

In particular, the deposits level at time t can be found as follows:

$$Deposits_t = Deposits_0 \left(1 + \frac{\pi^{n+1} - \pi}{\pi - 1}\right)$$

where π is the rate of profit.

The analysis conducted here confirms that firms' access to bank credit is crucial for sustainable capital growth. Indeed, the functional relation between banks and firms allows for the creation of net values. Thanks to such a relation, whenever consumption-goods and instrumental-goods are produced, the population is provided with the income necessary to purchase the totality of consumption-goods. The profit made by any company, which defines the total for bank deposits belonging to the company, allows for the payment of dividends, taxes, and interests, but it allows especially for investment activity. The latter leads to the creation of a new value; that is, to the value of capital-goods.

Chapter 5

Profit, lending, and banking reforms

The bugbear of a new financial crisis

As well observed by Baily, Litan, and Johnson (2008: 14), at the very beginning of the 21st century, lending securities were issued mostly to prime borrowers, that is, clients with high credit scores. This is true, for instance, of 2001, when 85% of loans originated in the United States were of high-quality. As the authors recall, an expansion in credit lending occurred in the subsequent years: the value of loans increased from $2.2 trillion in 2001, to about $4 trillion in 2003 alone, with another $9 trillion issued in 2004, 2005, and 2006. What is worth noting is that, over a few years, there was an important increase in the amount of non-prime loans, which were made of 'subprime, Alt-A and home equity lending' (Baily, Litan, and Johnson 2008: 14). In 2006, subprime loans – a very risky type of lending products consisting in credit securities issued to borrowers with poor credit scores and a poor income documentation – represented almost one half percent of the total credit issued in the United States. The expansion in the amount of loans led to an increase in the real home price index, with harsh consequences on households' purchasing power. Indeed, many individuals found themselves incapable of affording a house. Real estate values in the United States collapsed in 2007. This was the beginning of the Global Financial Crisis, the worst financial turmoil since the Great Depression of 1929.

It is often believed that the Global Financial Crisis might have been brought about by errors in regulations and a high-risk attitude of financial actors toward subprime loans especially. As well observed by Lavoie (2014: 1), a number of financial institutions went bankrupt or were bailed out by government intervention: for instance, in 2008 Freddie Mac and Fannie Mae were bailed out by the US government, and certain banks, such as Washington Mutual and Wachovia, were saved through State acquisition; the Canadian and US governments considered it necessary to bail out General Motors; the insurer AIG was bailed out by the US government; the bankruptcy of Lehman Brothers, in September 2008, proved to be the most disastrous event. In an era of financial market globalization, the crisis soon spread to Europe as well. One of the key problems for certain European economies (the so-called PIIGS, namely Portugal, Ireland, Italy, Greece, and Spain) was the high ratio of debt/GDP.

Subsequently, American and European banks made significant reductions in lines of credit to companies and loans to families. If it is certainly true that the growth in loans has slowed down starting from 2008–9, lending activities since the Global Financial Crisis have followed different paths in the United States and in Europe, as explained by Naceur and Roulet (2017: 7–9). In particular, the two authors show that commercial, retail, and other loans have followed different trends in the two geographical areas. Commercial loans include loans to trade and industry, to commercial real estate, to construction, to agriculture, and to funds in the money market. Retail and other loans are made of credit card loans; loans to installments, to residential real estate, to municipalities, and to governments; and other loans. Data provided by Naceur and Roulet (2017: 7–9) show that the credit market has recovered more quickly in the United States than in Europe. The United States experienced a fall in the growth rate of commercial loans from 2008 to 2010, followed by a continuous increase from 2011 to 2015. The growth rate in retail and other loans dropped in the United States from 2008 to 2011, when it started going upward. In Europe, the growth rate in commercial loans started decreasing in 2009. Over the following year, 2010, the Old Continent saw a slight commercial credit crunch, which was followed by a small increase in the growth rate in commercial loans that lasted until 2013, when Europe experienced a significant crunch in commercial credit (reaching almost –10% starting from 2014). A similar trend has been followed by retail and other loans in Europe, where their growth rate has decreased from 2009 to 2011 and, again, starting from 2013. European banks have faced a crunch in retail and other loans starting from 2014 (reaching a negative growth of almost 10%).

A decade after the Global Financial Crisis, a number of countries have not fully recovered, despite many of them being better off now than ten years ago. The gross domestic product, unemployment, stock prices, and real estate prices clearly show that world economies have taken different paths since the crisis. For instance, according to Manibog and Foley at *The Financial Times* (2017), the real gross domestic product in 2017, compared to the gross domestic product in 2007, was higher in the United States, Germany, the United Kingdom, France, Japan, Spain, Iceland, Ireland, and China, but lower in Portugal, Italy, and Greece. Full economic recovery and sustained growth may be a mirage for many years to come. Some experts warn in fact against the risks of another financial downturn. One of them is, for instance, Frank Partnoy, Professor at the University of San Diego and author, among other works, of *F.I.A.S.C.O.: Blood in the Water on Wall Street* (2009). Writing for *The Financial Times*, Partnoy (2017) argues that the instability of the financial system is nowadays being hidden by good credit ratings to collateralized loan obligations (CLOs), as happened in 2007. Then the financial crisis came.

Lending to high-risk borrowers is not the only potential cause of a new financial crisis. Indeed, the sovereign debt crisis in Europe and unconventional monetary policies have been said to be a major potential threat to financial recovery and stability in the Western World. According to the former Minister of Finance in Germany, Wolfgang Schäuble, for instance, increasing debts and the trillions of dollars pumped by central banks into banking systems may well be at the origin of a new crisis (see Chazan's 2017 contribution to *The Financial Times* on this). Schäuble indeed has been among the opponents of so-called 'quantitative easing', an expansionary monetary policy implemented by a number of central banks, including the Federal Reserve System and the European Central Bank. Through the purchase of bonds, central banks have sought to lower interest rates and to make credit cheaper, inducing companies and individuals to borrow money from financial institutions. The ultimate goal of quantitative easing is to prop consumption and investment. However, the endurance of a number of economies after the end of quantitative easing is yet to be proven.

Besides the sovereign debt crisis, another potential cause of new financial turmoil is the high level of debt contracted by the private sector in some major economies. Keen (2017), in particular, argues that a new crisis may soon be originated by the high level of private debt in China, which amounts to twice the Chinese gross domestic product. Keen (2017) also argues that a bubble may soon burst in Australia, where, since the Global Financial Crisis, the private sector debt increased by about 180% to 200% of the gross domestic product. The Australian economy (the housing market in particular) behaved well after the crisis, thanks to public intervention and to foreign investment. Now, Keen (2017), argues, it may well be different. 'As Minsky said, it is only a matter of time before the next crisis arrives' (Chancellor 2017).

Yet, much has been done since the Global Financial Crisis to reform major financial systems worldwide. Indeed, national legislators and central banks have not been sitting on their hands. The United States is among the major countries that have vigorously reacted to the financial turmoil started in 2007. In this sense, an important banking reform has been signed into law in 2010 with the aim of promoting financial stability in the country. The reform addresses a number of issues, including bank lending. Accordingly, the reform seeks to clamp down on predatory credit. Important measures have also been adopted in the European Union, where the European Commission (2018), among others, has promoted, for instance, the creation of a fully functioning banking union.

Besides the United States and the European Union, many other countries have adopted new financial regulations in the aftermath of the crisis. In particular, many jurisdictions have implemented a series of recommendations known as Basel III or the 2010 Basel Accord, which has strengthened the capital and liquidity requirements of banks. Both sets of regulations in the United States, in the European Union, and in the countries that have adopted the Basel rules have been largely endorsed, but also highly criticized for several reasons. The debate is still going on in the highest institutional circles.

It is interesting to note that, broadly speaking, the limits on lending, set by financial regulations, are made on an individual basis; that is, on the credit rating of each potential borrower. We shall argue that further measures should be taken by banks to ensure the financial stability of the system. It is certainly true in fact that banks, running their business activities, are becoming more and more efficient and transparent; however, we shall argue that banks, as pure intermediaries between companies and households, should build a better system of national payments. A reform of the system of national payments shall be proposed, as it was developed by Bernard Schmitt in the 1970s and 1980s. The reform advocates the creation of three bank departments, where record is kept of monetary transactions over each accounting period, of savings, and of invested profit. The ultimate goal of such a reform is to settle sustainable lending levels. In fact, the three departments together shall provide precise information about the overall amount of credit that banks can grant to their clients taken as a whole, not just as single individuals.

The fragility of regional regulations

The US Dodd-Frank Act

The Dodd-Frank Wall Street Reform and Consumer Protection Act (Public Law 111–203, 2010), which is named after Chris Dodd (then Chair of the Senate Banking Committee) and Barney Frank (who served as Chairman of the House Committee for Financial Services), became effective on July 21, 2010. The reform was meant to avoid new episodes of financial instability. The goal of the act was, in fact,

> [t]o promote the financial stability of the United States by improving accountability and transparency in the financial system, to end 'too big to fail', to protect the American taxpayer by ending bailouts, to protect consumers from abusive financial services practices, and for other purposes.
>
> (Public Law 111–203, 2010)

The Dodd-Frank reform is of particular interest, since it clearly shows the financial issues to which the public authority has been sensitive and willing to regulate in recent times. The Dodd-Frank Act defines the set of rules and procedures to be followed by different long-established, as well as new, actors as stated in a number of Titles, which address, among others, the following issues.

Prudential regulation, which aims to protect depositors from bank insolvency, is high on the agenda of financial authorities since the Global Financial Crisis of 2007–8 (see Tirole and Dewatripont 1993 on the topic). The Dodd-Frank regulation has been thought for sure, among other goals, to guarantee the prudence of financial actors when carrying out their daily activities, so as to foster financial stability. Accordingly, the reform regulates the Financial Stability Oversight Council (FSOC) and the Office of Financial Research (OFR) at the Department of the Treasury.

> The purposes of the Council are [. . .] (A) to identify risks to the financial stability of the United States that could arise from the material financial distress or failure, or ongoing activities, of large, interconnected bank holding companies or nonbank financial companies, or that could arise outside the financial services marketplace; (B) to promote market discipline, by eliminating expectations on the part of shareholders, creditors, and counterparties of such companies that the Government will shield them from losses in the event of failure; and (C) to respond to emerging threats to the stability of the United States financial system.
>
> (Public Law 111–203, 2010)

> The purpose of the Office is to support the Council in fulfilling the purposes and duties of the Council [. . .] and to support member agencies, by [. . .] (1) collecting data on behalf of the Council, and providing such data to the Council and member agencies; (2) standardizing the types and formats of data reported and collected; (3) performing applied research and essential long-term research; (4) developing tools for risk measurement and monitoring; (5) performing other related services; (6) making the results of the activities of the Office available to financial regulatory agencies; and (7) assisting such member agencies in determining the types and formats of data authorized by this Act to be collected by such member agencies.
>
> (Public Law 111–203, 2010)

The reform defines the powers given to the Office of the Comptroller of the Currency (OCC), to the Federal Deposit Insurance Corporation (FDIC), and to the Federal Reserve (FED), so as

> (1) to provide for the safe and sound operation of the banking system of the United States; (2) to preserve and protect the dual system of Federal and State-chartered depository institutions; (3) to ensure the fair and appropriate supervision of each depository institution,

> regardless of the size or type of charter of the depository institution; and (4) to streamline and rationalize the supervision of depository institutions and the holding companies of depository institutions.
>
> (Public Law 111–203, 2010)

The OCC, a Bureau of the Department of the Treasury, was created to supervise national and foreign banks in the United States, as well as federal savings associations, so as to guarantee the fairness, safety, and soundness of the financial system (Office of the Comptroller of the Currency 2018a). As supervisor, the OCC works proactively to promote 'a vibrant and diverse banking system that benefits consumers, communities, businesses, and the U.S. economy' (Office of the Comptroller of the Currency 2018b).

The FDIC is the major actor in charge of the liquidation of financial institutions, including banks, insurance, and nonbank financial companies. Also, the Federal Insurance Office at the Treasury Department has been conceived as the major authority in the insurance industry.

Among the other major goals of the Act are, for instance, the regulation of advisers to hedge funds and others, the transparency and accountability of Wall Street intermediaries – operating in the swap market in particular – and the enhancement of the supervision of the payment, clearing, and settlement system through the Federal Reserve.

The Act includes the so-called Volcker Rule, named after Paul Volcker, Chair of the President's Economic Recovery Advisory Board from 2009 to 2011 and Chair of the Federal Reserve from 1979 to 1987. According to the Federal Reserve (2017b),

> Section 619 of the Dodd-Frank Wall Street Reform and Consumer Protection Act, commonly referred to as the Volcker rule, generally prohibits insured depository institutions and any company affiliated with an insured depository institution from engaging in proprietary trading and from acquiring or retaining ownership interests in, sponsoring, or having certain relationships with a hedge fund or private equity fund. These prohibitions are subject to a number of statutory exemptions, restrictions, and definitions. The Federal Reserve Board is working closely with the other agencies charged with implementing the requirements of section 619, including the Office of the Comptroller of the Currency, the Federal Deposit Insurance Corporation, the Securities and Exchange Commission, and the Commodity Futures Trading Commission.

The Bureau of Consumer Financial Protection (CFPB) was created in 2012 so as to 'protect consumers from unfair, deceptive, or abusive practices and take action against companies that break the law' (Consumer Financial Protection Bureau 2018). The Bureau (2018) publicly recognizes its goals, which include: providing consumers with the tools, the information, and the knowledge required to make sound financial choices; taking action in case of misconduct by financial actors to the harm of consumers; educating both consumers and financial companies about financial markets, financial products, and financial laws. The supervision of financial markets, law enforcement, financial education and research, and the monitoring of financial markets and agents are all major goals of the Consumer Financial Protection Bureau.

The reform aims also to improve access to mainstream financial institutions to all those individuals that traditionally are left out of financial markets, by encouraging 'initiatives for financial products and services that are appropriate and accessible for millions of Americans who are not fully incorporated into the financial mainstream' (Public Law 111–203, 2010). Further, the Dodd-Frank Act includes other regulatory measures such as the 'Pay It Back Act', 'Miscellaneous Provisions', and 'Section 1256 Contracts'.

Given the large amount of credit extensions in the real estate sector, especially before the 2008 crisis, the Dodd-Frank Act seeks to reform the mortgage market and to avoid predatory lending. In particular, limits have been put on bank credit in the United States. According to the Office of the Comptroller of the Currency (U.S. Department of the Treasury 2017), 'lending limits protect the safety and soundness of national banks, promote diversification of loans, and help ensure equitable access to banking services'. Loans to the clients of national banks are set on individual bases. 'These limits prevent excessive loans to one person, or loans to related persons who are financially dependent. The lending limits regulation (12 CFR 32) applies to all loans and extensions of credit made by national banks and their domestic operating subsidiaries'. In particular, pursuant Section 32.2 of Title 12 (Banks and Banking) of the Code of Federal Regulations (CFR), banks must abide by a 'combined general limit', which goes as follows.

> A national bank's total outstanding loans and extensions of credit to one borrower may not exceed 15 percent of the bank's capital and surplus, plus an additional 10 percent of the bank's capital and surplus, if the amount that exceeds the bank's 15 percent general limit is fully secured by readily marketable collateral [. . .].

According to the Consumer Financial Protection Bureau (2017a), any lender must be aware of any borrower's records, such as her/his income, any asset, whether she/he is employed, her/his documented credit, and her/his consumption behavior. Before granting a loan, lenders should detect any potential cause of insolvency by the borrower. In other words, lenders must check objective factors indicating whether the borrower is able to repay her/his debt. In the case of real estate loans, lenders must grant so-called Qualified Mortgages, provided they have checked whether borrowers meet specific requirements (Consumer Financial Protection Bureau 2017b). In particular, some risky lending activities are forbidden, the amount of any loan must be settled on the basis of the borrower's income, fees are ruled by the Law, and, to some extent, lenders must be legally protected (Consumer Financial Protection Bureau 2017b).

Now, it must be observed that the Dodd-Frank Act has been frequently attacked over the years, especially a decade after the Global Financial Crisis, when the Republicans won the White House.

As well explained by Jopson for *The Financial Times* (2017), attempts have been made by the White House Republican administration, since its early days, to loosen the rules regulating the financial system. More than that, as Jopson observes, the President has been backed by some regulators, who have endorsed, among other actions, a revamp of the Volcker rule. According to Jopson's 2018 contribution to the same journal, on March 14, 2018, the Senate passed a set of rules to relax the Dodd-Frank Act. The rules, which moved to the House of Representatives, were thought to sweep bank deregulation. The rules were approved by the House on May 22, 2018, together with amendment 67–31, and became law following the signature of the US President on May 24, 2018. The law is known as the Economic Growth, Regulatory Relief, and Consumer Protection Act.

As observed by Alan Rappeport and Emily Flitter for *The New York Times* (2018), the Act of May 22 is a big rollback for the first time since the Dodd-Frank Act was signed into law. The importance of the new Act was remarkable, because it exempted banks with less than $250 billion in assets from the strictest supervision. The Dodd-Frank Act imposed strict supervision on those institutions with assets values exceeding $50 billion. This means that the Law of May 24 left 'fewer than 10 big banks in the United States subject to stricter federal oversight' (Rappeport and Flitter 2018). 'Republicans, and some Democrats, say the Dodd-Frank law has [. . .] cut off the flow of credit to many Americans who depend on smaller banks for business and personal loans' (Rappeport and Flitter 2018). On this ground, many opponents of the Dodd-Frank Act argue that the Republican legislation should ease the burden of financial rules carried by small and medium banks. In particular, the legislature was expected to intervene to limit the applications of the Volcker rule, 'which bans banks from making risky bets with depositor's money' (Rappeport and Flitter 2018).

The European banking union

The European Central Bank, which aims to be the central bank of all national central banks in the Euro-area, has played an active role as banking authority in the aftermath of the Global Financial Crisis. To act efficiently and with transparency, the European Central Bank needs the banking systems in the Eurozone to be grouped as a banking union. This has been particularly true after the economic and financial turmoil of 2007–8. It was in fact clear, for instance, that bank supervision was not strong enough in a number of banking systems worldwide. A full supervision of banks in the Euro-area can be achieved only if national banking systems are part of a banking union, with shared and common supervisory rules and procedures, possibly legally binding. Broadly speaking, the banking union 'allows for the consistent application of EU banking rules in the participating countries', being transparency and safety of banks among the major goals to be achieved by the union (European Central Bank 2018a). The development of a banking union was particularly endorsed by top EU institutions following the Global Financial Crisis and the sovereign debt crises that hit many economies ever since: a fully operational banking union would indeed reduce the likelihood that national problems in finances and in the banking sector would be transmitted to other nations (European Central Bank 2018a). Hence, as explicitly stated by the European Central Bank (2018a), thanks to the banking union, European banking would achieve greater transparency, 'by consistently applying common rules and administrative standards for supervision, recovery and resolution of banks'; national banking systems would also reach unification, 'by treating national and cross-border banking activities equally and by delinking the financial health of banks from the countries in which they are located'; banking in Europe would also be safe, 'by intervening early if banks face problems in order to help prevent them from failing, and – if necessary – by resolving banks efficiently'.

The banking union relies on two mechanisms: the Single Supervisory Mechanism (SSM) and the Single Resolution Mechanism (SRM). The European Central Bank and the national authorities in charge for banking supervision adopt the SSM, which was created as a new form of supervision in Europe after the crisis of 2007–8; the SRM was thought as a means to 'ensure the efficient resolution of failing banks with minimal costs for taxpayers and to the real economy' (European Central Bank 2018a). The European Central Bank shall supervise the banking system and shall determine the likelihood of a bank failure; the resolution of failed banks shall be enacted in a few days through measures adopted by the Single Resolution Board and financed by banks' contributions to the Single Resolution Fund (European Central Bank 2018a).

The two mechanisms are enacted in accordance with the single rulebook, that is, a series of regulations to be followed by the members of the European banking union. The rulebook 'provides legal and administrative standards to regulate, supervise and govern the financial sector in all EU countries more efficiently. It includes rules on capital requirements, recovery, and resolution processes and a system of harmonized national Deposit Guarantee Schemes' (European Central Bank 2018a).

As regards banking supervision, the SSM is of particular interest, because it has been conceived as a means to promote a safe and sound banking system in Europe as well as to allow for an integrated and stable financial environment where supervision is made consistently (European Central Bank 2018b). The European Central Bank (2018b) clearly explains the reasons, the goals, and the objects of the supervisory mechanism. Hereafter, they shall be briefly summarized, as reported by the Bank, given the importance of the supervisory mechanism, which is likely the most important attempt made in Europe to ward off a new crisis. The banking union is being conceived as a tool to create a trusted and resilient banking system in Europe, motivated by the spreading of financial troubles from one monetary system to the others, as happened during the Global Financial Crisis. The creation of a banking union would give full supervisory powers to the European Central Bank, which, on a daily basis, would act and take measures shared by all participants to the union. The European Central Bank also makes sure that all the supervisory agents in Europe are to provide their functions consistently and effectively. The European Central Bank, as head of supervision over the banking union, conduces 'supervisory reviews, on-site inspections and investigations', 'grant or withdraw banking licenses', 'assess banks' acquisition and disposal of qualifying holdings', ensure compliance with EU prudential rules', 'set higher capital requirements ("buffers") in order to counter any financial risks' (European Central Bank 2018b).

The European Central Bank itself (2018b) explains which countries belong to the Single Supervisory Mechanism and which banks fall under the direct supervision of the ECB. Participation in the SSM is automatic in the case of Eurozone members, while it is at the discretion of the other European countries. Whenever a European country is not part of the SSM, supervision should be guaranteed through cooperation between national supervisors and the European Central Bank. Under the mechanism, a number of banks are supervised by national authorities. Remaining banks are directly supervised by the European Central Bank. The ECB has direct supervisory authority over 118 banks under the SSM. The assets of these 118 banks altogether amount to 82% of banks' assets in the Eurozone. Banks that are directly supervised by the ECB are known as 'significant'.

Direct surveillance on significant banks is conceived under the SSM so as to prevent financial turmoil in the Eurozone, in an interconnected world where the troubles of one single institution may soon and quickly propagate all around. None excluded: the Global Financial Crisis has taught indeed that no financial institution is 'too big to fail'. The Regulation of the SSM and the Single Supervisory Mechanism Framework Regulation thus lists the criteria according to which a bank is deemed 'significant' (European Central Bank 2018c). As stated by the European Central Bank (2018c), a bank is given significant status whenever it meets at least one of the following criteria: total assets value over 30 billion euros; the bank is highly important in its country and/or in the European Union (national top three banks may always be deemed significant); total asset value of over 5 billion euros and important cross-border activities; the bank makes request for funds or actually does receive funds from the European Stability Mechanism or from the European Financial Stability Facility.

Banks participating in the SSM may change status, being deemed significant or less significant whenever they meet, or do not meet, the criteria for being directly supervised by the European Central Bank or by national supervisory authorities (European Central Bank 2018c): as soon as one or more of the significance criteria are met by the bank, the European Central Bank is entrusted by national supervisors with the supervision of such bank; vice versa, whenever a significant bank does not meet the significance criteria for three years in a row, supervision can be competence of national authorities (European Central Bank 2018c).

Supervision of significant banks is made, in rotation, by members of the European Central Bank and of national supervisory institutions, gathered in a number of Joint Supervisory Teams, any of which is formed to supervise one single bank at a time (European Central Bank 2018d). Broadly speaking, the purpose of Joint Supervisory Teams is to spread a common and consistent supervisory model throughout Europe, the highest output of cooperation between Frankfurt and European banks within the SSM (European Central Bank 2018d). Any significant bank is directly supervised by one Joint Supervisory Team, which is assigned the following tasks: 'perform the Supervisory Review and Evaluation Process', 'propose the supervisory examination programme, including a plan of on-site inspections', 'implement the approved supervisory examination programme and any supervisory decisions', and 'ensure coordination with the on-site inspection teams and liaise with the national supervisors' (European Central Bank 2018d). The members of each Joint Supervisory Team are chosen in number proportionally 'to the size, business model and risk profile' of the significant bank they are called to supervise, and they are both employees in Frankfurt and national supervisors established in any of the countries where the bank has its headquarters, its branches, and its subsidiaries (European Central Bank 2018d). Joint Supervisory Teams are formed by a coordinator in Frankfurt who is in charge of the team for a period between three and five years, other coordinators at the national level who supervise specific regions and on specific themes, and a number of professionals (European Central Bank 2018d).

Yet, despite all the work done so far by European authorities to build a banking union, much effort is still needed to achieve full financial stability. The limits of European banking and a call for action have been addressed by the European Commission to the European Parliament in October 2017 (European Commission 2018). Despite that the SSM and the SRM are working correctly, banking in Europe still lacks a single deposit protection and tools to eliminate all the financial risks connected, for instance, to credit lending and diversification in sovereign bond investment (European Commission 2018). Euclid Tsakalotos, Greece's finance minister, on January 7,

2018, has contributed to *The Financial Times*, raising some acute questions about the reach of a banking union in Europe. In particular, Tsakalotos (2018) argued that a banking union may not be enough to guarantee the financial safeness of single national economies.

The Vice-Chair of the Supervisory Board of the European Central Bank, Sabine Lautenshchäger, who has also been appointed member of the Executive Board of the same institution, made an interesting speech in Brussels, on March 22, 2018, regarding 'Financial Fragmentation or Integration' (European Central Bank 2018e). Lautenshchäger observed that financial regulation and supervision have been improved in Europe, and a rulebook on banking in Europe has been developed. Yet, the fragmentation of the national banking systems was still relevant in 2018, 'to a degree that makes it hard to reap the full benefits of the European banking supervision' (European Central Bank 2018e). What still needs to be fully and better addressed by legislation regard large investment companies and their branches in third countries, since they are still out of the scope of supervision, as well as 'national discretions', 'proper assessments', 'tools for crisis management', 'insolvency laws', and 'moratoriums' (European Central Bank 2018e).

Challenges to Basel III

The Bank for International Settlements in Basel, Switzerland, hosts the Basel Committee on Banking Supervision (BCBS), the Committee on the Global Financial System, the Committee on Payments and Market Infrastructures, the Markets Committee, the Central Bank Governance Forum, and the Irving Fisher Committee on Central Bank Statistics. They are 'responsible for financial stability by providing background analysis and policy recommendations' (Bank for International Settlements 2018a).

In particular, the BCBS is responsible for setting global standards concerning prudential regulation of banking systems, promoting cooperation on banking supervision (Basel Committee on Banking Supervision 2018a). Supervisory groups, international agencies, and other bodies work closely with the Committee and include the Bank for International Settlements, the Basel Consultative Group, the European Banking Authority, the European Commission, and the International Monetary Fund.

The BCBS was established in 1974 in response to 'serious disturbances in international currency and banking markets (notably the failure of Bankhaus Herstatt in West Germany)' (Basel Committee on Banking Supervision 2018a). The BCBS included the Governors of the Central Banks of the Group of Ten (G-10) countries, namely Belgium, Canada, France, Germany, Italy, Japan, the Netherlands, Sweden, Switzerland, the United Kingdom, and the United States. Over time, the number of members grew significantly, coming at present from Argentina, Australia, Belgium, Brazil, Canada, China, the European Union, France, Germany, Hong Kong SAR,

India, Indonesia, Italy, Japan, Korea, Luxembourg, Mexico, the Netherlands, Russia, Saudi Arabia, Singapore, South Africa, Spain, Sweden, Switzerland, Turkey, the United Kingdom, and the United States.

In 2018, the BCBS was made of institutional representatives of central banks and of the following regulatory authorities: the Australian Prudential Regulation Authority, the Canadian Office of the Superintendent of Financial Institutions, the China Banking Regulatory Commission, the European Central Bank Single Supervisory Mechanism, the French Prudential Supervision and Resolution Authority, the German Federal Financial Supervisory Authority (BaFin), the Indonesian Financial Services Authority, the Japanese Financial Services Agency, the Korean Financial Supervisory Service, the Mexican *Comisión Nacional Bancaria y de Valores*, the Swedish *Finansinspektionen*, the Swiss Financial Market Supervisory Authority (FINMA), the Turkish Banking Regulation and Supervision Agency, the British Prudential Regulation Authority, and, in the United States, the Office of the Comptroller of the Currency and the Federal Deposit Insurance Corporation. Observers include Chile, through the Central Bank of Chile and the Banking and Financial Institutions Supervisory Agency, Malaysia, through the Central Bank of Malaysia, and the United Arab Emirates, through the Central Bank of the United Arab Emirates.

In 1988, the BCBS issued a set of rules known as Basel I or Basel Capital Accord, which set the minimum requirements on banks' capital and risk-weighted assets (Basel Committee on Banking Supervision 2018a). A new accord, known as Basel II, was issued by the Basel Committee on Banking Supervision in 2004. The Accord was founded on three pillars: minimum requirements on banks' capital, the supervision of capital adequacy and the internal assessment of any institution, and disclosures so as to promote discipline and soundness in the banking system (Basel Committee on Banking Supervision 2018a). The Global Financial Crisis started in 2007–8 proved that many banking systems were far from being stable and led to a new accord in 2010, known as Basel III.

The 2010 Accord, which was a direct response of central bankers to the Global Financial Crisis, was thought as a set of standards to be implemented and applied by the countries or jurisdictions members of the BCBS, so as to strengthen regulatory financial frameworks, to supervise, and to better manage the risk incurred by banks (Basel Committee on Banking Supervision 2018a). As well described by the Basel Committee on Banking Supervision (2018b), the 2010 Basel Accord was meant to strengthen the requirements on the capital and on the liquidity of all banks, as well as to limit the risks associated to the interconnection of financial institutions. Particular attention is paid to 'globally systemic important banks (G-SIBs)', for which the Committee drew up ad-hoc regulations: 'should they fail, they can be automatically recapitalised by bailing in investors, without troubling taxpayers' (The Economist 2017).

The recommendations of Basel III that concern capital are based on three pillars. Pillar 1 regards the quality and the level of capital as well as the capacity of any bank to absorb losses. It also includes measures among which: a revision of the standards adopted to calculate many risks including credit, market, and operational risks; constraints on internal models so as to 'reduce unwarranted variability in banks' calculations of risk-weighted assets'; and 'capital requirements for exposures to central counterparties [. . .] and equity investments in funds' (Basel Committee on Banking Supervision 2018b). Pillar 1 also aims to contain leverage. The recommendations included in Pillar 2 were developed so as to manage and supervise risks arising, for instance, from 'off-balance sheets exposures' and 'compensation practices' (Basel Committee on Banking Supervision 2018b). Pillar 3 regards the discipline of the market, introducing, for instance, 'a dashboard of banks' key prudential metrics' (Basel Committee on Banking Supervision 2018b).

The Basel III Accord also regulates the liquidity of banks, by means, in particular, of a series of metrics and of two ratios: namely, the Liquidity Coverage Ratio (LCR) and the Net Stable Funding Ratio (NSFR) (Basel Committee on Banking Supervision 2018b). The two ratios possibly represent the most important constraints worldwide to banking liquidity and capital management introduced after the Global Financial Crisis. We shall propose here their main features and purposes, following the Bank for International Settlements (2018b, 2018c,d).

The Liquidity Coverage Ratio (LCR) has been conceived so as to reduce to the minimum the risk of a bank's shortage of liquidity in the short-run – that is, in thirty calendar days – by requiring any bank to hold so-called 'high-quality liquid assets' (HQLA), which are easily convertible into cash, in case the bank was in trouble (Bank for International Settlements 2018b). High-quality liquid assets, which are unencumbered, are made of cash or items that can be sold in the private market, with no substantial change in their value, whenever a bank finds itself in liquidity stress or shortage (Bank for International Settlements 2018c). In particular, the Liquidity Coverage Ratio is calculated as the ratio between high-quality liquid assets and '[t] otal net cash outflows over the next 30 calendar days', and it must be higher than or equal to 100% (Bank for International Settlements 2018c).

As well explained by the BIS (2018c), the Liquidity Coverage Ratio must be respected under normal circumstances, that is, when the bank experiences no liquidity stress. Therefore, any bank is usually required to hold high-quality liquid assets valued more than total net cash outflows in the short-term. Whenever situation of liquidity shortage sets in, the bank is allowed to reduce the amount of total net cash outflows, which are sold to private agents and converted into liquid assets such as cash. High-quality liquid assets should be turned into cash over a maximum period of 30 calendar days and, more precisely, over the minimum time required by the size of the shortage of liquidity faced by the bank. High-quality assets should also 'be eligible for use in central bank operations. Certain types of assets within HQLA are subject to a range of haircuts' (Bank for International Settlements 2018c).

As regards their composition, high-quality liquid assets consist of two categories of assets, so-called Level 1 and Level 2, which are described by the BIS (2018c) as follows. The first type of assets is made of 'cash, central bank reserves, and certain marketable securities backed by sovereigns and central banks, among others'. The second one is made, among others, of 'certain government securities, covered bonds and corporate debt securities' (Level 2A) and 'lower rated corporate bonds, residential mortgage backed securities and equities that meet certain conditions' (Level 2B). Basel III requires that Level 2 and Level 2B assets do not exceed 40% and 15%, respectively, of high-quality liquid assets (Bank for International Settlements 2018c).

Total net cash outflows constitute an important part of the Liquidity Coverage Ratio, together with high-quality liquid assets. Total net cash outflows are given by the difference between cash outflows and cash inflows in the first thirty calendar days of potential liquidity shortage (Bank for International Settlements 2018c). The definitions of cash outflows and cash inflows, which are precisely written in the Basel III Accord, are conceived so as to guarantee a sustainable value of HQLA over time, being cash inflows 'subject to an aggregate cap of 75% of total expected outflows' (Bank for International Settlements 2018c).

The other major ratio under the Basel III Accord is the Net Stable Funding Ratio (NSFR), which was conceived as a tool to guarantee the stability of a bank's sources on and off its balance sheet, with the purpose of safeguarding liquidity and reducing the spreading of a bank's troubles into the banking system (Bank for International Settlements 2018d). The Bank for International Settlements (2018d) has well described the features of the Net Stable Funding Ratio, which can be summarized as follows.

While the Liquidity Coverage Ratio has been thought as a means to deal with liquidity shortage in the very short period of thirty calendar days, the Net Stable Funding Ratio should protect the banking system from potential funding risks in a year's time. The value of the NSFR, which must exceed or be equal to 100%, is defined as the ratio between the available stable funding and the required stable funding. The available stable funding is made of the capital and of the liabilities that the bank expects to be holding over one year. Any institution is required to hold an amount of stable funding that 'is a function of the liquidity characteristics and residual maturities of the various assets held by that institution as well as those of its off-balance sheet (OBS) exposures' (Bank for International Settlements 2014: 2). The amount of available stable funding depends on a number of magnitudes that concern the stability of funding sources and that include, for instance, the maturities of a bank's liabilities and the specific features of the various funding sources.

The required stable funding amount is instead a function, broadly speaking, of the risk of liquidity shortage connected to the assets of a bank and its off-balance sheet activities.

It must be noted that Basel III has been facing important challenges since 2010.

The Regulatory Consistency Assessment Programme (RCAP) is in charge of monitoring and assessing how members authorities enact Basel III at the national level, transposing the recommendations of the Committee on Banking Supervision into national regulations (Basel Committee on Banking Supervision 2018a). On March 22, 2018, the Vice-Chair of the Supervisory Board of the European Central Bank has remarked on this regard:

> With Basel III finalised, we have a global set of regulatory standards. As standards, they are not always detailed and they are not binding, of course. So they still need to be transposed into hard law. [. . .] Supervisors must faithfully apply the rules which transpose the Basel standards.
> (European Central Bank 2018e)

Revisions and implementation of the Accord are usually made over a few years and, as regards Basel III, the last regulations were planned to be implemented by all member jurisdictions in 2019. It must be noted, however, that the implementation of Basel III, which is particularly slow, has met some obstacles. Indeed, 'there are signs that the trend towards international regulation that gathered pace after the financial crisis may be going into reverse' (The Economist 2017).

A number of bankers and officials feel the weight of financial regulations on banking activities. For instance, the implementation of Basel III forces banks to increase, compared to Basel I and Basel II, the ratio of capital levels over risk-weighted assets (RWAs) such as real estate mortgages and loans to large corporations. This is likely to the detriment of European banks rather than to the American banking system, because the value of mortgages and business loans is higher in Europe than in America (The Economist 2017). A side effect of the strong Basel III requirements on capital and liquidity are likely to reduce lending activities or to increase their costs (Baldwin 2012). 'This is a problem in consumer-driven economies like we have in the West, as consumers put off major purchases due to their inability to qualify for credit' (Baldwin 2012).

Also, the Republican White House administration has backed a climate of hostility toward international financial regulations. For instance, as observed by *The Economist* (2017), Patrick McHenry, serving the House Financial Services Committee, wrote a letter addressed to Janet Yellen, head of the Federal Reserve, arguing that it is not acceptable for the Federal Reserve to keep on negotiating international financial regulations. 'In other words, stay out of Basel until you get new orders' (The Economist 2017).

If it is true that predatory lending may give rise to a financial crisis, as it did at the beginning of the 21st century, it is also true that an excessive reduction in corporate and consumer loans may be to the detriment of economic prosperity. It follows that regulation is likely inevitable, but it may also have a negative impact on lending activities and, ultimately, on economic growth. Therefore, the transposition of Basel III capital requirements into national laws, together with national financial regulations, may have good and bad consequences on lending activities. The United Kingdom may well be a good example in this regard.

In the aftermath of the Global Financial Crisis, the United Kingdom approved a series of changes in financial regulation through the Financial Services Act of 2012 (Bank of England 2018). In particular, the Financial Services Act has led to the creation of the Financial Policy Committee and the Prudential Regulation Authority, and it has also given new supervisory responsibilities to the central bank on a number of financial issues (Bank of England 2018). The Bank of England (BoE) has adopted new measures in this regard, by embittering the requirements of banks' clients to take out mortgages. It has been said that Mark Carney, Governor of the BoE, 'has become the first leading central banker to try to prevent a new credit boom from derailing the economic recovery after the Bank of England imposed limits on mortgage borrowing and predicted that surging house prices will rise further still' (Fleming and Giles for *The Financial Times*, 2014).

Yet, according to a study made by Bridges et al. (2014) for the Bank of England, increases in capital requirements over time do affect banking lending in different ways, which include the following. The authors focus on four economic sectors, that is, loans to households (secured and unsecured), 'lending to commercial real estate corporations', and 'lending to non-real estate non-financial corporations' (Bridges et al. 2014: 11). Following capital requirements increases, banking lending activities do react differently across the different sectors of the economy: interestingly, the growth in loans to real estate, both to households and companies, reduce more than the growth in other lending categories. From their study (2014), Bridges, Gregory, Nielsen, Pezzini, and Spaltro found that, in the United Kingdom, secured household loans as well as corporate loans, in particular to companies operating in the commercial real estate sector, temporarily fall down in response to a capital requirement increase. Therefore, the authors' findings

> contribute to the debate on whether the Modigliani-Miller propositions hold (i.e. whether changes in the composition of a bank's liabilities affect the bank's overall cost of funds and credit supply), in which case changing banks' capital requirements would not affect lending. In practice, the empirical literature has identified a range of friction (with taxation of debt versus equity being frequently mentioned) such that the debt/capital structure of banks may not be neutral for credit supply.

> Our paper confirms that regulatory requirements tend to affect capital ratios permanently and credit supply temporarily.
>
> (Bridges et al. 2014: 4)

Therefore, the effects of financial regulations on lending activities and, broadly, on economic growth, are controversial and objects of a harsh debate. All financial regulations appear to be fragile and doomed to be endlessly changed.

Moreover, financial regulations at large allow banks to grant credit on individual grounds, meaning that any loan to the borrower must be backed by securities, and provided banks' liabilities are always matched by the same amount in banks' assets. Lloyds Bank (2018), for instance, processes a loan request made by any of his clients by setting an individual or 'personal loan rate' which includes the history of repayments, the history of past accounts, and individual details recorded within the bank. HSBC (2018) evaluates a credit score of its clients, which concerns the borrowing histories and public information so as to understand whether the clients are likely to pay the debt back. As reported by HSBC (2018), banks and credit card agencies use credit scores, that is, numerical scores, and credit ratings, based on bandings, to evaluate whether their clients are creditworthy. The credit score is then used to produce a credit report or 'credit file', which contains all the information regarding the payments, loan history, and credit card use pertaining to the potential borrower (HSBC 2018).

It is certainly true that individual credit should be granted, as much as possible, to creditworthy borrowers. Not a single objection can be raised in this regard. A couple of questions can be made, though. Financial regulations, particularly lending requirements, are usually made at the discretion of national authorities and, ultimately, of political actors. Is there a further way to determine the sustainable amount of credit to be granted by any national bank? Also, is there any relationship between profit and sustainable lending levels? The reform originally proposed by Bernard Schmitt in 1984 provided pioneer answers in this regard.

A reform of the system of national payments

Money has been among the object of economic writing since classical times. For instance, one may think of the Plan for the Establishment of a National Bank (1824), where Ricardo made a study of money creation and credit. The study of money and credit is of particular interest still at present. On the one hand, banks use money as a means of payment. On the other hand, banks manage deposits, for instance, through lending activities. Indeed, banks play two different though related intermediations: the monetary and the financial intermediations. The former relates to money *per se*, that is, nominal money; the latter regards the management of income, that is, real money.

A logical dependency ties the one to the other, for vehicular money should always be used (the monetary intermediation) to allow for the increases and the decreases in income as a result of production and consumption, respectively, as well as for convoying income from one bank account to another (the financial intermediation). Nowadays, this logical dependency between the two kinds of intermediations is little understood. This gives room to inevitable monetary problems, such as inflation. An example may help to understand the issue at hand.

By way of example, consider Table 5.1. Suppose that the income of households amounts to $100 (entry 1). Monetary income is deposited in the bank system and constitutes households' savings. During their existence, savings are lent by banks to creditworthy borrowers. For the sake of explanation, we shall think here of the limit case in which borrowers are granted a $150 loan by Nantucket Bank to purchase the products from Seafarer Co., a client of the same bank. Surprisingly enough, the bank may grant loans to an extent that exceeds the amount of income in the system. Indeed, financial regulations require banks to ensure that loans are matched by deposits of the same amount, independently of the income available in the system. Entry 2 in Table 1.3 shows that, when the loan finances the purchases from a company client of the same bank that grants the loan, it gives rise to a double-entry where the debt of the borrowers is perfectly matched by the deposits credited to the company, Seafarer Co. in our example. The rule according to which loans must always be covered by equivalent deposits is therefore complied with, despite the fact that the loan granted by Nantucket Bank is $50 greater than the amount of income generated by production. Banks have no real-time knowledge of the amount of income at their disposal prior to the end of the day. Therefore, loans may be partially financed by the creation of purely nominal money. Nominal money adds to money-income, thus decreasing the purchasing power of each money-unit. Each dollar buys fewer products than what it should. The process is thus inflationary. This example of monetary over-creation shows that inflation is a phenomenon in which a positive difference appears between total money-units and money-income.

Table 5.1 Consumer lending and inflation

Nantucket Bank (Massachusetts)			
Assets		*Liabilities*	
(1) Seafarer Co.	$100	Households	$100
(2) Borrowers	$150	Seafarer Co.	$150
(3) Borrowers	$150	Households	$100
		Seafarer Co.	$50

Source: Author's elaboration from Cencini and Rossi (2015).

This gives rise to an increase in the price level. It follows that a purely nominal profit forms in the hands of the company (entry 3). It must be observed that inflation is always unjustified on a logical ground. In fact, wage-income is necessary and sufficient for households to buy the entire stock of goods, for demand (monetary income) is always identical to supply (output value).

Borrowing Ricardo's words, '[w]hilst the Bank is willing to lend, borrowers will always exist, so that there can be no limit to their over-issues' (1809 [2004]: 17, III). When banks lend beyond the deposit level, they give rise to a mismatch between income as such (the monetized product) and monetary deposits – what can be defined as an inflationary phenomenon, given the fall in the purchasing power of money. Banks should not grant credit to consumption to their clients (the financial intermediation) by emitting nominal money (the monetary intermediation). In other words, bank lending to consumption should be regulated in order to impede banks' financial intermediation to be 'fed' through money creation.

In this light, it must be observed that Schmitt (1984) proposed a reform of the system of national payments that strictly dealt with lending activities. The reform would impede any confusion between the monetary and the financial intermediations of banks, thus allowing for a correct management of credit. The reform, unique in its kind, takes into account the strict relationship between nominal money, households' income, and corporate profits. The Schmitt plan thus foresees three banking departments accounting for the logical distinction between nominal money, savings, and invested profit and allowing for payments to be carried out in compliance with this logical distinction. Accordingly, the three departments are respectively:

(1) the department of monetary transactions or Issue Department (Department I);
(2) the Saving Department, also called Financial or Income Department (Department II); and
(3) the Capital Department, where records are made of invested profit (Department III).

Production and consumption

Let us resume the example made in Chapters 1 and 2 and think of Nantucket Bank as a commercial bank that functions as intermediary between the company Seafarer Co. and households. As accounting period between one balance and the next, we shall take the calendar month, meaning that, by assumption, wages are paid monthly. Table 5.2 regards a simple case in which wages are paid and fully spent before the closure of the accounting period and no profit is made. The first two entries (1 and 2) concern the creation of workers' income. The payment of wages entails the creation of $100, registered on the assets side of Department I, and an income of $100 on the

Table 5.2 Income and consumption (1)

Nantucket Bank (Massachusetts)			
Department I			
Assets		*Liabilities*	
(1) Seafarer Co.	$100	Department II	$100
(4) Department II	$100	Seafarer Co.	$100
(5)	$0		$0

Nantucket Bank (Massachusetts)			
Department II			
Assets		*Liabilities*	
(2) Department I	$100	Households	$100
(3) Households	$100	Department I	$100
(6)	$0		$0

Source: Author's elaboration from Cencini and Rossi (2015).

liabilities side of Department II. Meanwhile, Department I and Department II are debited-credited between each other. The two following entries (3 and 4) concern instead the definitive expenditure of income. The payment of households is registered on the assets side of Department II, while the company's credit is registered on the liabilities side of Department I. At the same time, the debt of Department I toward Department II is matched by the debt entered by Department II toward Department I, and the two entries cancel out. This allows for the settlement of the dual debit-credit relation between Seafarer Co. and households. Money and income are hence finally spent (balances 5 and 6). As long as the bookkeeping relationship between the two departments is not canceled out, it shows the maximum amount of loans ($100) that the bank is allowed to grant to its client during the accounting period.

Entries in Table 5.3 concern a case similar to the preceding one in which income is not entirely spent before the end of the accounting period. Supposing that workers have spent 60% of their wages without profit having been made, the payments registered in the two departments indicate a persistent company debt of $40, a households' credit for the same amount, and a credit-debit for the two departments equal to $40. The first four entries are similar to the first four in the previous case. Amounts and balances, however, differ. In fact, the new balances of the two departments (entries 5 and 6) show that, out of initial income, a $40 income has not yet been spent. At this point, according to Schmitt's reform proposals, the

Table 5.3 Income and consumption (2)

Nantucket Bank (Massachusetts)

Department I

Assets		*Liabilities*	
(1) Seafarer Co.	$100	Department II	$100
(4) Department II	$60	Seafarer Co.	$60
(5) Seafarer Co.	$40	Department II	$40
(8) Department II	$40	Seafarer Co.	$40
(9)	$0		$0

Nantucket Bank (Massachusetts)

Department II

Assets		*Liabilities*	
(2) Department I	$100	Households	$100
(3) Households	$60	Department I	$60
(6) Department I	$40	Households	$40
(7) Seafarer Co.	$40	Department I	$40
(10) Seafarer Co.	$40	Households	$40

Source: Author's elaboration from Cencini and Rossi (2015).

debt of Seafarer Co. is transferred from the first to the second Department, the rule being that at the end of each period, entries in Department I must cancel out. The rationale for this rule is that the income formed in any given period must not finance the purchase of the product of any other period. Households are free to spend their income when and how they like, but the system of payments must avoid the superposition of monetary flows pertaining to different periods. Generalized exchange is enough to allow households to purchase the products of their choice without jeopardizing the structure of the system. Transactions from 7 to 10 show that, after the first accounting period, income lasts over time in the form of a financial capital, because, even if it has not been definitively spent in the final purchase of produced output, it has been automatically lent by Nantucket Bank to Seafarer Co., which invests it in the formation of a real stock made up of the wage-goods yet to be sold on the market for products.

Once it forms, income is registered within the bank system and remains temporally available on the financial market. This means that savings will be spent by their legitimate holders or by borrowers (by households, broadly speaking). Department I is functional to avoid the occurrence of inflation, since it prevents money creation (void of any real content) to finance loans to (purchases of) bank clients. During the accounting period, Nantucket Bank is able to lend money up to $100. Whenever consumers decide to purchase goods and services, a portion of income will be spent on the products market, and deposits will thus decrease for the same amount. Once the accounting period is closed, households' saved-up income amounts to $40 and is matched by a debit of Seafarer Co. toward the bank, as recorded in Department II.

Observe that the entries studied in the two preceding cases do not involve Department III: entries in such department are made for net profit as well as for the payment of dividends and interests, so as to register the value of fixed capital. The next sections shall show the relationship between profit, fixed capital, and Department III.

Profit distribution and investment

Dividends, taxes, and interests

Let us study profit creation and its distribution to households (shareholders, tax recipients, rentiers, etc.). Table 5.4 gives the whole set of entries described hereafter.

We shall consider the entries in Department I concerning the sole payment of wages, so as to focus on those transactions that are registered in Departments II and III. Entries from 1 to 6 concern the payment of wages. Wages payment implies the creation of $100 and an income of the same amount: as previously observed, this implies the debit-credit of the first two departments (entries 1 and 2).

Let us suppose that, by the end of the accounting period, wages are not spent yet: saved-up income is recorded in Department II. The relationship between the two departments ceases to exist: the balance of the first department is null, because income is entirely spent in the formation of a stock of unsold goods; the balance of the second department amounts instead to

Table 5.4 Dividends, taxes, and interests

Nantucket Bank (Massachusetts)			
Department I			
Assets		*Liabilities*	
(1) Seafarer Co.	$100	Department II	$100
(4) Department II	$100	Seafarer Co.	$100
(5)	$0		$0

Nantucket Bank (Massachusetts)			
Department II			
Assets		*Liabilities*	
(2) Department I	$100	Households	$100
(3) Seafarer Co.	$100	Department I	$100
(6) Seafarer Co.	$100	Households	$100
(7) Households	$100	Seafarer Co.	$20 + $80
(8) Seafarer Co. (product)	$20	Seafarer Co. (profit)	$20
(9) Seafarer Co.	$20	Department III	$20
(11) Seafarer Co. (product)	$20	Department III	$20
(12) Department III	$5	Households	$5
(15) Seafarer Co. (product)	$20	Department III	$15
		Households	$5

Nantucket Bank (Massachusetts)			
Department III			
Assets		*Liabilities*	
(10) Department II	$20	Seafarer Co.	$20
(13) Seafarer Co.	$5	Department II	$5
(14) Department II	$15	Seafarer Co.	$15

Source: Author's elaboration from Cencini and Rossi (2015).

$100 (entries 3 to 6). Households' saved-up income (formed in the previous period) cannot be lent anymore.

Now, let us analyze wages expenditure and the existence of profit. For the sake of simplicity, we shall omit entries relative to Department I. Entry 7 regards the debit-credit of households and the company in the financial book (Department II) of the bank. This entry is important for two reasons. First, it shows the expenditure of $80 in the final purchase of a stock of goods valued by that same amount. The debt of Seafarer Co. toward Nantucket Bank is extinguished to the amount of $80. Further, this entry shows a profit of $20. Entry 8, which is the balance of Department II, shows the existence of company deposits (entered as a liability in the bank financial book) and the existence of a real stock stored in the company (registered as an asset in the same book).

A new department (Department III) must come to the fore. It is in this department that profit is recorded. Economic agents are still unaware of whether it will be invested entirely, whether it will be fully or partially distributed, or spent by the company to cover its costs of production. The deposit of profit in a proper department implies the entries (9 and 10) in the two Departments, II and III. The balance of the second department is thus as shown in entry 11.

Let us suppose that households receive dividends, taxes, and interests (any kind of rent, for instance) for $5. It is therefore necessary to credit households (entry 12 in Department II) and subtract the $5 corresponding to dividends, taxes, and other incomes of substitution from Department III (entry 13).

Profit, initially amounting to $20, has been partially distributed to households, whose deposits have hence increased by $5. Profit reduction is equivalent to an increase in households' deposits for an equal amount. Distributed as dividends, taxes, and interests, profit is back to the financial market in the form of income. The balance for Department III is therefore as shown in entry 14: the profit available for investment in the production of capital-goods (fixed capital) is therefore equivalent to $15.

The balance for Department II is as in entry 15. The balance for Department II shows that the product left unsold and stored at Seafarer Co. has a value of $20. The company's profit is recorded in Department III and households' savings are equal to $5.

Profit, once made by the company, is always registered in Department III. On the one hand, the portion of profit that is distributed as dividends, paid as interest, or spent by the company to purchase the stock yet to be sold, leaves Department III, and is again available in Department II. This means that dividends, taxes, and interests are again converted into income and, available on the financial market, will be spent on the products market, by their legitimate holders (shareholders, tax recipients, rentiers, etc.) or by borrowers. On the other hand, invested profit shall be definitively recorded into Department III.

The investment of profit

So far, we have described the accounting entries relative to production, profit creation, and profit distribution. We shall now proceed with an analysis of the entries relative to the investment of profit in a production of instrumental-goods (fishing rods, for instance). New wages are paid to the amount of $15. Let us suppose a selling price of chowder equal to its cost of production. Households will spend new wages to purchase the chowder, valued at $15, that is still warehoused at Seafarer Co. Households will also spend $5 paid by Seafarer Co. in the previous period as dividends, taxes, and interests, to purchase the other $5 chowder still to be sold by Seafarer Co. Instrumental capital consists of fishing rods belonging to Seafarer Co. Table 5.5 gives the complete sequence of accounting entries regarding investment.

Department I is always involved – i.e. whenever a payment takes place – vehicular money being the means of each single payment. However, as

Table 5.5 Investment

Nantucket Bank (Massachusetts)

Department I

Assets		*Liabilities*	
(16) Seafarer Co.	$15	Department II	$15
(19) Department II	$15	Seafarer Co.	$15
(20)	$0		$0

Nantucket Bank (Massachusetts)

Department II

Assets		*Liabilities*	
(15) Seafarer Co. (product)	$20	Department III	$15
		Households	$5
(17) Department I	$15	Households	$15
(18) Seafarer Co.	$15	Department I	$15
(21a) Seafarer Co. (product)	$20	Department III	$15
		Households	$5
(21b) Seafarer Co. (investment-goods)	$15	Households	$15
(22) Households	$20	Seafarer Co. (product)	$20
(23) Seafarer Co.	$15	Department III	$15

Source: Author's elaboration from Cencini and Rossi (2015).

previously stated, in this study, we chose to consider entries in Department I just as far as wage payments are concerned. Profit investment falls into such a type of payment. Entries 16 and 17 are related to the new payment of wages, amounting to $15. The first two departments are thus involved in monetary and financial transactions.

Over the accounting period, the money level amounts to $15 (recorded in Department I). This means that Nantucket Bank is allowed to grant credit to a maximum extent of $15. It has to be observed that the income level amounts to $20 (recorded in Department II). Supposing that wages are not spent, at the end of the accounting period we will register entries 18 and 19 in Departments I and II, since money does not survive the accounting period. The balance for the first department at the end of the accounting period is thus null (entry 20). Income survives, to be precise, as a temporal capital that will be finally spent as soon as consumption will be effective. Hence, the balance of Department II is as follows (entries 21a–21b).

The expenditure of wages, dividends, taxes, and interests to purchase the product left unsold is recorded as in entry 22. The final balance for the

Table 5.6 Department balances

Nantucket Bank (Massachusetts)			
Department I			
Assets		*Liabilities*	
(20)	$0		$0

Nantucket Bank (Massachusetts)			
Department II			
Assets		*Liabilities*	
(23) Seafarer Co.	$15	Department III	$15

Nantucket Bank (Massachusetts)			
Capital department III			
Assets		*Liabilities*	
(14) Department II	$15	Seafarer Co.	$15

Source: Author's elaboration from Cencini and Rossi (2015).

second department is therefore as in entry 23. At the end of the accounting period, there is no longer any consumption-good stored in the company, and the value of fixed capital is recorded in Department III.

The balances of the three departments for the overall accounting periods are shown in Table 5.6. Instrumental capital, which belongs to Seafarer Co., is now registered on the books at Nantucket Bank.

Following the analysis of income distribution and investment, one discovers that a reform of national payment systems is urgently needed. In particular, if one wants to preserve the current institutional order, as well as create a sound capitalism, a reform based on bank bookkeeping practice must be implemented in order to fully keep a record of money, income, and fixed capital levels. This will allow for a correct and objective management of bank credit that shall be built on macroeconomic grounds.

Conclusion

Of all the topics that economists have written about, profit is without any doubt one of the most controversial. Being true that microeconomic profits are made from the sale of goods at a mark-up, things are not as straightforward when one attempts to determine the ontology of macroeconomic profits. A number of scholars, from the Classicals to Keynesians, have always argued that macroeconomic profits constitute a positive income. Yet, economists have failed to provide a clear explanation of the origins of macroeconomic profits. Even worse, the great majority of economic theorists has come to ignore this subject. Inevitably, as more and more economists dodge the matter, it is increasingly important to clear the haze around it.

Economists' inability to share a common opinion on macroeconomic profits likely stems from a smoky understanding of the basic laws underlying economic phenomena. If academics failed to carry out a unitary theory of profits, such a failure is likely due to the lack of a full knowledge of the laws of production, consumption, and banking. Economics is a newborn science compared to the others, and as such, much research work is required to provide new answers to economic issues. Therefore, drawing from Bernard Schmitt's contribution to economic research, this volume has sought to clear the way for a new understanding of macroeconomic profits, by dwelling, since the very first pages, on the intertwined realm of production, consumption, and banking.

To understand the theoretical backdrop of profit analysis, one should think of companies as pure intermediaries. Indeed, companies are intermediaries in so far as they convey goods and services, thanks to the use of money, from workers-producers to households-consumers. The national product, in fact, is always produced by workers and temporarily stocked by companies. Through consumption, the product is subsequently sold to its final users. So as to allow for the production and the allocation of output in the hands of its final users, money is always injected and rejected by banks into the economy. Through the payment of wages, money as a currency is issued by banks as the numerical form of goods and services. Such an event gives rise to a positive wage-income which is temporarily credited on the bank accounts of workers. Monetary wages are then transferred from workers to households broadly speaking, either directly or indirectly. Through consumption, conversely, wage-income is definitely spent. Such an event allows firms to cover their production costs and pay back their debt toward the bank system.

Money, as a vehicular means of payment, is injected and rejected, credited and debited, in every payment. Therefore, money can be conceived as a numerical flow, a tool to be used to credit and debit companies and individuals, by means of bookkeeping entries in banks' books. The *raison d'être* of vehicular money abides in the need to provide products with a homogeneous form, a unit of account, from their very production to their final purchase. As soon as money 'covers' the physical product, money must be thought as a numerical stock, a positive income which is duly registered on banks' accounts, the duration of which is logically tied to the act of consumption. Indeed, it is worth observing that income is nothing but a financial capital, the nature of which is only temporary.

Through this volume, it has been observed that economic activities rely on the long-standing expertise of commercial banks, which are in charge of managing monetary transactions and deposits. Yet, it has also been argued that national monetary systems cannot be founded on commercial banks alone. Indeed, if it is true that production and trade are backed up by commercial banks, the management of interbank payments must be entrusted to the central bank. Historically, central banks have played various roles, aiming for instance to stem economic and financial turmoil, to guarantee the stability of monetary systems, and to manage the currency in circulation. This is what happened, for example, in the United Kingdom and in the United States, where the central banks were created in 1694 and 1913, respectively. In particular, through these pages, it has been argued that the orderly functioning of interbank transactions is allowed by the central bank through the management of interbank payments. Any central bank, in fact, has been envisioned to process, settle, and clear the payments issued by any commercial bank to other commercial banks operating within the same national economy. Acting as the intermediary of commercial banks, the central bank allows for the correct resolution of interbank payments through the use of the national currency.

Notes and coins in circulation, being IOUs issued from the central bank, are always entered in the books of banks. Therefore, they can never be concealed from the monetary system. Importantly, the use of cash or its abandonment does not affect at all the physiology of the monetary system. In fact, regardless of the individual preference or aversion to notes and coins, cash is nothing but the forefather of modern means of payments. The expansion of debit and credit cards and the increasing use of electronic means of payments testify that, in practice as much as in theory, modern economies can do without banknotes and coins in circulation. More than this, through paying by smartphones, debit and credit cards, or e-banking platforms, consumers act in place of bank clerks. Indeed, through the use of technology, payments are instantly made by consumers, without any assistance from bank employees. Therefore, the time should be ripe to understand that money is just a numerical means of payment independently of the medium used to represent it.

Being true that firms act as intermediaries between workers-producers and households-consumers, it is as much true that firms, making profits, must also be conceived as income-earners. Yet, the origin and the existence of profits at the macroeconomic level has always been a burning issue in economic theory, being a source of pitfalls and discord among economists.

The Classicals, from Adam Smith and James Steuart in Scotland, from Jean-Baptiste Say in France to David Ricardo in England, groped for a proper explanation of profit, conceived as the income of the capitalist class. Leafing through the pages of the Classicals, the term 'capitalist' acquires three meanings, referring to the capitalist, the entrepreneur, and the company. In the classical view, no conceptual distinction is to be made between the capitalists, entrepreneurs, and firms. Therefore, time and again the Classicals assumed profits to be an adjunct product belonging to the capitalist-entrepreneur-company. Yet they failed to contentedly reach a common theory of profits. Indeed, they all provided their own analyses, but not one of them was able to explain the laws of profit monetization.

Karl Marx made the most important attempt in this regard. Marx had longed to determine how monetary profits are made in the hands of the capitalists. Yet, despite thorough intuitions, on the nature of money for instance, the Prussian political economist could not undo the entangled strings of his theory. Indeed, assuming that workers are paid wages in exchange for their labor force, under the hypothesis that workers gratuitously produce profit-goods, Marx faced the logical impossibility to explain the way in which profit-goods are monetized.

If it is true that the Classicals were enthused about the study of profits, things briskly changed with Léon Walras, the founder of the neoclassical school. Profit was no longer conceived as the income of the capitalist-entrepreneur-company monad, but rather as the interest paid to the capitalist. The nub of Walras's argument was a simple one. The three figures of the capitalist, the entrepreneur, and the company were divided into two conceptual groups, the owners of capital and entrepreneurs-firms. The shift from the Classicals was significant: profit, defined as the aggregate income of the entrepreneur-company, was necessarily nil, for it was the counterpart of loss. Conceiving profit as the remuneration of the capitalist, the more recent neoclassical models of growth and fluctuations, developed since the 1950s, have been faithful to Walras' thinking. Therefore, no significant contribution to the neoclassical theory of profit has been made since the 19th century.

The neoclassical theory of distribution, since Walras, has been entirely carried out through the use of differential calculus. The laws of output allocation were the effect of a number of hypotheses made to satisfy mathematical requirements. Yet, such assumptions soon proved to be weak when put to the test. In particular, for instance, the neoclassical equality between the marginal product of capital and the rate of profit was seriously cast into doubt by the studies of Knut J. Wicksell, who paved the way to the research work of John Maynard Keynes and Keynesian economics.

The theory of profit was revived in the 1930s, when the contributions of Keynes came to the fore as an alternative to neoclassical economics. Having written on profits in the 1920s, Keynes was not new to the topic. Yet, the time that passed between 1930 and 1936, the publication years of *A Treatise on Money* and *The General Theory*, was a turning point in the history of economic thought. At that time, a number of notable scholars in Cambridge, United Kingdom, fed up discussions about the existence of profits which contributed to the shaping of *The General Theory*. Interestingly enough, the British economist argued that, labor being the sole source of value, the value of national output should be measured entirely in wages. In 1936, reminiscent of the Classicals, Keynes argued that the profits of entrepreneurs, together with wages, make up total national income. *The General Theory*, far from explaining unequivocally the laws of income distribution, prompted a number of new research lines.

Starting from 1937, notable economists, including Roy F. Harrod, John R. Hicks, James E. Meade, Oskar R. Lange, Franco Modigliani, Paul A. Samuelson, Alvin H. Hansen, and Axel Leijonhufvud, proposed 'orthodox' versions of *The General Theory*, which merged into the neo-Keynesian theory. This stream of thought was based on the IS-LM model of the late 1930s, which, later on, was also adopted by new Keynesian economists. Importantly, both neo-Keynesian and new Keynesian theories are built around the non-neutrality of money, but, given their theoretical constructs and the methodology adopted by their proponents, they are akin to the neoclassical theory rather than to the theory originally proposed by Keynes.

Unsatisfied with the 'orthodox' versions of *The General Theory*, post-Keynesian economists have developed further lines of inquiry. In particular, the seminal studies of Nicholas Kaldor and Luigi L. Pasinetti, which led to the neo-Pasinetti theorem, were followed by numberless reactions. The debates were cause of particular strain between economists in both the United Kingdom and the United States. Famous is indeed a controversy on capital, which, bringing to light the two phenomena known as 'reswitching of techniques' and 'capital reversing', undermined the neoclassical production function and the neoclassical theory of profit. In more recent times, musings have given birth to a number of post-Keynesian research lines. Several contributions have been made in fact by post-Keynesian scholars, who undertook to explain, among other topics, the existence of macroeconomic profits. Researchers have pointed out a series of solutions to the problem of profit realization. Models in this regard assume, for instance, the reliance of companies on foreign trade, public intervention, and the advance of profits through bank lending, and they hypothesize the subdivision of the economy into subsectors, supposing the existence of consumption- and investment-goods. Yet, consensus on the existence of profits has yet to emerge.

Given this state of things, this volume has sought to contribute to the theory of profits, aiming to pay close attention to the allocation of wage-goods and profit-goods in the hands of households and in the hands of companies. In many respects, the theory developed by Bernard Schmitt has many ties to classical and Keynesian economics, in so far as it is based, for instance, on the idea that labor alone is the sole source of value. Accordingly, the point of departure of the inquiry has been the fact that monetary wages constitute the right of workers on the goods and services temporarily stocked by companies. Being logically impossible for them to be made out of any excess of revenues over costs of production, macroeconomic profits must necessarily consist in a new allocation of produced goods and services.

Consistently, through the volume, it has been observed that profits form out of the transfer of monetary and real income from households to companies. Following this line of inquiry, it has been shown that profit is made as a real stock and simultaneously realized as money. The existence of monetary profits allows companies, taken as a whole, to finally purchase profit-goods for their own sake, to distribute profits to stakeholders, or to retain them for future investment activities. In the end, monetary wages and monetary profits turn out to be spent in the final purchase of goods and services, at the disposal of households and companies. Money, through the intermediation of banks, is always injected and rejected, so as to permit the origin, the distribution, and the expenditure of monetary incomes, as well as to allow for the final purchase of produced output, which ends up in the hands of households and companies. Worth observing is the fact that the existence of macroeconomic profits, conceived as the profits of firms taken as a set, allows us to thoroughly understand the nature of microeconomic profits, conceived as the gain made by any single firm in terms of revenues over costs of production.

The analysis of macroeconomic profits shows that profits and investment are strictly related to each other. In fact, retained profits become a financial source for firms to invest in the production of instrumental or capital-goods. The fundamental message of the positive analysis is straightforward. The value of total output is necessarily equal to the sum of *wages* paid for the production of consumption-goods and *invested profit*. This is tantamount to arguing that the value of wage-goods plus the value of investment-goods always makes up total income.

Profits are also strictly tied to the analysis of interest rates. Indeed, the interest on fixed capital appears to have a macroeconomic nature, just like in the case of macroeconomic profits. More than this, there seems to be a correlation between the profit (or natural interest) rate and the market interest rate, which is determined by central banks. In particular, the market interest rate would depend on the rate of profit. The analysis of profits and investment also leads to simple, far-reaching conclusions on the accumulation of capital in the long-term. Indeed, the volume has shown that bank deposits, resulting from infinite productions of consumer- and investment-goods, tend to reach an upper limit at quite a fast pace. Accordingly, an exact limit has been determined to the accumulation of capital and to the growth of monetary deposits over time.

The analysis of profits also allows us to trace out important conclusions in terms of economic policy, as a way out of economic and financial troubles. Economic crises have leapt out many times over the last two hundred years. The circumstances of the crises have always been disparate, but they have often resulted in increasing unemployment, in price changes, or in bankruptcies. The Global Financial Crisis of 2007–8, for instance, was mainly caused by unbiased lending activities to high-risk borrowers and led to the failure of important financial institutions, a high increase in involuntary unemployment, housing market crashes, and so on. Worrisome enough, many economists have an inkling that, a decade later, another crisis may swiftly hit the world economies. Indeed, certain financial actors seem to have found their way to issue large amounts of risky securities, sovereign and private debts are frightfully increasing, and economic growth is slow to take off. Therefore, national, regional, and international regulations have been adopted by a number of countries worldwide in the attempt to fix the state of disarray brought about by the Global Financial Crisis.

The most famous set of national financial laws is likely the Dodd-Frank Act, which entered into force in 2010 to rule the US financial system. The reform covers a wide spectrum of issues and ultimately aims to protect financial consumers from wild financial conduct and to avert the comeback of financial turmoil. Alongside the United States, the European Union has firmly endorsed the development of the Banking Union in Europe in the aftermath of the Global Financial Crisis, so as to bolster the financial stability of its member countries. The European Banking Union represents a striking example of regulation adopted at the regional level as a reaction to the 2007–8 crisis. In particular, the architects of the Union have come up with a supervisory structure where the European Central Bank acts as guarantor of the good behavior of financial institutions. At the international level, the Basel III Accords have replaced the previous sets of rules known as Basel I and Basel II. The new norms, which become legally binding only at the discretion of national legislators, in the same way as national and regional reforms, have been conceived as an answer to the Global Financial Crisis.

Yet, the future of financial regulations seems to be perilous. In fact, blind to the faults of unregulated financial systems, a number of politicians and financial experts have always felt shackled by regulations. Accordingly, legal foray has been made against the reforms. However, aside from politics and economic interests, the weakness of financial regulations lies in the lack of a strong management of bank credit on macroeconomic grounds. Therefore, attention of policy-makers should be drawn to the macro-management of credit, rather than to the sole ability of individuals to repay their debts. If it is true that individual credit should always be granted on well-defined criteria, financial institutions should also be instructed on the amount of credit to be granted to the entire set of their clients.

Accordingly, the volume contains the outlines of the plan of reform of the system of national payments that was originally drafted by Bernard Schmitt in the 1970s and 1980s. The plan, which was never implemented, was aimed to clear the misgivings about the unbiased management of bank credit at the national level. Given the financial turmoil of the early 21st century, the proposal is likely the most suitable at settling objective lending criteria at the macroeconomic level. One of the virtues of the Schmitt plan, proposed in 1984, lies in the fact that the reform would have a purely monetary nature, rather than financial. This means that the proposal foresees a reform of the structure of the system of national payments which, by its own nature, would never interfere with the usual activities of economic agents. The outstanding trait of the reform is worth mentioning. Entering monetary transactions, savings, and invested profits into three distinct though inter-related departments, banks would have a real-time knowledge of the amount of credit to be granted to the entirety of their clients over a given period of time. More precisely, this goal is achieved through the distinction between the first department, the Issue or Monetary department, and the second, the Savings or Financial department. On the other hand, the distinction between Department II and Department III, the Fixed Capital department, is what allows fixed capital to form in an orderly way, avoiding a process of duplication that leads to the formation of a pathological capital feeding speculation and leading to the consequent financial turmoil that accompanies inflation and unemployment.

Bibliography

Akerlof, G.A. (1969), "Relative Wages and the Rate of Inflation", *The Quarterly Journal of Economics*, 83 (August), pp. 353–74.

Akerlof, G.A. and Yellen, J.I. (1985), "A Near-Rational Model of the Business Cycle, with Wage and Price Inertia", *The Quarterly Journal of Economics*, 100 (Supplement), pp. 823–38.

Allais, M. (1947), *Economie et intéret*, Paris: Imprimerie National.

Arrow, K. and Debreu, G. (1954), "Existence of Equilibrium for a Competitive Economy", *Econometrica*, 22 (3), pp. 265–90.

Atkinson, A.B. (1975), *The Economics of Inequality*, Oxford: Clarendon Press.

Atkinson, A.B. (ed.) (1980), *Wealth, Income & Inequality*, Oxford and New York: Oxford University Press, 2nd edition.

Atkinson, A.B. (2011), "The Restoration of Welfare Economics", *American Economic Review*, 101 (3), pp. 157–61.

Atkinson, A.B. (2015), *Inequality: What Can Be Done?* Cambridge, MA: Harvard University Press.

Atkinson, A.B. and Piketty, T. (2010), *Top Incomes: A Global Perspective*, Oxford and New York: Oxford University Press.

Bailly, J-L., Cencini, A., and Rossi, S. (eds.) (2017), *Quantum Macroeconomics: The Legacy of Bernard Schmitt*, London and New York: Routledge.

Baily, M.N., Litan, R.E., and Johnson, M.S. (2008), "The Origins of the Financial Crisis", *The Brookings Institution*, Paper 3, November, www.brookings.edu/wp-content/uploads/2016/06/11_origins_crisis_baily_litan.pdf., retrieved May 30, 2018.

Baldwin, J.W. (1959), "The Medieval Theories of the Just Price: Romanists, Canonists and Theologians in the Twelfth and Thirteenth Centuries", *Transactions of the American Philosophical Society*, 49, Part 4.

Baldwin, S. (2012), "Basel Barriers: How Capital Requirements Would Impede Progress in the Sovereign Debt Crisis", *Forbes*, October 15, www.forbes.com/sites/shawnbaldwin/2012/10/15/basel-barriers/, retrieved June 20, 2018.

Bank of England. (2018), "Our History", www.bankofengland.co.uk/about/history, retrieved July 1, 2018.

Bank for International Settlements (BIS). (2003), "Payment Systems in the United States", www.bis.org/cpmi/paysys/unitedstatescomp.pdf, retrieved July 8, 2017.

Bank for International Settlements (BIS). (2012a), "Payment, Clearing and Settlement Systems in the United States", www.bis.org/cpmi/publ/d105_us.pdf, retrieved July 8, 2017.

Bank for International Settlements (BIS). (2012b), "Payment, Clearing and Settlement Systems in the United Kingdom", www.bis.org/cpmi/publ/d105_uk.pdf, retrieved July 4, 2018.

Bank for International Settlements (BIS). (2014), "Basel III: The Net Stable Funding Ratio", October, www.bis.org/bcbs/publ/d295.pdf, retrieved June 12, 2018.

Bank for International Settlements (BIS). (2018a), "About Committees and Associations", www.bis.org/stability.htm, retrieved June 12.

Bank for International Settlements (BIS). (2018b), "Basel III: The Liquidity Coverage Ratio and Liquidity Risk Monitoring Tools", www.bis.org/publ/bcbs238.htm, retrieved June 12.

Bank for International Settlements (BIS). (2018c), "Summary Description of the LCR", www.bis.org/press/p130106a.pdf, retrieved June 12.

Bank for International Settlements (BIS). (2018d), "Basel III: The Net Stable Funding Ratio", www.bis.org/bcbs/publ/d295.htm, retrieved June 12.

Bank of Italy (2017), "Lira-euro Conversion: Update as at 30 June 2017", www.bancaditalia.it/servizi-cittadino/servizi/cambio-banconote/cambio-lira-euro/index.html?com.dotmarketing.htmlpage.language=1, retrieved August 1.

Baragar, F. and Chernomas, R.J. (2013), "Profit without Accumulation", *International Journal of Political Economy*, 41 (3), pp. 24–40.

Baranzini, M.L. (1975), "The Pasinetti and the Anti-Pasinetti Theorems: A Reconciliation", *Oxford Economic Papers*, 27 (3), pp. 470–3.

Baranzini, M.L. (1991a), "The Pasinetti and Anti-Pasinetti Theorems: A Reply to K. Miyazaki and P.A. Samuelson", *Oxford Economic Papers*, 43 (2), pp. 195–8.

Baranzini, M.L. (1991b), *A Theory of Wealth Distribution and Accumulation*, Oxford: Clarendon Press.

Baranzini, M.L. (2001), "Sir John Hicks's Contribution in the Field of Income Distribution, Profit Determination and Differentiated Behavior of Economic Classes", in K. Puttaswamaiah (ed.), *John Hicks: His Contributions to Economic Theory & Application*, New Brunswick and London: Transaction Publishers, pp. 215–34.

Baranzini, M.L. and Harcourt, G.C. (eds.) (1994), *Dynamics of the Wealth of Nations: Growth Distribution and Structural Change (Essays in Honour of L.L. Pasinetti)*, London and New York: Palgrave Macmillan and St. Martin's Press.

Baranzini, M.L. and Mirante, A. (2013), "The Cambridge Post-Keynesian School of Income and Wealth Distribution", in G.C. Harcourt and P. Kriesler (eds.), *The Oxford Handbook of Post-Keynesian Economics, Vol. I: Theory and Origins*, Oxford: Oxford University Press, pp. 288–361.

Baranzini, M.L. and Mirante, A. (2018), *Luigi L. Pasinetti: An Intellectual Biography: Leading Scholar and System Builder of the Cambridge School of Economics*, series *History of Economic Thought*, London: Palgrave Macmillan.

Barkai, H. (1959), "Ricardo on Factor Prices and Income Distribution in a Growing Economy", *Economica*, 26 (103), pp. 240–50.

Barkai, H. (1965), "Ricardo's Static Equilibrium", *Economica*, 32 (125), pp. 15–31.

Barrére, A. (1979), *Déséquilibres Economiques et contre-Révolution Keynésienne*, Paris: Economica.

Barrére, A. (1990a), "Signification Générale du Circuit: une Interprétation", *Economie et Sociétés*, série *Monnaie et Production*, pp. 9–34.

Barrére, A. (1990b), *Macroéconomie Keynésienne: le Projet Economique de John Maynard Keynes*, Paris: Dunod.

Basel Committee on Banking Supervision. (2018a), "The Basel Committee – Overview", *Bank for International Settlements*, www.bis.org/bcbs/index.htm, retrieved May 30.

Basel Committee on Banking Supervision. (2018b), "Basel Committee on Banking Supervision reforms – Basel III", www.bis.org/bcbs/basel3/b3_bank_sup_reforms.pdf, retrieved May 30.

Baumol, W.J. and Becker, G.S. (1950), "The Classical Monetary Theory: The Outcome of the Discussion", *Economica*, 19 (76), pp. 355–76.

Baxter, M. and King, R.G. (1993), "Fiscal Policy in General Equilibrium", *American Economic Review*, 83 (3), pp. 315–34.

Bellofiore, R. (2005), "Monetary Economics after Wicksell: Alternative Perspectives within the Theory of the Monetary Circuit", in G. Fontana and R. Realfonzo (eds.), *The Monetary Theory of Production: Tradition and Perspectives*, Basingstoke and New York: Palgrave Macmillan, pp. 39–51.

Bernanke, B. (ed.) (2009), *Essays on the Great Depression*, Princeton, NJ: Princeton University Press.

Birner, J. (2002), *The Cambridge Controversies in Capital Theory: A Study in the Logic of Theory Development*, London and New York: Routledge.

Blanchard, O.J. (1991), "Neoclassical Synthesis", in J. Eatwell, M. Milgate, and P. Newman (eds.), *The World of Economics*, London: Palgrave Macmillan.

Blanchard, O.J. and Fischer, S. (1989), *Lectures in Macroeconomics*, Cambridge, MA: MIT Press.

Blanchard, O.J. and Galì, J. (2007), "Real Wage Rigidities and the New Keynesian Model", *Journal of Money, Credit, and Banking*, 39 (1) (Supplement), pp. 35–66.

Blanchard, O.J. and Quah, D. (1989), "The Dynamic Effects of Aggregate Demand and Supply Disturbances", *American Economic Review*, 79 (4), pp. 655–73.

Blinder, A.S. (1988), "The Fall and Rise of Keynesian Economics", *Economic Record*, 64 (4), pp. 278–94.

Bliss, C.J. (1975), *Capital Theory and the Distribution of Income*, Amsterdam and New York: North-Holland and American Elsevier.

Böhm-Bawerk, E. (1884–1921 [1959]), *Capital and Interest*, South Holland: Libertarian Press, 3 vols.

Boughton, J.M. (2000), "Northwest of Suez: The 1956 Crisis and the IMF", *International Monetary Fund Working Paper* No. 00/192, www.imf.org/en/Publications/WP/Issues/2016/12/30/Northwest-of-Suez-The-1956-Crisis-and-the-IMF-3899, retrieved September 7, 2018.

Bradley, X. (2003), "Involuntary Unemployment and Investment", in L-P. Rochon and S. Rossi (eds.), *Modern Theories of Money: The Nature and Role of Money in Capitalist Economies*, Cheltenham, UK and Northampton, MA: Edward Elgar, pp. 384–408.

Bridges, J., Gregory, D., Nielsen, M., Pezzini, S., Radia, A., and Spaltro, M. (2014), "The Impact of Capital Requirements on Bank Lending", *Bank of England*, Working Paper No. 486, www.bankofengland.co.uk, retrieved June 22, 2018.

Brown, M. (1969), "Substitution-Composition Effects, Capital Intensity Uniqueness and Growth", *The Economic Journal*, 79 (314), pp. 334–47.

Brunner, K. and Meltzer, A.H. (1971), "The Uses of Money in the Theory of an Exchange Economy", *American Economic Review*, 61 (December), pp. 784–805.

Bruno, M., Burmeister, E., and Shesinski, E. (1966), "The Nature and Implications of the Reswitching of Techniques", *The Quarterly Journal of Economics*, 80 (4), pp. 526–53.

Burmeister, E. (1980), *Capital Theory and Dynamics*, Cambridge: Cambridge University Press.

Caplin, A.S. and Spulber, D.F. (1987), "Menu Costs and the Neutrality of Money", *The Quarterly Journal of Economics*, 102 (November), pp. 703–25.

Carrera, A. (2015), "Studies in Profit and Capital Formation: An Alternative Theory of Distribution", *Cuadernos de Economía – Spanish Journal of Economics and Finance*, 38 (106), pp. 1–10.

Carrera, A. (2016a), "Money, Income, and Capital: A Reform of the System of National Payments", *Cuadernos de Economía – Spanish Journal of Economics and Finance*, 39 (111), pp. 189–202.

Carrera, A. (2016b), *Profit Theory: A New Macroeconomic Analysis*, doctoral thesis, Lugano: Università della Svizzera italiana, mimeo.

Carrera, A. and Rossi, S. (2015), "Money, Income, and Profit: Lessons from the Monetary Theory of Production", *Iberian Journal of the History of Economic Thought*, 2 (1), pp. 48–60.

Casarosa, C. (1978), "A New Formulation of the Ricardian System", *Oxford Economic Papers*, 30 (1), pp. 38–63.

Cass, D. (1965), "Optimum Growth in an Aggregative Model of Capital Accumulation", *The Review of Economic Studies*, 32 (3), pp. 233–40.

Cencini, A. (1982), "The Logical Indeterminacy of Relative Prices", in M.L. Baranzini (ed.), *Advances in Economic Theory*, Oxford: Basil Blackwell, pp. 126–36.

Cencini, A. (1984 [2013]), *Time and the Macroeconomic Analysis of Income*, with a *Preface* by Meghnad Desai, London, New Delhi, New York and Sydney: Bloomsbury.

Cencini, A. (1988), *Money, Income and Time*, with a *Preface* by Meghnad Desai, London and New York: Pinter Publishers. Published in 2013 by Bloomsbury.

Cencini, A. (1997), *Monetary Theory, National and International*, London and New York: Routledge.

Cencini, A. (2001), *Monetary Macroeconomics: A New Approach*, London and New York: Routledge.

Cencini, A. (2003), "IS-LM: A Final Rejection", in L-P. Rochon and S. Rossi (eds.), *Modern Theories of Money: The Nature and Role of Money in Capitalist Economies*, Cheltenham, UK and Northampton, MA: Edward Elgar, pp. 295–321.

Cencini, A. (2005), *Macroeconomic Foundations of Macroeconomics*, London and New York: Routledge.

Cencini, A. (2015), *Elementi di Macroeconomia Monetaria*, Padova: CEDAM.

Cencini, A. and Rossi, S. (2015), *Economic and Financial Crises: A New Macroeconomic Analysis*, London: Palgrave Macmillan.

Cencini, A. and Schmitt, B. (1977), *La pensée de Karl Marx: Critique et synthèse*, Vol. II, *La plus-value*, Albeuve: Castella.

Cencini, A. and Schmitt, B. (1991), *External Debt Servicing: A Vicious Circle*, London and New York: Pinters Publishers.

Champernowne, D.G. (1953–54), "The Production Function and the Theory of Capital: A Comment", *The Review of Economic Studies*, 21 (2), pp. 112–35.

Champernowne, D.G. (1973), *The Distribution of Income between Persons*, Cambridge, UK: Cambridge University Press.

Champernowne, D.G. and Cowell, F.A. (1998), *Economic Inequality and Income Distribution*, Cambridge, UK and New York: Cambridge University Press.

Chancellor, E. (2017), "Review: Can We Avoid Another Financial Crisis?" *Reuters*, May 5, www.reuters.com/article/us-review-crisis-breakingviews-idUSKBN1811XP, retrieved May 7, 2018.

Chazan, G. (2017), "Wolfgang Schäuble Warns of Debt-Driven Global Financial Crisis", *The Financial Times*, October 8, www.ft.com/content/9de0533c-aab8-11e7-93c5-648314d2c72c, retrieved February 22, 2018.

Christiano, L.J. and Eichenbaum, M.S. (1992), "Current Real-Business-Cycle Theories and Aggregate Labor-Market Fluctuations", *American Economic Review*, 82 (3), pp. 430–50.

Cobb, C.W. and Douglas, P.H. (1928), "A Theory of Production", *American Economic Review*, 18 (Supplement), pp. 139–65.

Coddington, A. (1976), "Keynesian Economics: The Search for First Principles", *Journal of Economic Literature*, 14 (4), pp. 1258–73.

Cohen, D., Piketty, T., and Saint-Paul, G. (2002), *The Economics of Rising Inequalities*, Oxford and New York: Oxford University Press.

Compaijen, B. (1981), *Kapitaal, rendement en tijd*, Groningen: Wolters-Noordhoff.

Consumer Financial Protection Bureau. (2017a), "What Is the Ability-to-Repay Rule? Why Is It Important to Me?" *Bureau of Consumer Financial Protection*, www.consumerfinance.gov/ask-cfpb/what-is-the-ability-to-repay-rule-why-is-it-important-to-me-en-1787/, retrieved April 15, 2018.

Consumer Financial Protection Bureau. (2017b), "What Is a Qualified Mortgage?" *Bureau of Consumer Financial Protection*, www.consumerfinance.gov/askcfpb/what-is-a-qualified-mortgage-en-a789/, retrieved April 15, 2018.

Consumer Financial Protection Bureau. (2018), "The Bureau", *Bureau of Consumer Financial Protection*, www.consumerfinance.gov/about-us/the-bureau/, retrieved February 7.

Cooper, A.S. (2011), *The Oil Kings: How the U.S., Iran, and Saudi Arabia Changed the Balance of Power in the Middle East*, New York, London, Toronto, Sydney and New Delhi: Simon & Schuster Paperbacks.

Coppock, D.J. (1961), "The Causes of the Great Depression, 1873–96", *Manchester School*, 29 (3) (September), pp. 205–32.

Cottin-Euziol, E. and Rochon, L-P. (2013), "Circuit with Multi-period Credit", *Review of Political Economy*, 25 (3), pp. 461–75.

Davenport-Hines, R. (2015), *Universal Man: The Seven Lives of John Maynard Keynes*, London: Harper Collins.

Davidson, P. (1959), "A Clarification of the Ricardian Rent Share", *Canadian Journal of Economics and Political Science*, 25 (2), pp. 190–5.

Davidson, P. (1965), "Keynes' Finance Motive", *Oxford Economic Papers*, 17 (1), pp. 47–65.

Davidson, P. (1972), *Money in the Real World*, New York: John Wiley & Sons.

Davidson, P. (1982), "Expectations: A Fallacious Foundation for Studying Crucial Decision Making Processes", *Journal of Post Keynesian Economics*, 5 (Winter), pp. 182–97.

Davidson, P. (1991), "Is Probability Theory Relevant for Uncertainty? A Post Keynesian Perspective", *Journal of Economic Perspectives*, 5 (Winter), pp. 129–43.

Davidson, P. (1992), "Would Keynes Be a New Keynesian?" *Eastern Economic Journal*, 18 (4), pp. 449–63.

Deane, P. (1978), *The Evolution of Economic Ideas*, Cambridge: Cambridge University Press.

Debreu, G. (1959), *Theory of Value: An Axiomatic Analysis of Economic Equilibrium*, New York: Wiley.

Deleplace, G. and Nell, E.J. (eds.) (1996), *Money in Motion: The Post Keynesian and Circulation Approaches*, London and New York: Palgrave Macmillan and St. Martin's Press.

De Roover, R. (1958), "The Concept of the Just Price: Theory and Economic Policy", *Journal of Economic History*, 18 (4), pp. 418–34.

Desai, M. (1981), *Testing Monetarism*, London, New Delhi, New York and Sydney: Bloomsbury.

Diamond, P. (1965), "National Debt in a Neoclassical Growth Model", *American Economic Review*, 55 (5), pp. 1126–50.

Dimand, R.W. (1983), *From the Treatise to The General Theory: The Formulation of Keynes' Theory of Employment and Output*, doctoral dissertation, New Haven, CT: Yale University.

Dimand, R.W. (1986), "The Macroeconomics of the Treatise on Money", *Eastern Economic Journal*, 12 (4), pp. 431–41.

Dimand, R.W. (1988), *The Origins of the Keynesian Revolution*, Aldershot, UK: Edward Elgar and Stanford, CA: Stanford University Press.

Dobb, M.H. (1929), "A Skeptical View of the Theory of Wages", *The Economic Journal*, 39 (156), pp. 506–19.

Dobb, M.H. (1973), *Theories of Value and Distribution Since Adam Smith: Ideology and Economic Theory*, Cambridge, UK: Cambridge University Press.

Domar, E.D. (1946), "Capital Expansion, Rate of Growth and Employment", *Econometrica*, 14 (2), pp. 137–47.

Dornbusch, R. and Frenkel, J.A. (1982), "The Gold Standard and the Bank of England in the Crisis of 1847", December, *National Bureau of Economic Research Working Paper* No. 1039, reprint No. R0503.

Douglas, P.H. (1934), *The Theory of Wages*, New York: Palgrave Macmillan.

Dow, S.C. (1996), *The Methodology of Macroeconomic Thought*, Cheltenham, UK and Brookfield: Edward Elgar.

Eatwell, J. and Milgate, M. (1983), *Keynes's Economics and the Theory of Value and Distribution*, London and New York: Duckworth.

Eatwell, J. and Milgate, M. (2011), *The Fall and Rise of Keynesian Economics*, New York: Oxford University Press.

The Economist. (2017), "Basel 3, An International Capital-Adequacy Standard, Is Unloved but Much Needed", May 4, www.economist.com/special-report/2017/05/04/basel-3-an-international-capital-adequacy-standard-is-unloved-but-much-needed, retrieved June 2.

Eichengreen, B. and Flandreau, M. (eds.) (1985), *The Gold Standard in Theory and History*, New York: Methuen Inc.

European Central Bank. (2018a), "Banking Union", www.bankingsupervision.europa.eu/about/bankingunion/html/index.en.html.

European Central Bank. (2018b), "Single Supervisory Mechanism", www.bankingsupervision.europa.eu/about/thessm/html/index.en.html, retrieved June 4.

European Central Bank. (2018c), "What Makes a Bank Significant?" www.bankingsupervision.europa.eu/banking/list/criteria/html/index.en.html, retrieved June 4.

European Central Bank. (2018d), "Joint Supervisory Teams", www.bankingsupervision.europa.eu/banking/approach/jst/html/index.en.html, retrieved June 4.

European Central Bank. (2018e), "Financial Fragmentation or Integration", March 22, www.ecb.europa.eu/press/key/date/2018/html/ecb.sp180322.en.html, retrieved June 4.

European Central Bank. (2018f), "How Quantitative Easing Works", www.ecb.europa.eu/explainers/show-me/html/app_infographic.en.html, retrieved September 20.

European Commission. (2018), "What Is the Banking Union", https://ec.europa.eu/info/business-economy-euro/banking-and-finance/banking-union/what-banking-union_en#completing-the-banking-union, retrieved June 23.

Febrero, E. (2008), "The Monetization of Profits in a Monetary Circuit Framework", *Review of Political Economy*, 20 (1), pp. 111–25.

Federal Reserve. (2006), "Report to the Congress on Practices of the Consumer Credit Industry in Soliciting and Extending Credit and their Effects on Consumer Debt and Insolvency", www.federalreserve.gov/boarddocs/rptcongress/bankruptcy/bankruptcybillstudy200606.pdf, retrieved June 23, 2017.

Federal Reserve. (2016a), "Selected Assets and Liabilities of Commercial Banks in the United States", July 15, www.federalreserve.gov/releases/h8/current/, retrieved July 21.

Federal Reserve. (2016b), "Quarterly Report on Federal Reserve Balance Sheet Development", May, www.federalreserve.gov/monetarypolicy/files, retrieved July 21.

Federal Reserve. (2017a), "History of the Federal Reserve", www.federalreserveeducation.org, retrieved June 2017.

Federal Reserve. (2017b), "Volcker Rule", www.federalreserve.gov/supervisionreg/volcker-rule.htm, retrieved August 6.

Federal Reserve Bank of Boston. (2017), "Credit History: The Evolution of Consumer Credit in America", www.bostonfed.org/-/media/Documents/ledger/spring . . . /credhistory.pdf, retrieved June 23.

Federal Reserve Bank of San Francisco. (2016), "The State of Cash: Preliminary Findings from the 2015 *Diary of Consumer Payment Choice*", authored by W. Matheny, S. O'Brien, and C. Wang. www.frbsf.org/cash/publications/fed-notes/2016/november/state-of-cash-2015-diary-consumer-payment-choice, retrieved July 2, 2017.

Fels, R. (1949), "The Long-Wave Depression, 1873–97", *The Review of Economics and Statistics*, 31 (1) (February), pp. 69–73.

Ferguson, C.E. (1969), *The Neo-Classical Theory of Production and Distribution*, Cambridge: Cambridge University Press.

Ferguson, C.E. and Allen, R.F. (1970), "Factor Prices, Commodity Prices, and Switches of Technique", *Western Economic Journal*, 8 (2), pp. 95–109.

Fleming, S. and Giles, C. (2014), "Bank of England Limits Mortgages to Protect Recovery", *The Financial Times*, June 26, www.ft.com/content/ef06b7fc-fd13-11e3-8ca9-00144feab7de?mhq5j=e3, retrieved July 3, 2017.

Fontana, G. (2006), "Keynesian Uncertainty and Money", in P. Arestis and M. Sawyer (eds.), *A Handbook of Alternative Monetary Economics*, Cheltenham, UK and Northampton, MA: Edward Elgar, pp. 438–53.

Fontana, G. and Realfonzo, R. (eds.) (2005), *The Monetary Theory of Production: Tradition and Perspectives*, Basingstoke and New York: Palgrave Macmillan.

Forstater, M. (2013), "Time of Production, Time of Circulation and Turnover Time: Exploring the Guts of Marx's Circuits of Capital", in L-P. Rochon and M. Seccareccia (eds.), *Monetary Economies of Production: Banking and Financial Circuits and the Role of the State*, Cheltenham, UK and Northampton, MA: Edward Elgar.

Friedman, M. and Schwartz, A.J. (1963), *A Monetary History of the United States. 1867–1960*, Princeton, NJ: Princeton University Press.

Galbraith, J.K. (1987), *A History of Economics: The Past as the Present*, London: Hamish Hamilton.

Galbraith, J.K. (2012), *Inequality and Instability: A Study of the World Economy Just before the Great Crisis*, New York: Oxford University Press.

Galbraith, J.K. (2014), *The End of Normal: The Great Crisis and the Future of Growth*, New York: Simon and Schuster.

Gallaway, L. and Shukla, V. (1974), "The Neoclassical Production Function", *American Economic Review*, 64 (3), pp. 348–58.

Galpern, S.G. and Keefer, E.C. (eds.) (2012), *Energy Crisis, 1974–1980*, Washington, DC: United States Government Printing Office.

Garegnani, P. (1960 [1972]), *Il Capitale nelle Teorie della Distribuzione*, Milan: Giuffré Editore.

Garegnani, P. (1966), "Switching of Techniques", *The Quarterly Journal of Economics*, 80 (4), pp. 554–67.

Garegnani, P. (1970), "Heterogeneous Capital, the Production Function and the Theory of Distribution", *The Review of Economic Studies*, 37 (3), pp. 407–36.

Garegnani, P. (1976), "The Neoclassical Production Function: Comment", *American Economic Review*, 66 (3), pp. 424–7.

Garegnani, P. (1990), "Quantity of Capital", in J. Eatwell, M. Milgate, and P. Newman (eds.), *Capital Theory*, London: Palgrave Macmillan, pp. 1–78.

Georgescu-Roegen, N. (1986), "Man and Production", in M.L. Baranzini and R. Scazzieri (eds.), *Foundations of Economics: Structures of Inquiry and Economic Theory*, Oxford and New York: Basil Blackwell, pp. 247–80.

Glasner, D. (1997), "Crisis of 1873", in D. Glasner (ed.), *Business Cycles and Depressions: An Encyclopedia*, New York: Garland Publishing, pp. 132–3.

Gnos, C. (2003), "Circuit Theory as an Explanation of the Complex Real World", in L-P. Rochon and S. Rossi (eds.), *Modern Theories of Money*, Cheltenham, UK and Northampton, MA: Edward Elgar, pp. 322–98.

Gnos, C. (2005), "Circuit Theory and the Employment Issue", in G. Fontana and R. Realfonzo (eds.), *The Monetary Theory of Production: Tradition and Perspectives*, Basingstoke and New York: Palgrave Macmillan, pp. 173–83.

Gnos, C. (2006), "French Circuit Theory", in P. Arestis and M. Sawyer (eds.), *A Handbook of Alternative Monetary Economics*, Cheltenham, UK and Northampton, MA: Edward Elgar, pp. 87–104.

Gnos, C. (2009), "Circuit Theory Supplementing Keynes's Genuine Analysis of the Monetary Economy of Production", in J-F. Ponsot and S. Rossi (eds.), *The*

Political Economy of Monetary Circuits: Tradition and Change in Post-Keynesian Economics, Basingstoke: Palgrave Macmillan, pp. 1–20.

Gnos, C. (2013), "A Historical Perspective on the Theory of the Monetary Circuit: From Schumpeter to Parguez", in L-P. Rochon and M. Seccareccia (eds.), *Monetary Economies of Production: Banking and Financial Circuits and the Role of the State*, Cheltenham, UK and Northampton, MA: Edward Elgar, pp. 23–32.

Godley, W. and Lavoie, M. (2007), *Monetary Economics: An Integrated Approach to Credit, Money, Income, Production and Wealth*, Baskingstoke and New York: Palgrave Macmillan.

Goodhart, C. (1988), *The Evolution of Central Banks*, Cambridge, MA and London: MIT Press.

Gordon, R. (2016), *The Rise and Fall of American Growth: The U.S. Standard of Living since the Civil War*, Princeton, NJ: Princeton University Press.

Graziani, A. (1983), "Moneta Senza Crisi", *Materiali Filosofici*, 7, pp. 95–112.

Graziani, A. (1989), "The Theory of the Monetary Circuit", *Thames Papers in Political Economy*, Spring, pp. 1–26. Reprinted in M. Musella and C. Panico (eds.) (1995), *The Money Supply in the Economic Process*, Aldershot, UK and Brookfield: Edward Elgar, pp. 1–26.

Graziani, A. (1996), "Money as Purchasing Power and Money as a Stock of Wealth in Keynesian Economic Thought", in G. Deleplace and E.J. Nell (eds.), *Money in Motion: The Post Keynesian and Circulation Approaches*, London and New York: Palgrave Macmillan and St. Martin's Press, pp. 139–54.

Graziani, A. (2003), *The Monetary Theory of Production*, Cambridge, UK: Cambridge University Press.

Hagenauer, S. (1931), "Das 'Justum Pretium' bei Thomas von Aquino: Ein Beitrag zur Geschichte der Objective Wettheorie", in *Vierterljahrscrift für Sozial und Wirtschaftsgeschichte*, 24, Stuttgart: W. Kohlhammer.

Hamouda, O.F. (1993), *John R. Hicks: The Economist's Economist*, Oxford and Cambridge, USA: Bsil Blackwell.

Hansen, A.H. (1949), *Monetary Theory and Fiscal Policy*, New Delhi, Bombay and Calcutta: Oxford and IBH Publishing Company.

Hansen, A.H. (1953), *A Guide to Keynes*, New York, Toronto and London: McGraw-Hill and Tokyo: Kogakusha Company, Ltd.

Hansen, G.D. (1985), "Indivisible Labor and the Business Cycle", *Journal of Monetary Economics*, 16 (3), pp. 309–27.

Hansson, B.A. (1987), "Forced Saving", in J. Eatwell, M. Milgate, and P. Newman (eds.), *The New Palgrave: A Dictionary of Economics*, Volume 1, London: Palgrave Macmillan, pp. 398–400.

Harcourt, G.C. (1969), "Some Cambridge Controversies in the Theory of Capital", *The Journal of Economic Literature*, 7 (2), pp. 369–405.

Harcourt, G.C. (1972), *Some Cambridge Controversies in the Theory of Capital*, Cambridge, UK: Cambridge University Press.

Harcourt, G.C. and Kriesler, P. (eds.) (2013), *The Oxford Handbook of Post-Keynesian Economics, Vol. I: Theory and Origins*, Oxford: Oxford University Press.

Harrod, R.F. (1937), "Mr. Keynes and Traditional Theory", *Econometrica*, 5 (1), pp. 74–86.

Harrod, R.F. (1939), "An Essay in Dynamic Theory", *The Economic Journal*, 49 (193), pp. 14–33.

Harrod, R.F. (1948), *Towards a Dynamic Economics*, London: Palgrave Macmillan.

Hayek, F.A. (1931), "Reflections on the Pure Theory of Money of Mr. J.M. Keynes", *Economica*, 33 (August), pp. 270–95.

Hayek, F.A. (1932), "Reflections on the Pure Theory of Money of Mr. J.M. Keynes (continued)", *Economica*, 35 (February), pp. 22–44.

Hicks, J.R. (1934), "Leon Walras", *Econometrica*, 2 (4), pp. 338–48.

Hicks, J.R. (1937), "Mr. Keynes and the 'Classics': A Suggested Interpretation", *Econometrica*, 5 (2), pp. 147–59.

Hicks, J.R. (1965), *Capital and Growth*, Oxford: Oxford University Press.

Hicks, J.R. (1973), *Capital and Time*, Oxford: Clarendon Press.

Hicks, J.R. (1975), "Revival of Political Economy: The Old and the New", *Economic Record*, 51 (3), pp. 365–67.

Hicks, J.R. (1977), *Economic Perspectives: Further Essays on Money and Growth*, Oxford: Clarendon Press.

Hicks, J.R. (1980–81), "IS-LM: An Explanation", *Journal of Post Keynesian Economics*, 3 (2), pp. 139–55.

Hicks, J.R. (1986), "Is Economics a Science?" in M.L. Baranzini and R. Scazzieri (eds.), *Foundations of Economics: Structures of Inquiry and Economic Theory*, Oxford and New York: Basil Blackwell, pp. 91–101.

Hirschman, A.O. (1984), "Against Parsimony: Three Easy Ways of Complicating Some Categories of Economic Discourse", *American Economic Review*, 74 (2), pp. 89–96.

HSBC. (2018), "What Is a Credit Score", www.hsbc.co.uk/1/2/tools-and-guides/credit-cards/what-is-a-credit-score, retrieved March 30, 2018.

Hughes, J.R. (1956), "The Commercial Crisis of 1857", *Oxford Economic Papers*, 8 (2) (June), pp. 194–222.

Johannessen, J-A. (2016), *Innovations Lead to Economic Crises*, London: Palgrave Macmillan.

Jopson, B. (2017), "Regulators Back Trump on Looser Financial Rules", *The Financial Times*, June 22, www.ft.com/content/843ad85c-5758-11e7-80b6-9bfa4c1f83d2, retrieved June 2, 2018.

Jopson, B. (2018), "House Republicans Push for More Sweeping Bank Deregulation", *The Financial Times*, March 15, www.ft.com/content/9559a52a-27e4-11e8-b27e-cc62a39d57a0, retrieved May 15.

Kahn, R.F. (1931), "The Relation of Home Investment to Unemployment", *The Economic Journal*, 41 (162), pp. 173–98.

Kahn, R.F. (1984), *The Making of Keynes' General Theory*, Cambridge, UK: Cambridge University Press.

Kaldor, N. (1951), "Mr. Hicks on the Trade Cycle", *The Economic Journal*, 61 (244), pp. 832–47.

Kaldor, N. (1956), "Alternative Theories of Distribution", *The Review of Economic Studies*, 23 (2), pp. 83–100.

Kaldor, N. (1957), "A Model of Economic Growth", *The Economic Journal*, 67 (268), pp. 591–624.

Kaldor, N. (1960), "Keynes' Theory of the Own-rates of Interest", in *Essays on Economic Stability and Growth*, Glencoe, IL: Free Press.

Kaldor, N. (1961), "Capital Accumulation and Economic Growth", in D.C. Hague and F.A. Lutz (eds.), *The Theory of Capital*, London: Palgrave Macmillan, pp. 177–222.

Kaldor, N. (1966), "Marginal Productivity and the Macro-Economic Theories of Distribution: Comment on Samuelson and Modigliani", *Review of Economic Studies*, 33 (4), pp. 309–19.

Kaldor, N. (1970), "The New Monetarism", *Lloyds Bank Review*, 97 (July), pp. 1–17.

Kaldor, N. (1982), *The Scourge of Monetarism*, New York: Oxford University Press.

Kalecki, M. (1935), "A Macrodynamic Theory of Business Cycles", *Econometrica*, 3 (3), pp. 327–44.

Kalecki, M. (1939 [1990]), *Essays in the Theory of Economic Fluctuations*, London: Allen & Unwin, from M. Kalecki: *Collected Works of Michal Kalecki*, Vol. 1, *Capitalism, Business Cycles and Full Employment*, Oxford: Clarendon Press, pp. 233–318.

Kalecki, M. (1942), "A Theory of Profits", *The Economic Journal*, 52 (206–7), pp. 258–67.

Kalecki, M. (1951), *Theory of Economic Dynamics: An Essay on Cyclical and Long Run Changes in Capitalist Economy*, London: Allen and Unwin.

Keen, S. (2017), *Can We Avoid Another Financial Crisis*, Cambridge, UK and Malden: Polity Press.

Kelton, S. and Nell, E.J. (eds.) (2003), *The State, the Market, and the Euro: Chartalism versus Metallism in the Theory of Money*, Cheltenham, UK and Northampton, MA: Edward Elgar.

Keynes, J.M. (1923), *A Tract on Monetary Reform*, London: Palgrave Macmillan.

Keynes, J.M. (1930a [1971]), "A Treatise on Money, Vol. I", in D. Moggridge (ed.) (1971–89), *The Collected Writings of John Maynard Keynes*, London and Basingstoke: Palgrave Macmillan.

Keynes, J.M. (1930b [1971]), "A Treatise on Money, Vol. II", in D. Moggridge (ed.) (1971–89), *The Collected Writings of John Maynard Keynes*, London and Basingstoke: Palgrave Macmillan.

Keynes, J.M. (1931), "The Pure Theory of Money. A Reply to Dr. Hayek", *Economica*, 34 (November), pp. 387–97.

Keynes, J.M. (1933 [1979]), "Draft of the General Theory", in D. Moggridge (ed.) (1971–89), *The Collected Writings of John Maynard Keynes, XXIX The General Theory and After: A Supplement*, London: Palgrave Macmillan, pp. 48–76.

Keynes, J.M. (1936 [1964]), *The General Theory of Employment, Interest and Money*, New York: Harvest and Harcourt.

King, J.E. (2009), *Nicholas Kaldor*, Hampshire: Palgrave Macmillan.

King, R.G. (1993), "Will the New Keynesian Macroeconomics Resurrect the IS-LM Model?" *Journal of Economic Perspectives*, 7 (1), pp. 67–82.

Koopmans, T. (1965), "On the Concept of Optimal Economic Growth", in *Scientific Papers of Tjalling C. Koopmans*, New York: Springer, pp. 485–547.

Kregel, J.A. (1971), *Rate of Profit, Distribution, and Growth: Two Views*, Chicago: Aldine Atherton.

Krugman, P.R. (2016), "Why Monetarism Failed", *New York Times*, April 13.

Kunz, D.B. (1991), *The Economic Diplomacy of the Suez Crisis*, Chapel Hill and London: The University of North Carolina Press.

Kurz, H.D. and Salvadori, N. (1995), *Theory of Production: A Long-Period Analysis*, Cambridge: Cambridge University Press.

Kydland, F.E. and Prescott, E.C. (1982), "Time to Build and Aggregate Fluctuations", *Econometrica*, 50 (6), pp. 1345–70.

Lange, O.R. (1938), "The Rate of Interest and the Optimum Propensity to Consume", *Economica*, 5 (17), pp. 12–32.

Lavoie, M. (1987), "Monnaie et Production: Une Synthèse de la Théorie du Circuit", *Économie et Sociétés*, 21 (9), pp. 65–101.

Lavoie, M. (1996), "Monetary Policy in an Economy with Endogenous Credit Money", in G. Deleplace and E.J. Nell (eds.), *Money in Motion: The Post Keynesian and Circulation Approaches*, London and New York: Palgrave Macmillan and St. Martin's Press, pp. 532–45.

Lavoie, M. (2003), "A Primer on Endogenous Credit-Money", in L-P. Rochon and S. Rossi (eds.), *Modern Theories of Money: The Nature and Role of Money in Capitalist Economies*, Cheltenham, UK and Northampton, MA: Edward Elgar, pp. 506–43.

Lavoie, M. (2006a), *Introduction to Post-Keynesian Economics*, Houndmills and New York: Palgrave Macmillan.

Lavoie, M. (2006b), "Endogenous Money: Accomodationist", in P. Arestis and M. Sawyer (eds.), *A Handbook of Alternative Monetary Economics*, Cheltenham, UK and Northampton, MA: Edward Elgar, pp. 17–34.

Lavoie, M. (2013), "The State, the Central Bank and the Monetary Circuit", in L-P. Rochon and M. Seccareccia (eds.), *Monetary Economies of Production: Banking and Financial Circuits and the Role of the State*, Cheltenham, UK and Northampton, MA: Edward Elgar, pp. 11–22.

Lavoie, M. (2014), *Post-Keynesian Economics: New Foundations*, Cheltenham, UK: Edward Elgar.

Leijonhufvud, A. (1967), "Keynes and the Keynesians: A Suggested Interpretation", *American Economic Review*, 57 (2), pp. 401–10.

Levhari, D. (1965), "A Nonsubstitution Theorem and Switching of Techniques", *The Quarterly Journal of Economics*, 79 (1), pp. 98–105.

Lloyds Bank. (2018), "Personal Loan", www.lloydsbank.com/loans/loan-personal.asp#tab-row-1, retrieved February 3, 2018.

Long, J.B. and Plosser, C.I. (1983), "Real Business Cycles", *Journal of Political Economy*, 91 (1), pp. 39–69.

Lowenstein, R. (2016), *America's Bank: The Epic Struggle to Create the Federal Reserve*, New York: Penguin Books.

Lucas, R.E. (1972), "Expectations and the Neutrality of Money", *Journal of Economic Theory*, 4 (2), pp. 103–24.

Lucas, R.E. (1988), "On the Mechanics of Economic Development", *Journal of Monetary Economics*, 22 (1), pp. 3–42.

Manibog, C. and Foley, S. (2017), "The Long and Winding Road to Economic Recovery", *The Financial Times*, August 10, www.ft.com/content/c8d1d150-7869-11e7-a3e8-60495fe6ca71, retrieved December 10.

Mankiw, N.G. (1990), "A Quick Refresher Course in Macroeconomics", *Journal of Economic Literature*, 28 (4), pp. 1645–60.

Mankiw, N.G. (2015), *Principles of Economics*, Stamford, CT: Cengage Learning, 7th edition.

Marshall, A. (1920 [1961]), *Principles of Economics*, London: Palgrave Macmillan.
Marx, K. (1857–61 [1973]), *Grundrisse: Foundations of the Critique of Political Economy*, London: Penguin Books in association with New Left Refiew. Translated by Martin Nicolaus.
Marx, K. (1867 [1982]), *Capital: A Critique of Political Economy*, Harmondsworth, Middlesex, England: Penguin. First edited in 1867 by Verlag von Otto Meisner, Hamburg, 3 vols.
Marx, K. (1898 [1969]), *Value, Price and Profit*, New York: International Co., Inc.
Marx, K. (1925), *Histoire des doctrines économiques*, Paris: Alfred Costes Ed.
Mas-Colell, A., Whinston, M.D., and Green, J.R. (1995), *Microeconomic Theory*, New York and Oxford: Oxford University Press.
Meade, J.E. (1937), "A Simplified Model of Mr. Keynes' System", *The Review of Economic Studies*, 4 (2), pp. 98–107.
Meade, J.E. (1963), "The Rate of Profits in a Growing Economy", *The Economic Journal*, 73 (292), pp. 665–74.
Meade, J.E. (1966a), "The Outcome of the Pasinetti Process: A Note", *The Economic Journal*, 76 (301), pp. 161–5.
Meade, J.E. (1966b), "Life-Cycle Savings, Inheritance and Economic Growth", *The Review of Economic Studies*, 33 (1), pp. 61–78.
Meek, R.L. (1954), "Adam Smith and the Classical Concept of Profit", *Scottish Journal of Political Economy*, 1 (2) (June).
Meek, R.L. (1962), *The Economics of Physiocracy*, London: Allen & Unwin.
Minsky, H.P. (1957), "Central Banking and Money Market Changes", *The Quarterly Journal of Economics*, 71 (2), pp. 171–87.
Minsky, H.P. (1964), "Longer Waves in Financial Relations: Financial Factors in the More Severe Recessions", *The American Economic Review*, 54 (3), pp. 324–35.
Minsky, H.P. (1975), *John Maynard Keynes*, New York: Columbia University Press.
Minsky, H.P. (1977), "A Theory of Systemic Financial Fragility", in E.I. Altman and A.W. Sametz (eds.), *Financial Crises: Institutions and Markets in a Fragile Environment*, New York: John Wiley & Sons.
Minsky, H.P. (1982), *Can "It" Happen Again?* Armonk: M.E. Sharpe.
Minsky, H.P. (1993), "Financial Integration and National Economic Policy", in *Post Keynesian Workshop*, July, Knoxville: University of Tennessee.
Mints, L.W. (1965), *A History of Banking Theory in Great Britain and the United States*, Chicago and London: University of Chicago Press. Fourth impression. First published in 1945.
Mishan, E.J. (1981), *Introduction to Normative Economics*, New York and Oxford: Oxford University Press.
Mishkin, F. (2016), *The Economics of Money, Banking, and Financial Markets*, Harlow, UK: Pearson Education Limited, 11th edition.
Miyazaki, K. (1991), "On the Neo-Keynesian Interpretation of the Anti-Pasinetti Theory", *Oxford Economics Papers*, 43 (2), pp. 187–94.
Modigliani, F. (1944), "Liquidity Preference and the Theory of Interest and Money", *Econometrica*, 12 (1), pp. 45–88.
Modigliani, F. (1966), "The Life Cycle Hypothesis of Saving, the Demand for Wealth and the Supply of Capital", *Social Research*, 33 (2), pp. 160–217.

Modigliani, F. and Papademos, L.D. (1990), "The Supply of Money and the Control of Nominal Income", in B.M. Friedman and F.H. Hahn (eds.), *Handbook of Monetary Economics*, Amsterdam: North-Holland, pp. 398–494.

Moggridge, D.E. (ed.) (1971–89), *The Collected Writings of John Maynard Keynes*, London and Basingstoke: Palgrave Macmillan, 30 vols.

Moggridge, D.E. (1973), "From the Treatise to the General Theory: An Exercise in Chronology", *History of Political Economy*, 5 (1), pp. 72–88.

Moggridge, D.E. (1992), *Maynard Keynes: An Economist's Biography*, London and New York: Routledge.

Moore, B.J. (1988), *Horizontalists and Verticalists: The Macroeconomics of Credit Money*, Cambridge, UK: Cambridge University Press.

Mosak, J.L. (1944), *General Equilibrium Theory in International Trade*, Cowles Commission Monograph n. 7, Bloomington, IN: Principia Press.

Mosler, W. (2010), *Seven Deadly Innocent Frauds of Economic Policy*, United States: Valance.

Musson, A.E. (1959), "The Great Depression in Britain, 1873–1896: A Reappraisal", *The Journal of Economic History*, 19 (2) (June), pp. 199–228.

Myrdal, K.G. (1939), *Monetary Equilibrium*, London: William Hodge & Co.

Naceur, S.B. and Roulet, C. (2017), "Basel III and Bank-Lending: Evidence from the United States and Europe", *IMF WP/17/XX*, www.imf.org/en/Publications/WP/Issues/2017/11/15/Basel-III-and-Bank-Lending-Evidence-from-the-United-States-and-Europe-45345, retrieved May 23, 2018.

National Archives. (2018), "Economic Slump", www.nationalarchives.gov.uk/cabinetpapers/themes/economic-slump.htm, retrieved September 7.

Neal, L. (1998), "The Financial Crisis of 1825 and the Restructuring of the British Financial System", *Review*, May/June, Federal Reserve of St. Louis, https://files.stlouisfed.org/files/htdocs/publications/review/98/05/9805ln.pdf, retrieved September 6, 2018.

Nell, E.J (1996), "The Circuit of Money in a Production Economy", in G. Deleplace and E.J. Nell (eds.), *Money in Motion: The Post Keynesian and Circulation Approaches*, London: Palgrave Macmillan.

Nell, E.J. (2002), "On Realizing Profits in Money", *Review of Political Economy*, 14 (4), pp. 519–30.

Nell, E.J. (2004), "Monetising the Classical Equations: A Theory of Circulation", *Cambridge Journal of Economics*, 28 (2), pp. 173–203.

Office of the Comptroller of the Currency. (2017), "Banks and Banking", www.gpo.gov/fdsys/pkg/CFR-2004-title12-vol1/content-detail.html, retrieved July 8, 2017.

Office of the Comptroller of the Currency. (2018a), "Who We Are", www.occ.treas.gov/about/who-we-are/comptroller-of-the-currency/comptroller-joseph-otting.html, retrieved February 18.

Office of the Comptroller of the Currency. (2018b), "About", www.occ.treas.gov/about/what-we-do/mission/index-about.html, retrieved February 18.

Ohlin, B. (1937), "Some Notes on the Stockholm Theory of Savings and Investment", *The Economic Journal*, 47 (185), pp. 53–69.

Orphanides, A. and Solow, R.M. (1990), "Money, Inflation and Growth", in B.M. Friedman and F.H. Hahn (eds.), *Handbook of Monetary Economics*, vol. I, Amsterdam: North Holland, pp. 223–61.

Palley, T. (1996), *Post Keynesian Economics: Debt, Distribution, and the Macro Economy*, Houndmills, Basingstoke, Hampshire, and London: Palgrave Macmillan and New York: St. Martin's Press.
Papademos, L.D. (2005), "Teoria Macroeconomica e Politica Monetaria: Contributi di FM e il Dibattito in Corso", *Moneta e Credito*, 58 (230–1), pp. 203–32.
Parguez, A. (1975), *Monnaie et Macroéeconomie*, Paris: Economica.
Parguez, A. (1996), "Beyond Scarcity: A Reappraisal of the Theory of the Monetary Circuit", in G. Deleplace and E. Nell (eds.), *Money in Motion: The Post Keynesian and Circulation Approaches*, London and New York: Palgrave Macmillan and St Martin's Press, pp. 155–99.
Parguez, A. (2001), "Money without Scarcity: From the Horizontalist Revolution to the Theory of the Monetary Circuit", in L-P. Rochon and M. Vernengo (eds.), *Credit, Interest Rates and the Open Economy*, Cheltenham, UK and Northampton, MA: Edward Elgar, pp. 69–103.
Parkin, M. (1986), "The Output-Inflation Tradeoff When Prices Are Costly to Change", *Journal of Political Economy*, 94 (February), pp. 200–24.
Partnoy, F. (2009), *F.I.A.S.C.O.: Blood in the Water on Wall Street*, New York and London: W. W. Norton & Company.
Partnoy, F. (2017), "The Sequel to the Global Financial Crisis Is Here", *The Financial Times*, July 31, www.ft.com/content/95808118-662e-11e7-9a66-93fb352ba1fe, retrieved June 15, 2018.
Pasinetti, L.L. (1960), "A Mathematical Formulation of the Ricardian System", *The Review of Economic Studies*, 27 (2), pp. 78–98.
Pasinetti, L.L. (1962), "Rate of Profit and Income Distribution in Relation to the Rate of Economic Growth", *The Review of Economic Studies*, 29 (4), pp. 267–79.
Pasinetti, L.L. (1966), "Changes in the Rate of Profit and Switches of Techniques", *The Quarterly Journal of Economics*, 80 (4), pp. 503–17.
Pasinetti, L.L. (1973), "La Teoría de Cambridge Sobre la Tasa de Beneficio, y Sus Precedentes Teóricos", *Cuadernos de Economía – Spanish Journal of Economics and Finance*, 1 (2), pp. 221–34.
Pasinetti, L.L. (1974), *Growth and Income Distribution: Essays in Economic Theory*, Cambridge, UK: Cambridge University Press.
Pasinetti, L.L. (1981), *Structural Change and Economic Growth: A Theoretical Essay on the Dynamics of the Wealth of Nations*, Cambridge: Cambridge University Press.
Pasinetti, L.L. (1986), "Theory of Value – A Source of Alternative Paradigms in Economic Analysis", in M.L. Baranzini, and R. Scazzieri (eds.), *Foundations of Economics: Structures of Inquiry and Economic Theory*, Oxford and New York: Basil Blackwell, pp. 409–31.
Pasinetti, L.L. (1989), "Ricardian Debt/Taxation Equivalence in the Kaldor Theory of Profits and Income Distribution", *Cambridge Journal of Economics*, 13 (1), pp. 25–36.
Pasinetti, L.L. (2000), "Critique of the Neoclassical Theory of Growth and Distribution", *BNL Quarterly Review*, 53 (215), pp. 383–431.
Pasinetti, L.L. (2005), "How Much of John Maynard Keynes Can We Find in Franco Modigliani?", *BNL Quarterly Review*, 58 (233–4), pp. 21–39.

Pasinetti, L.L. (2007), *Keynes and the Cambridge Keynesians: A 'Revolution in Economics' to Be Accomplished*, Cambridge, UK: Cambridge University Press.

Pasinetti, L.L. and Solow, R.M. (eds.) (1994), *Economic Growth and the Structure of Long-Term Development*, Houndsmills, Basingstoke, Hampshire, and London: Palgrave Macmillan.

Peacock, A.T. and Rowley, C.K. (1972), "Pareto Optimality and the Political Economy of Liberalism", *Journal of Political Economy*, 80 (3), pp. 476–90.

Phelps, E.S. (1961), "The Golden Rule of Economic Growth", *American Economic Review*, 51 (4), pp. 638–43.

Phelps, E.S. (1968), "Money-Wage Dynamics and Labor-Market Equilibrium", *Journal of Political Economy*, 76 (4), pp. 678–711. Published in 1970 in E.S. Phelps et al. (eds.), *Microeconomic Foundations of Employment and Inflation Theory*, New York: Norton.

Phelps, E.S. and Taylor, J.B. (1977), "Stabilizing Powers of Monetary Policy under Rational Expectations", *Journal of Political Economy*, 85 (February), pp. 163–90.

Ponsot, J-F. and Rossi, S. (eds.) (2009), *The Political Economy of Monetary Circuits: Tradition and Change in Post-Keynesian Economics*, Basingstoke: Palgrave Macmillan.

Porta, P. (ed.) (1992), *Notes on Malthus's "Measure of Value"*, Cambridge and New York: Cambridge University Press.

Prescott, E.C. (1986), "Theory Ahead of Business Cycle Measurement", *Federal Reserve Bank of Minneapolis Quarterly Review*, (Fall), pp. 9–22.

Public Law 111–203, 2010, "Dodd-Frank Wall Street Reform and Consumer Protection Act", U.S. Government Publishing Office, www.gpo.gov/fdsys/pkg/PLAW-111publ203/html/PLAW-111publ203.htm, retrieved August 3.

Ramsey, F.P. (1928), "A Mathematical Theory of Saving", *The Economic Journal*, 38 (152), pp. 543–59.

Rappeport, A. and Flitter, E. (2018), "Congress Approves First Big Dodd-Frank Rollback", *The New York Times*, May 22, www.nytimes.com/2018/05/22/business/congress-passes-dodd-frank-rollback-for-smaller-banks.html, retrieved June 23.

Realfonzo, R. (1998), *Money and Banking: Theory and Debate (1900–1940)*, Cheltenham, UK and Northampton, MA: Edward Elgar.

Renaud, J-F. (2000), "The Problem of the Monetary Realization of Profits in a Post Keynesian Sequential Financing Model: Two Solutions of the Kaleckian Option", *Review of Political Economy*, 12 (3), pp. 285–304.

Ricardo, D. (1809 [2004]), "The Price of Gold: Three Contributions to the Morning Chronicle", in P. Sraffa and M.H. Dobb (eds.), *The Works and Correspondence of David Ricardo*, Vol. III, Indianapolis: Liberty Fund, pp. 13–46. First edited in 1951 by Cambridge, UK: Cambridge University Press.

Ricardo, D. (1815 [2004]), "An Essay on The Influence of a Low Price of Corn on the Profits of Stock", in P. Sraffa and M.H. Dobb (eds.), *The Works and Correspondence of David Ricardo*, Vol. IV, Indianapolis: Liberty Fund, pp. 1–41. First edited in 1951 by Cambridge, UK: Cambridge University Press.

Ricardo, D. (1817 [2004]), "On the Principles of Political Economy and Taxation", in P. Sraffa and M.H. Dobb (eds.), *The Works and Correspondence of David Ricardo*, Vol. I, Indianapolis: Liberty Fund. First edited in 1951 by Cambridge, UK: Cambridge University Press.

Ricardo, D. (1823 [2004]), "Note on Absolute Value and Exchangeable Value", in P. Sraffa and M.H. Dobb (eds.), *The Works and Correspondence of David Ricardo*, Vol. IV, Indianapolis: Liberty Fund, pp. 357–412. First edited in 1951 by Cambridge, UK: Cambridge University Press.

Ricardo, D. (1824 [2004]), "Plan for the Establishment of a National Bank", in P. Sraffa and M.H. Dobb (eds.), *The Works and Correspondence of David Ricardo*, Vol. IV, Indianapolis: Liberty Fund, pp. 271–300. First edited in 1951 by Cambridge, UK: Cambridge University Press.

Robbins, L. (1934), *The Great Depression*, New York: Palgrave Macmillan.

Robinson, A.E. (1977), "Keynes and His Cambridge Colleagues", in D. Patinkin and L.J. Clark (eds.), *Keynes, Cambridge and 'The General Theory'*, London: Palgrave Macmillan, pp. 25–38.

Robinson, J.V. (1942), *An Essay on Marxian Economics*, London and Basingstoke: The Macmillan Press.

Robinson, J.V. (1953), "The Production Function and the Theory of Capital", *The Review of Economic Studies*, 21 (2), pp. 81–106.

Robinson, J.V. (1956), *The Accumulation of Capital*, London: Palgrave Macmillan.

Robinson, J.V. (1960), *Exercises in Economic Analysis*, London: Palgrave Macmillan. French translation by Bernard Schmitt as *Exercices d'Analyse Économique*, Paris: Presses Universitaires de France (1963).

Robinson, J.V. (1962), *Essays in the Theory of Economic Growth*, London and Basingstoke: Palgrave Macmillan.

Rochon, L-P. (2003), "On Money and Endogenous Money: Post Keynesian and Circulation Approaches", in L-P. Rochon and S. Rossi (eds.), *Modern Theories of Money: The Nature and Role of Money in Capitalist Economies*, Cheltenham, UK and Northampton, MA: Edward Elgar, pp. 115–41.

Rochon, L-P. (2005), "The Existence of Monetary Profits within the Monetary Circuit", in G. Fontana and R. Realfonzo (eds.), *The Monetary Theory of Production: Tradition and Perspectives*, Basingstoke and New York: Palgrave Macmillan, pp. 125–38.

Rochon, L-P. (2009), "The Existence of Profits within the Monetary Circuit: Some Unanswered Questions Revisited", in J-F. Ponsot and S. Rossi (eds.), *The Political Economy of Monetary Circuits: Tradition and Change in Post-Keynesian Economics*, Basingstoke: Palgrave Macmillan, pp. 56–76.

Rochon, L-P. and Rossi, S. (eds.) (2003), *Modern Theories of Money: The Nature and Role of Money in Capitalist Economies*, Cheltenham, UK and Northampton, MA: Edward Elgar.

Rochon, L-P. and Rossi, S. (2013), "Endogenous Money: The Evolutionary versus Revolutionary Views", *Review of Keynesian Economics*, 1 (2), pp. 210–29.

Rochon L-P. and Rossi, S. (2018), "The Relationship between Inflation and Unemployment: A Critique to Friedman and Phelps", *Review of Keynesian Economics*, 6 (4), pp. 533–44.

Rochon, L-P. and Seccareccia, M. (eds.) (2013), *Monetary Economies of Production: Banking and Financial Circuits and the Role of the State*, Cheltenham, UK and Northampton, MA: Edward Elgar.

Rodrigues, J. (2009), "The Bank of England: A Brief History", *The Guardian*, January 8, www.theguardian.com/business/2009/jan/08/central-bank-england, retrieved February 1, 2018.

Romer, C.D. (1988), "World War I and the Postwar Depression. A Reinterpretation Based on Alternative Estimates of GNP", *Journal of Monetary Economics*, 22 (1) (July), pp. 91–115.

Romer, D.H. (2001), *Advanced Macroeconomics*, New York: McGraw-Hill and Irwin, 2nd edition.

Romer, P.M. (1986), "Increasing Returns and Long-Run Growth", *Journal of Political Economy*, 94 (5), pp. 1002–37.

Romer, P.M. (1990), "Endogenous Technological Change", *Journal of Political Economy*, 98 (5), pp. S71–S102.

Roncaglia, A. (2005), *The Wealth of Ideas: A History of Economic Thought*, Cambridge, UK: Cambridge University Press.

Rossi, S. (1997), *Modalités d'institution et de fonctionnement d'une banque centrale supranationale, le cas de la Banque Centrale Européenne*, Berne: Peter Lang.

Rossi, S. (2001), *Money and Inflation: A New Macroeconomic Analysis*, Cheltenham, UK: Edward Elgar.

Rossi, S. (2003), "Money and Banking in a Monetary Theory of Production", in L-P. Rochon and S. Rossi (eds.), *Modern Theories of Money: The Nature and Role of Money in Capitalist Economies*, Cheltenham, UK and Northampton, MA: Edward Elgar, pp. 339–59.

Rossi, S. (2005), "Central Banking in a Monetary Theory of Production: The Economics of Payment Finality from a Circular-Flow Perspective", in G. Fontana and R. Realfonzo (eds.), *The Monetary Theory of Production: Tradition and Perspectives*, Basingstoke and New York: Palgrave Macmillan, pp. 139–51.

Rossi, S. (2006), "The Theory of Money Emissions", in P. Arestis and M. Sawyer (eds.), *A Handbook of Alternative Monetary Economics*, Cheltenham, UK and Northampton, MA: Edward Elgar, pp. 121–38.

Rossi, S. (2007), *Money and Payments in Theory and Practice*, London and New York: Routledge.

Rossi, S. (2009), "Monetary Circuit Theory and Money Emissions", in J-F. Ponsot and S. Rossi (eds.), *The Political Economy of Monetary Circuits: Tradition and Change in Post-Keynesian Economics*, Basingstoke: Palgrave Macmillan, pp. 36–55.

Rossi, S. (forthcoming a), "Milton Friedman and the Monetarist School", in H. Bougrine and L-P. Rochon (eds.), *A Short History of Economic Thought: Major Contributions Since Adam Smith*, Cheltenham, UK and Northampton, MA: Edward Elgar.

Rossi, S. (forthcoming b), "Monetary Policy and Central Banks' Interventions: A Critical Investigation", in N. Karagiannis and J.E. King (eds.), *Handbook of Government Intervention*, Cheltenham, UK and Northampton, MA: Edward Elgar.

Rotemberg, J.J. (1982), "Sticky Prices in the United States", *The Journal of Political Economy*, 90 (6), pp. 1187–211.

Rothbard, M.N. (1963), *America's Great Depression*, Princeton, NJ: D. Van Nostrand.

Rothschild, E.G. (1992), "Commerce and the State: Turgot, Condorcet, and Smith", *The Economic Journal*, 102 (414), pp. 1197–210.

Rothschild, E.G. (2001), *Economic Sentiments: Adam Smith, Condorcet, and the Enlightenment*, Cambridge, MA and London: Harvard University Press.

Rothschild, E.G. (2011), *The Inner Life of Empires: An Eighteenth-Century History*, Princeton, NJ and Oxford: Princeton University Press.

Samuelson, P.A. (1948 [1980]), *Economics*, New York: McGraw-Hill.

Samuelson, P.A. (1959), "A Modern Treatment of the Ricardian Economy", *The Quarterly Journal of Economics*, 73 (1), pp. 1–35 and 79 (2), pp. 217–31.

Samuelson, P.A. (1962), "Parable and Realism in Capital Theory: The Surrogate Production Function", *The Review of Economic Studies*, 29 (3), pp. 193–206.

Samuelson, P.A. (1966), "Paradoxes in Capital Theory: A Symposium", *The Quarterly Journal of Economics*, 80 (4), pp. 503–83.

Samuelson, P.A. (1991), "Extirpating Error Contamination Concerning the Post-Keynesian Anti-Pasinetti Equilibrium", *Oxford Economics Papers*, 43 (2), pp. 177–86.

Samuelson, P.A. and Modigliani, F. (1966a), "The Pasinetti Paradox in Neoclassical and More General Models", *The Review of Economic Studies*, 33 (4), pp. 269–301.

Samuelson, P.A. and Modigliani, F. (1966b), "Reply to Pasinetti and Robinson", *The Review of Economic Studies*, 33 (4), pp. 321–30.

Sato, K. (1976), "The Neoclassical Production Function: Comment", *American Economic Review*, 66 (3), pp. 428–33.

Say, J-B. (1821 [1971]), *A Treatise on Political Economy*, New York: Augustus M. Kelley Publishers. Reprint of 1880, Philadelphia: Claxton, Remsen & Haffelfinger. First published in French in 1803 as *Traité d'Economie Politique*, Paris: Callmann-Lévy.

Scazzieri, R., Sen, A.K., and Zamagni, S. (eds.) (2008), *Markets, Money and Capital: Hicksian Economics for the Twenty-First Century*, Cambridge: Cambridge University Press.

Schmitt, B. (1960), *La formation du pouvoir d'achat*, Paris: Sirey.

Schmitt, B. (1966 [1975]), *Monnaie, salaires et profits*, Albeuve: Castella. First published in 1966 by Presses Universitaires de France, Paris.

Schmitt, B. (1972), *Macroeconomic Theory: A Fundamental Revision*, Albeuve: Castella.

Schmitt, B. (1973), *New Proposals for World Monetary Reform*, Albeuve: Castella.

Schmitt, B. (1975), *Théorie unitaire de la monnaie, nationale et internationale*, Albeuve: Castella.

Schmitt, B. (1984), *Inflation, Chômage et Malformations du Capital: Macroéconomie Quantique*, Paris and Albeuve: Economica and Castella.

Schmitt, B. (1986), "The Process of Formation of Economics in Relation to Other Sciences", in M.L. Baranzini and R. Scazzieri (eds.), *Foundations of Economics: Structures of Inquiry and Economic Theory*, Oxford and New York: Basil Blackwell, pp. 103–32.

Schmitt, B. (1996a), "Cours de théorie monétaire", University of Fribourg, mimeo.

Schmitt, B. (1996b), "A New Paradigm for the Determination of Money Prices", in G. Deleplace and E.J. Nell (eds.), *Money in Motion: The Post Keynesian and Circulation Approaches*, London and New York: Palgrave Macmillan and St. Martin's Press, pp. 104–38.

Schmitt, B. (2007), *Le thèorème de l'intérêt*, Lugano-Vezia: Research Laboratory in Monetary Economics.

Schmitt, B. (2014), "The Formation of Sovereign Debt. Diagnosis and Remedy", *Social Science Research Network (SSRN)*, https://papers.ssrn.com/sol3/papers.cfm?abstract_id=2513679, retrieved February 28, 2018.

Schmitt, B. and De Gottardi, C. (2003), "An Internal Critique of General Equilibrium Theory", in L-P. Rochon and S. Rossi (eds.), *Modern Theories of Money*, Cheltenham, UK and Northampton, MA: Edward Elgar, pp. 265–94.

Schumpeter, J.A. (1994 [1954]), *History of Economic Analysis*, London and New York: Routledge.

Seccareccia, M. (1996), "Post Keynesian Fundism and Monetary Circulation", in G. Deleplace and E.J. Nell (eds.), *Money in Motion: The Post Keynesian and Circulation Approaches*, London and New York: Palgrave Macmillan and St. Martin's Press, pp. 400–16.

Seccareccia, M. (2003), "Pricing, Investment and the Financing of Production within the Framework of the Monetary Circuit: Some Preliminary Evidence", in L-P. Rochon and S. Rossi (eds.), *Modern Theories of Money: The Nature and Role of Money in Capitalist Economies*, Cheltenham, UK and Northampton, MA: Edward Elgar, pp. 173–97.

Seccareccia, M. (2005), "Interest Rates, Interest Spreads and Monetary Circulation: Theoretical Framework and Empirical Implications for Macroeconomic Performance", in G. Fontana and R. Realfonzo (eds.), *The Monetary Theory of Production: Tradition and Perspectives*, Basingstoke and New York: Palgrave Macmillan, pp. 269–84.

Sen, A.K. (1970), "The Impossibility of a Paretian Liberal", *Journal of Political Economy*, 78 (1), pp. 152–7.

Sen, A.K. (1971), "The Impossibility of a Paretian Liberal: Reply", *Journal of Political Economy*, 79 (6), 1406–7.

Sen, A.K. (1977), "Rational Fools: A Critique of the Behavioral Foundations of Economics Theory", *Philosophy and Public Affairs*, 6 (Summer), pp. 317–44.

Sen, A.K. (1992), *Inequality Reexamined*, Cambridge, MA: Harvard University Press.

Sen, A.K. (1994), "Growth Economics: What and Why?" in L.L. Pasinetti and R.M. Solow (eds.), *Economic Growth and the Structure of Long-Term Development*, Houndsmills, Basingstoke, Hampshire, and London: Palgrave Macmillan, pp. 363–8.

Sen, A.K. (1997), *On Economic Inequality*, Oxford: Clarendon Press and New York: Oxford University Press. First published in 1973.

Sen, A.K. (1998), "Amartya Sen – Biographical", *The Sveriges Riksbank Prize in Economic Sciences in Memory of Alfred Nobel 1998*, www.nobelprize.org, retrieved March 24, 2017.

Skidelsky, R.J. (2003), *John Maynard Keynes. 1883–1946: Economist, Philosopher, Statesman*, London: Palgrave Macmillan.

Skidelsky, R.J. (2009), *Keynes: The Return of the Master*, London: Allen Lane.

Smith, A. (1776 [1981]), *An Inquiry into the Nature and Causes of the Wealth of Nations*, R.H. Campbell and A.S. Skinner (eds.), 2 vols, Indianapolis: Liberty Fund.

Smithin, J. (1997), "An Alternative Monetary Model of Inflation and Growth", *Review of Political Economy*, 9 (4), pp. 395–409.

Solow, R.M. (1955–56), "The Production Function and the Theory of Capital", *The Review of Economic Studies*, 23 (2), pp. 101–8.

Solow, R.M. (1956), "A Contribution to the Theory of Economic Growth", *The Quarterly Journal of Economics*, 70 (1), pp. 65–94.

Solow, R.M. (1990), *The Labour Market as a Social Institution*, Oxford: Basil Blackwell.

Solow, R.M. (2000), "The Neoclassical Theory of Growth and Distribution", *BNL Quarterly Review*, 53 (215), pp. 349–81.

Solow, R.M. (2010), "Building a Science of Economics for the Real World", United States House of Representatives, Committee on Science and Technology, Serial No. 111–106, www.gpo.gov/fdsys/pkg/CHRG-111hhrg57604/pdf/CHRG-111hhrg57604.pdf, retrieved January 26, 2016.

Solow, R.M. (2012), "On Pasinetti and the Unfinished Keynesian Revolution", in R. Arena and P. Porta (eds.), *Structural Dynamics and Economic Growth*, Cambridge: Cambridge University Press, pp. 267–73.

Sraffa, P. (1960), *Production of Commodities by Means of Commodities: Prelude to a Critique of Economic Theory*, Cambridge: Cambridge University Press.

Sraffa, P. and Dobb, M.H. (eds.) (2004), *The Works and Correspondence of David Ricardo*, Indianapolis: Liberty Fund, 11 vols. First edited in 1951 by Cambridge, UK: Cambridge University Press.

Stamp, J.C. (1931), "The Report of the Macmillan Committee", *The Economic Journal*, 41 (163), pp. 424–35.

Steil, B. (2013), *The Battle of Bretton Woods: John Maynard Keynes, Harry Dexter White, and the Making of a New World Order*, Princeton, NJ: Princeton University Press.

Steuart, J. (1767), *An Inquiry into the Principles of Political Economy: Being an Essay on Science of Domestic Policy in Free Nations*, 2 vols, London: A. Millar and T. Cadell.

Swan, T.W. (1956), "Economic Growth and Capital Accumulation", *Economic Record*, 32 (2), pp. 343–61.

Sylos Labini, P. (1995), "Why the Interpretation of the Cobb-Douglas Production Function Must Be Radically Changed", *Structural Change and Economic Dynamics*, 6 (4), pp. 485–504.

Taylor, J.B. (1979), "Staggered Wage Setting in a Macro Model", *American Economic Review*, 69 (May), pp. 108–13.

Terzi, A. (2002), *La Moneta*, Bologna: Il Mulino.

Tirole, J. and Dewatripont, M.F. (1993), *The Prudential Regulation of Banks*, Cambridge, MA and London: MIT Press.

Tobin, J. (1955), "A Dynamic Aggregative Model", *Journal of Political Economy*, 63 (2), pp. 103–15.

Tobin, J. (1956), "The Interest Elasticity of the Transactions Demand for Cash", *Review of Economics and Statistics*, 38 (3), pp. 241–7.

Tobin, J. (1963), "Commercial Banks as Creators of Money", in D. Carson (ed.), *Banking and Monetary Studies*, Homewood: Richard Irwin, pp. 408–19.

Tobin, J. (1965), "Money and Economic Growth", *Econometrica*, 33 (4), pp. 671–84.

Tobin, J. (1969), "A General Equilibrium Approach to Monetary Theory", *Journal of Money, Credit, and Banking*, 1 (1), pp. 15–29.

Tobin, J. (1971), "Phillips Curve Algebra", in *Essays in Economics*, Vol. 2, Amsterdam: North Holland Press.

Tobin, J. (1972), "Inflation and Unemployment", *American Economic Review*, 62 (1), pp. 1–18.

Tobin, J. (1974), "Friedman's Theoretical Framework", in R.J. Gordon (ed.), *Milton Friedman's Monetary Framework*, Chicago: University of Chicago Press.

Tobin, J. (1975), "Keynesian Models of Recession and Depression", *American Economic Review*, 65 (2), pp. 195–202.

Tobin, J. (1976), "Monetary Policies and the Economy: The Transmission Mechanism", *Southern Economic Journal*, 44 (3), pp. 421–31.

Tobin, J. (1980), *Asset Accumulation and Economic Activity*, Chicago: University of Chicago Press.

Tobin, J. (1982), "Money and Finance in the Macroeconomic Process", *Journal of Money, Credit, and Banking*, 14 (2), pp. 171–204.

Tobin, J. (1993), "Price Flexibility and Output Stability: An Old Keynesian View", *Journal of Economic Perspectives*, 7 (1), pp. 45–66.

Tsakalotos, E. (2018), "Banking Union Is Not Enough to Save the Eurozone", *The Financial Times*, January 7, www.ft.com/content/0096a770-f225-11e7-bb7d-c3edfe974e9f, retrieved June 23.

Ullmo, J. (1969), *Le Profit*, Paris: Dunod.

U.S. Department of the Treasury. (2017), "A Financial System That Creates Economic Opportunities: Banks and Credit Unions", www.treasury.gov/press-center/press-releases/ . . . /A%20Financial%20System.pdf, retrieved July 31.

U.S. Government (1948), *Proceedings and Documents of the United Nations Monetary and Financial Conference. Bretton Woods, New Hampshire. July 1–22, 1944*, Washington, DC: United States Government Printing Office, https://fraser.stlouisfed.org/files/docs/publications/books/1948_state_bwood_v1.pdf, retrieved September 17, 2018.

Vercelli, A. (1991), *Methodological Foundations of Macroeconomics: Keynes and Lucas*, Cambridge and New York: Cambridge University Press.

Walras, L. (1874 [1965]), *Elements of Pure Economics*, Homewood, IL: Richard D. Irwin.

Wells Fargo. (2013), "Wells Fargo Is No. 1 Originator of ACH Electronic Payments", April 11, www.wellsfargo.com/about/press/2013/20130411_WellsFargo ACHPayments/, retrieved July 12, 2017.

Wheatley, A. (2017), "Virtual Payments Are Fast Displacing Cash, but not Completely and not Everywhere", *International Monetary Fund*, June, *Finance and Development*, www.imf.org/external/pubs/ft/fandd/2017/06/pdf/wheatley.pdf, retrieved July 1, 2018.

Wicksell, J.K. (1898 [1965]), *Interest and Prices*, New York: Kelly.

Wicksell, J.K. (1901 [1934]), *Lectures on Political Economy*, vol. I, London: Routledge & Kegan Paul.

Wicksell, J.K. (1912 [1997]), "Kapital – und kein Ende. Reply to Docent Brisman", in B. Sandelin (ed.), *Knut Wicksell. Selected Essays in Economics*, London and New York: Routledge, pp. 15–25.

Wicksell, J.K. (1923), "Real Capital and Interest", *Ekonomisk Tidskrift*, 5-6, pp. 145–80, translated as "Appendix 2" in J.K. Wicksell (1934), *Lectures on Political Economy*, London: George Routledge & Sons, pp. 258–99.

Wieczner, J. (2017), "The Fortune 500's 10 Most Profitable Companies", *Fortune*, June 7, http://fortune.com/2017/06/07/fortune-500-companies-profit-apple-berkshire-hathaway/, retrieved July 31.

Wood, A.J. (1975), *A Theory of Profits*, Cambridge, UK: Cambridge University Press.

Wood, A.J. (1978), *A Theory of Wages*, Cambridge, UK: Cambridge University Press.

Wood, J.C. and Woods, R.N. (eds.) (1989), *Sir John Hicks: Critical Assessments*, London: Routledge, 4 vols.

World Bank. (2017), "Gross Domestic Product 2016", http://databank.worldbank.org/data/download/GDP.pdf, retrieved July 31.

Wray, R.L. (1996), "Money in the Circular Flow", in G. Deleplace and E.J. Nell (eds.), *Money in Motion: The Post Keynesian and Circulation Approaches*, London and New York: Palgrave Macmillan and St. Martin's Press, pp. 440–64.

Wray, R.L. (2013), "Is There Room for Bulls, Bears and States in the Circuit?" in L-P. Rochon and M. Seccareccia (eds.), *Monetary Economies of Production: Banking and Financial Circuits and the Role of the State*, Cheltenham, UK and Northampton, MA: Edward Elgar, pp. 54–69.

Yergin, D. (1991), *The Prize: The Epic Quest for Oil, Money, and Power*, New York: Simon & Schuster.

Zamagni Negri, V. (2017), *An Economic History of Europe Since 1700*, Newcastle Upon Tyne: Agenda Publishing.

Zazzaro, A. (2003), "How Heterodox Is the Heterodoxy of Monetary Circuit Theory? The Nature of Money and the Microeconomics of the Circuit", in L-P. Rochon and S. Rossi (eds.), *Modern Theories of Money: The Nature and Role of Money in Capitalist Economies*, Cheltenham, UK: Edward Elgar.

Zezza, G. (2003), "The Existence of Monetary Profits within the Monetary Circuit: Comments on Rochon", presented at a conference in honor of Augusto Graziani held in Benevento, Italy, December 5–6.

Name index

Subject index